SACRED RHETORIC

SACRED RHETORIC

or

A Course of Lectures on Preaching

❧

ROBERT L DABNEY, D.D.

THE BANNER OF TRUTH TRUST

THE BANNER OF TRUTH TRUST
3 Murrayfield Road, Edinburgh EH12 6EL
P.O. Box 621, Carlisle, Pennsylvania 17013, U.S.A.

*

First published 1870
First Banner of Truth Trust edition, 1979
ISBN 0 85151 290 9

*

Printed and bound in Great Britain
by W & J Mackay Limited, Chatham

THIS book is dedicated to my younger brethren, the Alumni and Students of Union Theological Seminary, as a mark of esteem and gratitude for that courtesy, kindness and propriety which, without a single exception in seventeen years, have governed their deportment toward me as their teacher; and as an affectionate effort to promote their efficiency in their blessed and solemn work.

R. L. DABNEY.

FEBRUARY 7, 1870.   3

PREFACE.

THIS little book is the fruit of study, reflection and teachings continued through twenty years. It would be hazardous for any one to claim originality in a department of literature which contains so many great works as sacred rhetoric. The most effectual disavowal of such pretensions will be to recite the titles of the books which I have read with most advantage, and which have contributed to my knowledge or opinions on this subject. If my readers are familiar with these treatises, they will probably find in them either the germs or the full forms of nearly all the ideas which I advance. The following treatises I have found exceedingly instructive:

Aristotle's *Rhetoric*.

Cicero, *De Oratore*.

Horace, *Epistle to the Pisos*.

Quinctilian, *De Institutione Oratoria*.

Campbell's *Philosophy of Rhetoric*.

Whateley's *Rhetoric*.

Vinet's *Homiletics*.

My studies have also included—

    Plato's *Gorgias*.

    Fénélon's *Dialogues on Eloquence*.

    Dr. G. Campbell's *Lectures on Pulpit Eloquence*.

    Porter's *Homiletics*.

    M. Bungener, *Priest and Preacher*.

    Abbé Bautain, *On Extempore Speech*.

    Dr. J. W. Alexander's *Thoughts on Preaching*.

    Theremin, *Eloquence a Virtue*.

    Shedd's *Homiletics*.

    Dr. Samuel Miller, *On Public Prayer*.

To the natural question, why I presume to add another to so long a catalogue (which might be indefinitely lengthened), I reply, that the task of teaching a course of Pulpit Rhetoric in Union Theological Seminary soon convinced me that none of these books are adapted to be sufficient text-books for classes. While several of them contain features of great value, they all lack others which should be essential. I was therefore compelled very early to attempt the construction of such a course as would be an adequate guide to the evangelical Protestant preacher. The approbation which my course has received from my pupils and brethren in the ministry, with their general and continued request for its publication, have encouraged me to attempt it. One object, at least, will be gained thereby, which is first with me—the throwing of my instructions into a form more useful to my pupils.

If this work has any peculiarities to which value may be attached, they are these: that the necessity of eminent Christian character is urged throughout as the foundation of the sacred orator's power, and that a theory of preaching is asserted, with all the force which I could command, that honours God's inspired word and limits the preacher most strictly to its exclusive use as the sword of the Spirit. If my readers rise from the perusal with these two convictions enhanced in their souls—that it is grace which makes the preacher, and that nothing is preaching which is not expository of the Scriptures—my work is not in vain.

I have preferred that the work should be issued by the publishing agency of my own denomination. But its doctrines are not denominational. The theory of preaching taught is equally adapted to all evangelical ministers. My hope and prayer are that my labour will be useful to all my brethren of every name, and will assist them to preach the glorious gospel of the Lord Jesus Christ more directly, more scripturally and more effectively, so that this divinely-ordained agency may resume its primitive power in the Church.

CONTENTS.

LECTURE XIX.

LECTURE XX.

LECTURE XXI.

LECTURE XXII.

LECTURE XXIII.

LECTURE XXIV.

LECTURES ON SACRED RHETORIC.

LECTURE I.

INTRODUCTORY.

My Young Brethren:

SOME well-meaning Christians meet us at the threshold of our subject, with objections to the application of an art of Rhetoric to sacred topics. These may appear plausible enough to need a reply. Not only do they advance the trite assertions, "*Poeta nascitur, non fit*," and, "Nature is a better teacher than art;" they draw peculiar pleas from the sanctity of the preacher's function and motive, and even from the word of God. They claim that the messenger, who bears the gospel of love to man, should be unaffected and sincere. They say that while those who argue less worthy causes may perhaps excuse their art, the preacher should be above all art. They cite against us the twice-repeated declaration of the apostle Paul, that his "speech and his preaching was not with enticing words of man's wisdom, but in demonstration of the Spirit and of power." [1]

To the first observation I answer, that if the orator

---

[1] See 1 Cor. ii. 4, 13.

is born, his oration is not. That, at least, must be made. Rhetoric does not profess to create a vigorous understanding, feeling, taste and genius, but only to teach their most effective use. The artisan does not make hands for his apprentice, but he shows him how to use the members Nature has given him. And the man of common mould is enabled, by means of this training, to make a better plough or cart than could be produced without it by the youth whose limbs matched those of the *Apollo Belvidere*. If it is urged that we not seldom hear the untaught son of Nature, by virtue of the original nobility of his faculties, speak with far more true eloquence than the assiduous rhetorician, the reply is obvious. Those excellent gifts of Nature should have been perfected by true culture, so that this fortunate man might have excelled his fellows of the common, but trained capacity, even farther than he did. For all that excellence he owed to his God, by the rule that we must "love him with all our heart, and soul, and mind, and strength." The unskillfulness of the professed rhetorician may also prove, not that his art is worthless, but that he has imperfectly acquired it. You will easily conceive how a system of real value, if only half mastered, and by reason of deficient experience in its application, employed without facility, may embarrass instead of aiding us. The royal armour of King Saul was doubtless of the best temper. We do not doubt that David used such with splendid advantage in his subsequent career of conquest. But when the raw shepherd-boy was clad with it, he found himself encumbered by it, "because he had not proved it."

The assumption that the preacher's sacred attitude is above rhetoric reveals ignorance of the nature of true art. Let us then, at the outset, seek a correct conception of it. And we may be led to this idea by considering the distinction between art and artifice. Art is but the rational adjustment of means to an end.[1] Art is adaptation; it employs proper means for a worthy end; it is but wisdom in application. Artifice is false; it adopts deceitful means for a treacherous end. When the benevolent physician compounds a drug, which his learning shows to be a specific cure for a disease, this is art. ·When the cunning seducer prepares a seeming attraction which is not indeed real, to inveigle his prey into the snare, this is artifice. There is a popular application of the word art which has also assisted to delude the judgment of these objectors. It is that which we express usually by the term "fine arts," in which the end of the skill employed is only to gratify taste, and not to evoke practical volition. I shall show that the art of eloquence is contrasted with these, in that its aim is ever intensely practical. And I shall urge that, whenever the preacher permits his aim to degenerate into that of the painter or musician, the mere pleasure of taste, he flagrantly violates both the principles of his art and of his religious duty. But I assert none the less that, since this duty is to convey gospel truth effectively to other souls, and since there are adapted means by which this end may be the better accom-

---

[1] Art, from *Ars* (root, *art*-is) which is from Greek αρω, to adjust, whence αρτυνω, αρτος, joined. *Art* is, therefore, adjustment. Webster's derivation, from W. *cerz* and Ir. *ceard*, carrying the rudimental idea of *strength*, is as far-fetched as absurd.

plished, there is a true art of preaching, which is not only lawful and honest, but sacredly obligatory.

The opponents whom we now consider love to contrast art with nature. I assert that all true art is natural. If man is by nature a creature of reason and conscience; if duty, forecast, judgment, will, desire of legitimate success, are natural to him, then surely he does not obey, but violates his nature when he discards the use of adapted means for his ends. If there are gifted souls who, without that detailed study of art which is necessary for us common mortals, are able to effectuate their ends more nobly than we with all our labour, then the explanation is that their more powerful genius has only made a quicker and easier intuition of their art. To reach that pinnacle of efficiency, they have ascended the common stairway, for there is no other. The difference is, that while we climb it step by step, their superior vigour enables them to bound up it with almost unconscious effort. Moreover, it is not true that these advocates of pure nature discard art. They are not naturally so natural as they claim to be. It was the fashion for the infidel school of Rousseau and the Encyclopædists to call savages "children of nature;" yet a savage is the least simple of men. He is the slave of his conventionalities, his fashions, his artifices. The only difference is, that they are unlike to, and more intense than, those of the civilized man. So, those speakers who profess to leave all to nature, are always most unnatural; they have not only art, but artifice and mannerism, and are more in bondage to them than the true artist. Art, I repeat, is but a well-adapted method, and the real option which we have is not between art and nature, but only between art wise and art foolish, art skilful, or art clumsy. Indeed, the result of true art is simply to assist Nature to perfect herself, and thus to open the way for her to her worthiest ends. Thus I retort the conclusion upon our objector. I assert that unless he holds men's faculties permit no employment of methods, and that their first untaught essays are necessarily their best, he must grant a legitimate art of sacred rhetoric. And it is not only the preacher's privilege, but sacred duty to seek and use it.

We easily escape the seeming disclaimer of the great Apostle, by asking what was that rhetoric which he repudiated, and whether he did not employ a method of his own? The Christian antiquary answers the first question. The spurious and unworthy art which is here rejected, was that of the Greek Sophists—a system of mere tricks of logic and diction, prompted by vanity and falsehood, and misguided by a depraved taste. It was the pretentious rhetoric so scathed by the sarcasm and reasoning of Socrates in the *Gorgias*. While the Apostle disclaimed this, surely he did not preach without any method! He adopted an appropriate one of his own. If you say that it was honest, as opposed to the deceitfulness of the Greeks; that it was simple, as opposed to the ambitious complexity of the Greeks; that it was modest, as opposed to their ostentation; that it was disinterested, as contrasted with their overweening selfishness, I assent, and I add that these are the things which made St. Paul's a true rhetoric. Let us then adopt the ascertaining of his method as the object of our search. Let us make our sacred rhetoric just his, so far as it was primarily taught him by the Holy Spirit, and taught him next by his high culture and pure devotion.

The objection drawn from the inhibition of previous care and preparation to the apostles, when brought before persecutors, can scarcely embarrass you for a moment. Our Saviour said to them, "Settle it in your hearts not to meditate before what you shall answer; for I will give you a mouth and wisdom which all your adversaries shall not be able to gainsay or resist." This command is based evidently upon the accompanying promise. It should be asked, Was the promise made to them as common ministers, or as inspired apostles? This is determined by the "signs which should follow;" speaking with tongues, healing the sick, casting out devils. It is, then, a mere wresting of the Scriptures, to claim for the uninspired preacher that extraordinary inspiration, superseding the necessity for premeditation, which is as truly miraculous as the divine works that attested its source. Our Saviour's prohibition seems to forbid immediate preparation for a particular discourse, even more clearly than the general study of the art of speaking. But who would now pretend that the minister ought not even to meditate upon the subject which he is about to expound? It is, surely, sufficient proof that the apostle Paul did not understand preparation to be unlawful, that we find him commanding Timothy " to give attendance to reading, to exhortation, to doctrine, to meditate upon these things, and give himself wholly to them, that his profiting might appear unto all."[1]

---

[1] Luke. xxi. 14; 1 Ep. to Tim. iv. 13–15.

Whateley[1] cites, as he says, from Aristotle, a very plain and conclusive illustration of the matter in debate. There are two men who have had equal opportunity to observe and comprehend a transaction. Each of them undertakes to relate it to his friends, who did not witness it. One of them so narrates it that his story is perspicuous and graphic, and is listened to, not only without effort, but with keen pleasure. The other so confuses his account of it, that his relation is irksome to the listeners, and fails to convey that apprehension of the matter which was designed. Do not such instances often occur in fact? Now, says Aristotle, the difference in the way in which these two men tell their story, is rhetoric. Wherein does that difference consist? This is just what we seek in this course.

It is not asserted that a course of sacred rhetoric can be made so extensive, or so fruitful of mental and spiritual culture to the student, as some branches of sacred science, which my colleagues teach. But in one respect it may be said to bear an important relation to all your other studies here, not unlike that which Lord Bacon[2] describes as the *vindemiatio* of inductions. The observation, comparing, classifying of *phenomena* are preparatory; the final inference from the comparison, leading us to the true law of causation, extracts that precious juice for the sake of which solely the clusters have been collected with so much care. In like manner I may claim, that as you come here to be made preachers of the gospel, and as its proclamation from the pulpit is to

---

[1] Rhetoric: introduc. Cicero de Orat. b. I., c. 14, §§ 63, 64.
[2] Nov. Organum, lib. II. § 20.

be your prominent task, all other studies are ancillary
to this which we now undertake.   It is sacred rhetoric
which teaches you to apply to the lips of perishing man
the expressed wine of all other acquisitions.

I design next, to introduce you into the consideration
of our subject by a brief outline of the history of
preaching.   The gift of speech is the most obvious at-
tribute which distinguishes man from the brutes.[1]   To
him, language is so important a handmaid of his mind
in all its processes, that we remain uncertain how many
latent faculties, which we are now prone to deny to the
lower animals, may not be lying inactive in them, because of their privation of this *medium*.   It is speech
which makes us really social beings; without it our instinctive attraction to our fellows would give us, not
true society, but the mere gregariousness of the herds.
It is by speech that the gulf is bridged over, which in-
sulates each spirit from others.   This is the great com-
municative faculty which establishes a communion between men in each other's experience, reasoning, wisdom
and affections.   These familiar observations are recalled
to your view, in order to suggest how naturally and
even necessarily oral address must be employed in the
service of religion.   If man's religious and social traits

---

[1] Quinctil., lib. II., c. 16, §§ 16, 17. "Nam. . . . opera quædam
nobis inimitibilia (qualia sunt cerarum et mellis) efficere, non nul-
lius fortasse rationis est; sed quia (animalia) carent sermone, quæ
id faciunt, muta atque irrationalia vocantur. Denique homines
quibus negata vox est, quantulum adjuvat amimus ille cœlestis?
Quare si nihil a diis oratione melius accepimus, quid tam dignum
cultu ac labore ducamus, aut in quo malimus præstare hominibus,
quam quo ipsi homines cæteris animalibus præstant? eo quidem
magis, quod nulla in parte plenius labor gratiam refert."

are regarded, we cannot but expect to find a wise God, from the beginning, consecrate His gift of speech to the end of propagating sacred knowledge and sentiments.

Accordingly, we learn that continuous, oral address has been so used from the earliest ages. In the little that is told us of the antediluvians, we read that God's will was preached among them. " Enoch, the seventh from Adam, prophesied of the ungodly." [1] Noah was " a preacher of righteousness." [2] When we descend to the Hebrew commonwealth we find three orders of official preachers, besides the patriarchal heads of households. On these a constant oral instruction of children was enjoined,[3] which probably assumed rather the familiar plainness of homiletical instruction,[4] than the formality of the sermon. But the prophets were beyond question, if occasional officers of the theocracy, yet public preachers of revealed truth. We read of such discourses from Moses, Aaron (who was both prophet and priest), Isaiah, Elijah, Elisha, Jonah, Jeremiah and the prophets of the restoration. Ezekiel aptly illustrates the responsibilities of his office by that of the watchman set to proclaim the coming of an enemy.[5] We read also of schools of the prophets, in which youth devoted to God's special service were assembled under the tuition of inspired men, not indeed to learn by rote that divine gift which can only be received by God's sovereign bestowal, but to prepare themselves for it by habits of devotion, and by familiarity with the Scriptures and worship of Israel.

The second order of preachers was the priest's. It

---

[1] Jude 14. [2] 2 Pet. ii. 5. [3] Deut. vi. 7.
[4] See proper sense of ὁμιλειν. [5] Ezek. xxxiii.

is clear that his stated duties were not only sacrificial—these occupied but a few weeks of his year—but also pastoral. The priests and Levites, when not employed at the sanctuary, were scattered throughout Israel, and were required to occupy themselves in teaching and preaching. This is intimated in the complaint of Azariah the son of Obed, in the reign of Asa, against their delinquency : " Now for a long season Israel hath been without the true God, and without a teaching priest," etc.[1] It is more expressly declared by Malachi : " For the priests' lips should keep knowledge, and they should seek the law at his mouth, for he is the messenger of the Lord of hosts." [2]

There is some evidence that the theocratic kings also included preaching among their legitimate functions. It may be remarked, in passing, that the early type of Mohammedanism shows how naturally this duty fell in with those of the divinely-appointed ruler. Mohammed, who embodied in his pretensions very accurately certain of the formal ideas of Oriental religion, announced himself as both prophet and theocratic head of his new commonwealth. The latter office was transmitted to his successors, and we find the early khalifs, before the military career of Islam had changed them into mere soldiers, and especially the first of them, Abubeker, constantly preaching in virtue of his position. But this is by the way. One of Solomon's titles was " preacher," [3] and we have abundant proof in the places cited and others that he was accustomed to exer-

---

[1] 2 Chron. xv. 3.   [2] Mal. ii. 7.
[3] Eccles i. 1; xii. 9, קֹהֶלֶת.

cise this function frequently. We cannot doubt that the same thing was done, at least during the seasons of greatest fidelity to the Hebrew institutions, by Asa, by Hezekiah and by the good Josiah.

But it was under Ezra that preaching assumed, by divine appointment, more nearly its modern place as a constant part of worship, and also its modern character as an exposition of the written Scriptures. This new impulse of the usage was given by the necessities of a great religious revival, and the disuse of the classic Hebrew language by the people as a vernacular tongue. Their seventy years' residence in Chaldea had taught them a modified dialect. Hence the necessity for accompanying the reading of the sacred text with explanations in the popular language. "And Ezra, the priest, brought forth the Law before the congregation. . . . So they read in the book of the law of God distinctly, and gave the sense, and caused them to understand the reading."[1] We shall seek in vain for a more apt and scriptural definition of the preacher's work than is contained in these words. Henceforth, as the Jewish antiquaries tell us, expository preaching prevailed as a regular exercise, following the reading of the Scriptures in the services of the synagogues. You are too familiar with that usage to need detailed accounts of it. The hints contained in the Gospels themselves[2] show that it was not the exclusive function of the "ruler of the synagogue," but at his invitation was performed by any learned and competent worshipper; that it was founded usually upon the lessons of the day, and that

---

[1] Neh. viii. 1–8.   [2] Luke iv. 16; Matt. xiii. 54; John xviii. 20.

while the reader stood in reading these passages of the Law and Prophets, he resumed his seat to pronounce his own discourse. The importance of these notices to us is that they show us our Saviour's sanction of preaching, as a part of the divine service, and that they connect the preaching of the old dispensation with that of the new.

The Redeemer, and after Him, the apostles, were constant preachers of the gospel. Whenever they were permitted, they availed themselves of the Sabbath worship and synagogues for this purpose. But they preached everywhere; in the temple-courts, in private houses, in the streets and highways, beside the sea, on the mountains. Preaching was the chief instrument of the Christian missionary and teacher, of whatever rank. " It pleased God by the foolishness of preaching to save them that believe." [1] And it is very plain from the Acts and Epistles, in both their preceptive and narrative parts, that this continued to be a regular part of the public service of all the Christian assemblies.

The literature of the Church which has reached us is extremely scanty until the middle of the second century. But the well-known testimony of Justin Martyr, the letter of Pliny to Trajan, and all the statements of the Fathers disclose to us the uniform continuance of preaching in the Church under its uninspired teachers. The sermons of the primitive pastors were rather expository than textual, usually founded on the portions of the Scripture read—inartificial, warm, and practical, seldom delivered from a manuscript, and often *extempore*.

---

[1] 1 Cor. i. 21.

As in the synagogue, so in the Christian assemblies, the duty was not confined to the bishops or pastors, but was performed, on their invitation, by the lower clergy, the catechists, and even by learned laymen. When Origen was filling Cæsarea with the fame of his sermons, he was only a lector and catechist.

As the Church gained members and worldly importance, and was able to migrate from the private chambers, where her early worship was held, to lordly temples and *basilicæ*, the style of preaching became more ambitious. The sacred orator, if a bishop, sat in the episcopal chair or throne while he spoke; or else upon the steps of the altar. The people meantime stood during the sermon; for the ancient churches were not furnished with seats. Pulpit eloquence was now cultivated with zeal; and many of the clergy acquired a distinguished fame as orators; among whom, as you know, Ambrose, Chrysostom, and Augustine stand foremost. If we may judge by the printed remains of the sermons of the last named, these Fathers held themselves free from a rule by which the moderns are sometimes mischievously constrained; they did not feel themselves bound to consume a fixed time in their discourses, but stopped when they had finished. Some of Augustine's discourses appear to have occupied six minutes, some sixty. There were still very few discourses read to the assemblies; but they were often written down as delivered, by stenographers; a custom which probably accounts for the existence of most patristic sermons now extant. The privilege of open applause was often claimed by the people, and not seldom granted by the preachers; and as religion became more ostentatious and corrupt, churches became scenes of gross disorder.

The approach of the Dark Ages was marked by a decline in preaching. By degrees the incapacity of the clergy led them to substitute homilies provided ready to their hand, for their own sermons; and then, to usurp the space before assigned to preaching, for the liturgies. Except when an epidemic excitement stirred some popular clerical demagogue to proclaim a crusade or a fast, the public worship included no sermon. Or if a more ambitious priest attempted to display his superiority by this exercise, his subject was superstitious, trivial, or even ludicrous; the vaunting of the virtues of a relic, the legend of his tutelar saint, the value of the indulgences sold by him, the terrors of purgatory, or the sin and danger of resisting Holy Church and her clergy. One famous preacher, of the age of Philip Augustus of France, exhausted his eloquence against the long points upon the fashionable shoes of the day. Another, of a previous age, debated the grave question whether the gold given by the Magi to the infant Saviour was coined or ingots. Another informed his audience of the edifying inquiry, with what weapon Cain slew his brother.

The great Reformation was emphatically a revival of gospel preaching. All the leading Reformers, whether in Germany, Switzerland, England, or Scotland, were constant preachers, and their sermons were prevalently expository. It is well known to you that Luther's commentary on Galatians, and many of the learned expositions of Calvin, were the fruits of their courses of exegetical sermons. We may assume with safety, that the instrumentality to which the spiritual power of that great revolution was mainly due, was the restoration of scriptural preaching. In the seventeenth century the Protestant churches of the continent witnessed another change in their pulpits. The preaching, instead of being evangelical, was prevalently polemical and technical, dealing rather in the exposition and defence of church symbols than of God's word. This innovation was soon followed by a decay in the piety of the age, from which the Lutheran churches were partially aroused by the Pietists. The English clergy and the Scotch, under the influence of Moderatism, lapsed into that method of preaching which justified the well-known sarcasm, that their texts were borrowed indeed from Paul, but their sermons from Seneca. Their ambition was to discuss ethics rather than Christianity, and with literary elegance rather than evangelical unction. The result was that benumbing flood of Socinianism, Deism, formality and vice which swept over the Church, until the Methodism of the eighteenth century arose to stay it.

You will not suppose, young gentlemen, that I intend this perfunctory sketch as an intrusion into the field of history. My purpose is only to recall to your minds such an outline of facts as will prepare you to understand the preacher's warrant and function. This review even will convince you that the state of the pulpit may always be taken as an index of that of the Church. Whenever the pulpit is evangelical, the piety of the people is in some degree healthy; a perversion of the pulpit is surely followed by spiritual apostasy in the Church. And it is exceedingly instructive to note, that there are three stages through which preaching has repeatedly passed with the same results. The first is that in which scriptural truth is faithfully presented in scriptural garb—that is to say, not only are all the doctrines asserted which truly belong to the revealed system of redemption, but they are presented in that dress and connection in which the Holy Spirit has presented them, without seeking any other from human science. This state of the pulpit marks the golden age of the Church. The second is the transition stage. In this the doctrines taught are still those of the Scriptures, but their relations are moulded into conformity with the prevalent human dialectics. God's truth is now shorn of a part of its power over the soul. The third stage is then near, in which not only are the methods and explanations conformed to the philosophy of the day, but the doctrines themselves contradict the truth of the Word. Again and again have the clergy traveled this descending scale, and always with the same disastrous result. The first grade is found in the primitive and in the Reformation churches of the first and the sixteenth centuries. The second grade may be seen in the scholasticism of Clement of Alexandria and his pupils, and in the symbolical discourses with which the continental pulpit echoed during the seventeenth century. The last is found in the Dark Ages and in Rationalism. This cycle is strikingly illustrated also by the history of the New Theology as it is completing itself in our day in America. When the Protestant churches of this country were founded, the ministry had not lost the Reformation impulse, and belonged to the first stage. The generation, unwittingly introduced by the great and good Jonathan Edwards,. marks the second; during which the doctrines of grace were not openly impugned, but they were successively stretched into the schemes of metaphysics—the "exercise scheme," the "light scheme," the "greatest benevolence scheme"—which fascinated a people of narrow and partial culture and self-confident temper. The next generation was called to witness the apostasy which turned the truth of God into a lie, and took both the methods and the dogmas of the Socinian and the Pelagian. Let us, my brethren, eschew the ill-starred ambition which seeks to make the body of God's truth a "lay figure" on which to parade the drapery of human philosophy. May we ever be content to exhibit Bible doctrine in its own Bible dress!

LECTURE II.

THE PREACHER'S COMMISSION.

SACRED RHETORIC is one branch of eloquence. It is of prime importance that the student should apprehend, first, what eloquence truly is, and, second, what is the difference between the secular department of it and ours. Eloquence is often named as one of the fine arts, but, as I have already forewarned you, there is an essential distinction made by the ends of the two. Music and the imitative arts are designed, primarily, to gratify the taste. Their immediate aim is at the sentimental affections of the soul. But the immediate end of eloquence is to produce in the hearer some practical volition. Its design is to evoke an act. When this is said, you will not understand me as indicating by the word action only the movement of the body and its members. I speak of the actions of the soul, of those matured determinations of the will in which man's rational and responsible activity consummates itself. And, I repeat, that wherever there is no direct purpose in the speaker to educe action of will in his hearers there is no proper oration.[1] True, the oration

---

[1] For instance, Aristotle (b. I., ch. 3) incorrectly classes orations under three *genera:* of the Statesman, of the Advocate, and of the Eulogist. The object of the first is always to cause the election or rejection of a given course of action. That of the second is to pro-

may, while it determines the soul to action, produce as a collateral effect much excitement of taste. But if it elevates this subordinate result into the place of its chief design, it has degenerated into a spurious poem without metre. So, a poem, and especially a lyric like the Marseillaise Hymn, may be addressed to the will, but in this it ceases to be mere poetry, and becomes a true metrical oration. The essay is directed to still another object, the elucidation and establishment of truth to the reason. It aims to propagate only opinion and not action.

Let me now recall your doctrines of ethics and psychology, so far as to gain the answer to this question, How is the soul determined to volition? You know that it is not by the sensibility alone, nor by the logical discernment alone. Volition is not a conclusion of any separate faculty of the soul, but of the soul itself, involving all its powers, whether active or passive, whether of cognition, sensibility or desire. The previous states of soul which have to volition the relation of cause to immediate effect are always complex, being both processes of intellection and appetency. Whence, it is manifest, eloquence deals with the hearer's soul through all its powers. But it is far more important to say that eloquence operates through all the powers of the speaker's soul likewise. Not only must the ora-

cure a verdict of acquittal or condemnation. That of the third, not so obviously active, is really so, for it aims to gain a moral verdict by which the hearer adopts the subject as his approved model of virtue. Aristotle knew nothing of our nobler department, that of evangelical eloquence. We may more clearly decide of this, that its end is always action of soul in the hearer, repentance, faith, or some other duty.

tor's reason perform the processes of perception and logic, his heart must be powerfully actuated by those processes of emotion which he seeks to propagate, his taste must thrill with those affections of sentiment which he would make ancillary to his main effect, and his will must go forth vehemently to that act to which he would decide the hearer. The last assertion is perhaps the most important of the four just made. For the power of the orator over his hearer is far more than intellectual, it is more than sentimental, it projects the force of his volition through these other powers upon the will of his hearer. And there is a sympathy of soul between man and his fellows, by which each power of the one operates upon the corresponding powers of the others; not, of course, without the *medium* of cognition, yet with its own proper force. Especially is this true of the will. How often do we see men swayed by the mere strength of a vigorous will in another beyond the legitimate influence of his logic?

I would, then, define eloquence as *the emission of the soul's energy through speech*. This view of its nature, as you perceive, justifies the judgment, that it is one of the finest exercises of the human faculties.

But that it may be worthy of the name of eloquence, it must have one more trait: the purpose of propagating in the soul a volition morally excellent. If you have understood my definitions and explanations, you are convinced that the powers of soul employed by the orator are even more the moral than the intellectual. If, therefore, he wrests these, which are the peculiar domain of conscience, to resist conscience, he is guilty of the most glaring perversion of the art. His spurious

is related to the true eloquence, as vice is related to virtue. For when man perpetrates a wicked act, he exercises the active powers of the soul, desire and choice,
which put themselves forth in the right act. The whole
difference is in their opposite direction to a vicious instead of a virtuous end. Artifices of persuasion, skill-
fully used to cause one to will amiss, have no more
claim to be true eloquence, because they are similar to
the means of the proper art, than evil volitions have to
be considered virtuous energy, because they are also exercises of man's spontaneity. I urge, moreover, that all
vice is a weakness of his nature. The perverted activities of the soul are depraved in energy as well as in moral quality. Hence, the man of wicked ends will never
exhibit the same power of soul, with the righteous man
of the same native force. But the crowning reason is,
that conscience herself is the mightiest power in man,
and the moral affections are not only the purest but the
most profound of all. The speaker, whose end is to
persuade men to violate their conscience, is therefore
not only enfeebled in the main forces of his own nature;
but he must act without, yea against, those forces in the
souls he would move. Thus I trace the true rhetorical
power to its source in a noble purpose. There must be
clear intellection, vivid sensibility, ardent emotion, vehement will; but chiefest of all, must be the virtuous
end. Well did Theremin speak in propounding as his
theorem, " Eloquence is a virtue."

Having found true eloquence to be the soul's virtuous
energy exerted through speech, I would remind you
that the sermon is a peculiar species of eloquence.
Like all other eloquence, it aims always to produce a

definite, practical volition in the hearer. This aim is, in the best sense, a worthy one; for the acts it evokes are the spiritual. But its peculiarity is chiefly this, that it applies to the will, the authority of God, the only Lord of the conscience. This alone, I repeat, makes the gospel discourse. Other orators bring to bear upon the understandings of their hearers the force of human testimony and natural reason; they apply to their hearts legitimate secular and moral inducements. The preacher relies alone upon evangelical inducements, and refers every conviction of the reason ultimately to God's testimony. I elaborate this all-important distinction carefully; perhaps my reasons for it are difficult to grasp, because of their simplicity. The end, I repeat, of every oration is *to make men do*. But the things which the sermon would make men do, are only the things of God. Therefore it must apply to them the authority of God. If your discourse urges the hearer merely with excellent reasons and inducements, natural, ethical, social, legal, political, self-interested, philanthropic, if it does not end by bringing their wills under the direct grasp of a " thus saith the Lord," it is not a sermon; it has degenerated into a speech.[1]

Were it necessary, young gentlemen, I would even beseech you to master these definitions of what eloquence is, and of what the sermon is. Fix them firmly in your minds, as the foundations of successful study in this course. As we proceed, you will meet many confirmations of their justice, and I trust that when we are done, you will think with me of them. One great dif-

---

[1] 1 Thess. ii. 13.

ficulty of the young preacher is caused by confusion of thought, upon the precise nature and aim of the sermon. Such was the testimony of Dr. Baxter's experience. If the true conception of preaching is that high and sacred one which I have presented, how inexpressibly does he enervate its proper force, who.confounds it with the moral oration!

The last subject of remark has introduced us to the fundamental question, What is the preacher's scriptural position and warrant? You will perceive a necessary connection between my theory here, and the theological system of the Protestant churches. It is our doctrine that "the Bible alone is the religion of Protestants." We eschew all "will-worship" as forbidden and mischievous. We admit no title to do anything as a part of the public, religious service of God, except those things which He hath appointed in his word. Hence, unless we can find such warrant for preaching, as an instituted part of divine service, we dare not introduce it. We hold likewise that "unto this catholic visible Church, Christ hath given the ministry, oracles, and ordinances of God, for the gathering and perfecting of the saints, in this life, to the end of the world."[1] It is also the creed of Protestants, as of the Bible, that this book is "all given by inspiration of God," and is our divine and supreme rule of faith and life. "The whole counsel of God concerning all things necessary . . . . for man's salvation, faith and life, is either expressly set down in Scripture, or by good and necessary consequence may be deduced from Scripture; unto

---

[1] Conf. of Faith, ch. xxv. § 3.

which nothing at any time is to be added."[1]   But this
word is only made effectual to the calling and sanctification of any rational adults, by the almighty inworking of God's Holy Spirit.[2]

For the warrant, then, of our office as preachers, we
point first to the example and precedent of the scriptural Church—teachers of both Testaments, and especially to the apostolic.   This precedent, being set, and
uniformly imitated, by divine authority, is to us of the
force of a command.   Next, we point to the express
precepts of our Saviour; " As ye go, preach ;"[3] and of
the Apostle: " Preach the word; be instant, in season,
out of season ; reprove, rebuke, exhort, with all long-
suffering and doctrine."[4]

The nature of the preacher's work is determined by
the word employed to describe it by the Holy Ghost.
The preacher is a herald ;[5] his work is heralding the
King's message.   Once, the apostles call themselves
Christ's ambassadors ; but of old, ambassadors were no
other than heralds.   Now the herald does not invent his
message; he merely transmits and explains it.   It is
not his to criticise its wisdom or fitness ; this belongs to
his sovereign alone.   On the one hand, he does not
carry it as a mere implement of sound, a trumpet or a
drum; he is an intelligent *medium* of communication
with the king's enemies; he has brains as well as a
tongue ; and he is expected so to deliver and explain
his master's mind, that the other party shall receive not
only the mechanical sounds, but the true meaning of the

---

[1] Conf. of Faith, ch. i. §§ 2, 6.   [2] Ibid., ch. x.

[3] Matt. x. 7 ; Luke x. 1 ; Acts x. 42.   [4] 2 Tim. ii. 2; iv. 2.

[5] Κηρυξ, κηρυσσειν, passim.   Υπερ Χριστου πρεσβευομεν. 2 Cor. v. 20.

message. On the other hand, it wholly transcends his office to presume to correct the tenour of the propositions he conveys, by either additions or change. These are the words of God's commission to an ancient preacher: "Arise; go unto Nineveh, that great city, and preach unto it the preaching that I bid thee."

The preacher's task may be correctly explained as that of (instrumentally) forming the image of Christ upon the souls of men. The plastic substance is the human heart. The die which is provided for the workman is the revealed Word; and the impression to be formed is the divine image of knowledge and true holiness. God, who made the soul, and therefore knows it, made the die. He obviously knew best how to shape it, in order to produce the imprint he desired. Now the workman's business is not to criticise, recarve, or erase anything in the die which was committed to him; but simply to press it down faithfully upon the substance to be impressed, observing the conditions of the work assigned him in his instructions. In this view, how plain is it, that preaching should be simply representative of Bible truths, and in Bible proportions! The preacher's business is to take what is given him in the Scriptures, as it is given to him, and to endeavour to imprint it on the souls of men. All else is God's work. The die is just such, so large, so sharp, so hard, and has just such an "image and superscription" on it, as God would have. Thus He judged, in giving it to us. With this, "the man of God is perfect, thoroughly furnished unto all good works."[1] This is enough for us.

---

[1] 2 Tim. iii. 17.

Here we have plain truths which no evangelical believer will dare dispute. But if I am not mistaken, they contain deductions adverse to some things in the practice of professed Protestant ministers. For instance, not only must Bible topics form the whole matter of our preaching, but they must be presented in scriptural aspects and proportions. The Bible was made to be the food of the people; it is not a raw material which the religious philosopher is to digest into new forms before they can assimilate it. This book is not like that of creation, a mixed mass of the ore of knowledge, which must be reduced by science before it can be applied to the uses of life. It is the great principle of Protestants that the Bible is for the people. And this implies that God, who knew best, has not only set forth such truths, but in such proportions and relations as really suit man's soul under the dealings of the Holy Spirit. There can be no other connections and forms of the truth so suitable as these, for these are they which God has seen fit to give. We may be guilty then of infidelity to our task, though we be not heterodox. We may preach only truths, and yet from an overweening temper make some truths relatively more prominent and others more retired than the Bible does. Our preaching must in this regard be conformed to the "proportion of faith."[1]

But there are many who shrink with fear from what they regard as so confined a walk of ministerial instruction. They think it necessary to take a more ample range in preaching than simply showing the people

---

[1] Rom. xii. 6.

what the Bible means, and imprinting that meaning on their souls. The secret feeling is: "This would not allow variety and interest enough. There would not be verge enough for the preacher to display his own powers. This is a business too simple and plodding for your profound theological philosopher. There is not mental *pabulum* enough for the intellects of enlightened hearers." So, in some pulpits, we have grandiloquent expositions of the "moral system of the universe." In others the Sabbaths of the people are wholly occupied with those polemics by which the outworks of Christianity should be defended against the foreign assaults of infidel philosophy; as though one would feed the flock within the fold with the bristling missiles which should have been hurled against the wolves without. Others deal in scholastic discussions of the propositions of church-symbols, cleaving the "bare bones of their orthodoxy" into splinters as angular and dry as the gravel of the desert. Others again offer metaphysical discussions of the psychology of religion, as though they would feed the babes of Christ with a sort of chemical resolution of the sincere milk of the Word into its ultimate elements, instead of the living, concrete nourishment provided for them by their Saviour. Now what is this but the very spirit of unbelief and self-seeking? The selection of such forms of truth is evidently not guided by the lowly, self-devoted spirit of the "servant" of the Church, but by a single eye to self-display. God puts the "sword of the Spirit" into this man's hand, and tells him that with this he shall conquer. He distrusts it, he will add something more trenchant. God tells him that the "Word is quick and

powerful, and sharper than any two-edged sword, piercing even to the dividing asunder of the soul and spirit,
and of the joints and marrow, and is a discerner of the
thoughts and intents of the heart."[1] "No," says the
unbelieving servant, "I can devise truths more piercing." These, my brethren, are not the men to do the
work of that God who "hath chosen the foolish things
of the world to confound the wise." Theirs is the
spirit of infidelity, and their preaching breeds infidelity.

I have explained to you what the true end of the
sermon is, what eloquence is, and by what means the
orator reaches that end. I wish you to infer hence this
most momentous of all conclusions, that the prime
qualification of the sacred orator is sincere, eminent
piety. Consider: nothing is an oration which does
not directly move the hearer to act. The main action
urged in every sermon is to believe and be saved. Eloquence we saw is the emission through speech of all the
soul's virtuous energies, of thought, of sensibility, and
especially of will. Now, unless the preacher's will is
ardently directed toward this end, the salvation of the
hearer, the main element of his power is lacking. But
what is this direction of the will, save love for souls?
And this is pre-eminently the spirit of Christ.

The scriptural doctrine of the preacher's mission and
warrant also decides at once against an abuse of the
pulpit, to which the clergy have always been prone. It
may be named with sufficient accuracy by the popular
phrase, "political preaching." Romanists hold a theory

---

[1] Heb. iv. 12.

of church power which if correct, would legitimate the practice. Although it is inconsistent with the principles of Protestants, they have since the Reformation been frequently seduced into it by a sophism. The prevalence of this error requires, therefore, that we consider it in this connection. Its tendency has always been, whether among Romanists or Protestants, to degrade the position and character of the clergy, to embitter party spirit, to provoke bloodshed, and to corrupt the hearts of the hearers. The reasons of these results are not difficult to find.

It was remarked (in substance) by Burke, that when parsons meddle publicly with state affairs they usually show nothing of the politician but his rancour. This charge is true. It is explained in part by the fact that clergymen are accustomed to deference and unused to contradiction, and in part, by their habit of urging the opinions they espouse from a conscientious point of view. They become accustomed to sanctifying their creeds in their own eyes, and regarding their quarrel as God's. Thus their very animosities become holy in their view.

The appropriate mission of the minister is to preach the gospel for the salvation of souls. The servant who by diverging into some other project not especially enjoined on him, nor essential for him to perform, precludes himself from his allotted task, is clearly guilty of disobedience to his master, if not of treason to his charge. Now, questions of politics must ever divide the minds of men; for they are not decided by any recognized standards of truth, but by the competitions of interest and passion. Hence, it is inevitable that he who embarks publicly in the discussion of these questions, must become the object of party animosities and obnoxious to those whom he opposes. How then can he successfully approach them as the messenger of redemption? By thus transcending his proper functions, he criminally prejudices his appointed work with half the community, for the whole of which he should affectionately labour.

God has reserved for our spiritual concerns one day from seven, and has appointed one place into which nothing shall enter, except the things of eternity, and has ordained an order of officers, whose sole charge is to remind their fellow-men of their duty to God. Surely, it is a tribute small enough to pay the transcendent weight of eternal things, to reserve the season and the place sacredly to them, which God has set apart for them. This surely is not too much for resisting the tendencies of man toward the sensuous and toward forgetfulness of the spiritual life. But when the world sees a portion or the whole of this sacred season abstracted from spiritual concerns, and given to secular agitations, and that by the appointed guardians of sacred things, it is the most emphatic possible disclosure of unbelief. It says to men, "Eternity is not of more moment than time; heaven is not better than earth; a man is profited if he gains the world and loses his soul, for do you not see that we postpone eternity to time, and heaven to earth, and redemption to political triumph—we who are the professed guardians of the former?" One great source, therefore, of political preaching may always be found in the practical unbelief of the preacher himself; as one of its sure fruits is infidelity among the people. He is not feeling the worth of souls, nor the " powers of the world to come," nor " the constraining love of Christ " as he should; if he were, no sense of the temporal importance of his favorite political measures, however urgent, would cause the wish to abstract an hour from the few allowed him for saving souls. We solemnly protest to every minister who feels the impulse to introduce the secular into his pulpit, that he thereby betrays a decadent faith and spiritual life in his own breast. Let him take care! He · is taking the first steps toward backsliding, apostasy, damnation.

Another motive which prompts ministers of the Gospel to preach politics is usually to be thus explained: The topics of redemption are dry and repulsive to the great world; and especially, when the public mind is absorbed by agitating questions of social interest. Hence, the minister's self-love and vanity feel the itching to enjoy some of the *éclat* of the exciting discussion; to see his ideas reflected from the faces of sympathizing crowds, and to hear the applause of approving supporters. This, to the carnal mind, is much more attractive and easy, than the holy, but difficult task, of recalling the hearts jaded and debauched by the engrossing passions of the world, to peaceful and heavenly themes. If the political preacher will candidly examine his own breast, he will surely detect this unworthy and pitiful motive, under his zeal for social reform.

This abuse of the pulpit tends directly to produce in the hearers, uncharitableness, spiritual pride, censoriousness, animosity, contempt of opponents, and violence, instead of humility, penitence, holy love, and holy liv-

ing. Your political parson is only such, when he has
an approving party to address; and usually it is the
majority in his own charge. This is accounted for by
the remarks just made. Moreover, when he sets out
on his crusade of social reform, it is always against the
sins or errors of some people to whom his approving
clique are opposed, that he bears his Pythonic testimony. To be eloquent against the social heresies or
crimes of his own party would not exactly answer the
purposes of his self-love. Thus, the amount of his
Sunday-ministrations is to invite the hearts of his hearers to the consideration of their neighbours' sins and not
their own. On the contrary, everything tends to suggest their own superior virtue and orthodoxy. Their
vain glory is pleasantly stimulated by the comparison;
and their hearts gratified with the luxury of self-righteous hatred and carping, instead of being summoned to
those irksome, impertinent, old-fashioned exercises, self-
examination and repentance. Whereas the Gospel in-
sulates each sinner, directs his eyes within, to his own
sins, reminds him of his own solemn responsibility, calls
him to contrition and self-reformation, and ever says to
him, " Thou art the man," this religion of party strife
diverts men's eyes from their own faults, (by sorrowing
for which their hearts might be made better,) to the
faults of others, by gloating over which they become
full of all uncharitableness, pride, and hatred. Thus,
the result of such a perversion of the pulpit is, uniformly, an outburst of corruption in the bosom of the
nominal Christianity which is cursed by it. The tendency of the human heart is ever to the worse; there is
no wonder that when the appointed restraints of Gos-

pel truth are withdrawn, and this ministration of pride and spite is applied at the same time, the progress in depravity should be frightfully rapid. Witness the effect on public morals of the preaching of the crusades against the Albigenses, of the Romish clergy in France during the *Ligue*, of the Puritans in England against the Royalists, of the radical clergy of this country against the Union and the Constitution.

Weak defences of this abuse have been attempted. It is asked, "Is not the minister also a citizen?" The answer is: "He is a citizen only at the hustings, and on a secular day. In the pulpit he is only the ambassador of Christ." It is urged again, that Peter, Paul, and the Lord Jesus Christ, taught political duties. We reply: Would that these pests of modern Christianity had truly imitated them; had taken not only their texts, but their discourses from them, instead of deriving the latter from the newspapers. Let them do as the sacred writers do: teach the duties of allegiance from the Christian side and motive only, "that the word of God and his Gospel be not blasphemed." Another plea is, that Christianity is designed to produce important collateral results on the social order of nations; as that social order reacts on Christianity. The answer is twofold: that these secular results are the minor, the eternal redemption of souls is the chief end of God in his Gospel. He is a criminal servant who wilfully sacrifices the less to the greater. Second, the only innocent way (as the most efficient) in which the minister of religion can further these secular results, is so to preach each man's own sins and redemption to him as to make him personally a holy man. When society is thus purified, by cleansing the integral individuals who compose it, then, and then only, will the social corruptions of commonwealths be effectually purged away.

If the example of Christ and his apostles were correctly weighed, it would be a sufficient guide to all other ministers. They lived in a time of intense party agitation. The Jewish commonwealth was then divided by a question, the most momentous that could fire the heart of a nation—whether their divinely-ordained constitution was compatible with their subjugation by a Pagan empire? This question was everywhere hotly debated; it was rapidly growing into that war which a generation later brought the end of the Hebrew commonwealth. We know that neither Jesus nor Paul was insensible to patriotism. The former wept over the approaching ruin of his country; the latter declared himself ready to die for his compatriots; yet, such is their reserve on the question in their religious teachings, that the unlearned reader of the New Testament is left in actual ignorance of its existence, except that once it is forced upon our Saviour's attention by a direct inquiry. And then so small does this great secular interest appear beside the eternal errand which he came to subserve, he devotes only a part of one sentence to the former, reverting even before he ends it to the more absorbing concerns of the soul.[1] Let his ministers imitate him.

The experience of the Church sustains this plea for the exclusive preaching of redemption. The pomps of a liturgical drama may attract occasional crowds to

---

[1] Matt. xxii. 16–21.

the cathedral of the ritualist. Party rage may for a
time cause the multitude to throng the steps of the
clerical demagogue; yet the permanent hold upon the
popular mind and heart is possessed by the evangelical
preacher. Sooner or later, the mere moralist, the Socinian, the political preacher, the philosophizer, the
choir of ghostly pantomimists, are all seen performing
to empty benches, while from age to age the multitude
of Christians surrounds those who preach "Christ and
him crucified." May not even we perceive a reason
for this? The conceit and self-love of the natural
mind persuade the would-be pulpit philosopher that his
newly-coined ideas are wondrously attractive, because
they are the bantlings of his own invention. Perhaps
he is not fully aware of his own motive, but it is his
intellectual vanity which selects them as his clerical
hobbies. Now he forgets a very simple fact, that his
hearers have toward these favourite topics not a particle
of his pride of paternity. They are thoroughly conscious that they did not beget them; that they are the
preacher's only. Hence he is perpetually disappointed
by finding that he cannot sustain the enthusiasm of the
people for his favourite topics. He never wearies of
them; his hearers do. But God's topics, the fall, the
curse, sin, death, immortality, duty, redemption, faith,
hope, judgment, hell, heaven, these transcendent subjects have an abiding, an overmastering common interest. All men share it, because they are men. These
assert their power over the human soul under every
condition, and in spite of man's natural carnality, with
a force akin to their vastness. Honour God then, my
young brethren, by urging no other truths than those

he has given you, urging them with disinterested fidelity, and he will honour your ministry.

In conclusion, few words are needed to show that this peculiar mission of the preacher will dictate a method of its own which will differ from that of the secular orator. It will communicate a peculiar earnestness, tenderness and authority. Its influence will extend to the structure, the style, the utterance and the gesture, making · all more serious, more paternal, more elevated than they are in him who pleads the affairs of earth.

LECTURE III.

DISTRIBUTION OF SUBJECTS.

RHETORIC or the science of the orator has been tritely called *the art of persuasion*. Its usual distribution has been into the three parts of *Invention, Disposition,* and *Elocution*.[1] The last word, you must know, is taken here in a sense much wider than our popular usage gives to it, including the whole subjects of diction and style. The first two parts, then, treat of the matter of the discourse. The last discusses everything pertaining to the verbal *medium,* by which this matter is conveyed to the hearer's mind. Invention discovers and selects this matter. Disposition arranges it in its proper place. Upon this classification there are two obvious remarks. One is, that to the sacred orator, the work of invention cannot be what it is to the secu-

---

[1] Cicero de Orat. Lib. II. c. 19, § 79 : Denique quinque faciunt quasi membra eloquentiæ, invenire quid dicas, inventa disponere, deinde ornare verbis, post memoriæ mandare, tum ad extremum agere ac pronuntiare. See also Lib. I. c. 31, § 142.

Quinctilian, L. III. c. 3, § 1 : Omnis autem orandi ratio, ut plurimi maximique auctores tradiderunt, quinque partibus constat, inventione, dispositione, elocutione, memoria, pronunciatione sive actione.

The moderns, against the protest of Quinctilian, reduce the division to the first three, including the pronunciation, under elocution, and treat the memorizing as rather an instrument than a constituent part of rhetoric.

lar, because, as has been shown above, the whole matter which we are to handle is given to us by the Scriptures. If we restrict invention to selection, still the principles of systematic and pastoral theology rather than rhetoric, will be, in this, the student's guide. The other remark is that made by *Vinet*, that invention is a work not confined to the matter. The method, the style, the diction, the gesticulation, all must be invented. His meaning is not that they may be artificial; but that they must, in order to be appropriate, be discovered and selected by the same exertions of the mind which give the speaker his thoughts. You will not find me, then, attempting to impose this distribution, throughout, upon the body of this course. Several of the subjects, which we shall next consider together, may be regarded as falling partially under the head of invention. The other two divisions, disposition and elocution, we can more accurately apply.

It is now necessary to undertake a question of classification of a different sort. It is this: Are there more species of sermons than one? And if so, what are they? One answer divides them, according to the extent of the passage of Scripture upon which they are founded, into topical and expository; another, according to their matter, into doctrinal, practical, and narrative. Let us consider the latter classification first.

By a doctrinal sermon is not intended one of those peculiar discussions so named in the popular phrase of the last generation, where the points which distinguish Calvinism from the lower systems of theology, and especially the points of predestination, were discussed. But we intend the treatment of all the doctrines which make up the system of revealed theology, not exclusive of those just named. Doctrinal preaching is that which aims to instruct the people methodically in the truths of the Gospel. It should also be distinguished from "theological preaching." In the latter, the strict methods of science rather than the claims of rhetoric prevail. Analysis and abstraction are freely employed, in disregard of the difficulty and even of the repulsiveness of the discussion. The object is neither the pleasure of taste nor the immediate movement of the will, but the exact ascertainment of truth by the understanding. Theological teaching, therefore, properly requires of its pupils laborious attention, and demands the effort to grasp what may be abstruse. It seeks to be logical and exhaustive of its subject. Manifestly this method can rarely be appropriate to the pulpit, because the multitude to be instructed there do not think abstractly, but delight in the concrete; because they are unaccustomed to scientific rigour; because truth dressed in this form will be unintelligible and repulsive to them. President Dwight is said to have delivered his work in sermons (expositions of the plainer doctrines and reasonings of theology) to his students. Dr. Ashbell Green prepared his lectures on the Shorter Catechism for the advanced catechumens of his charge, educated young persons. Unless you have a peculiar and select audience like these, you will not often attempt theological sermons. Your doctrinal teachings should be science made popular. They will set forth some theses of your theology; they will, of course, not be deficient in sound logic; they will address themselves with masculine strength to the understandings of your hearers : systematic divinity will inform and enrich them from its stores. But its form will be popular, and in the concrete, rather than abstractly scientific. And you will consult that plainness of argument and paucity of separate points suitable to those who only listen to the fleeting words, instead of poring over the permanent page. It may be supposed, at the first glance, that if it is of the essence of the oration to aim at a practical movement of the will, this instructiveness of the doctrinal sermon is inconsistent with the rhetorical treatment. The reply is, first, that we have not asserted the pastor must always be expressly the orator, or that every discourse must needs be a true oration. His teaching may sometimes properly be homiletic rather than rhetorical. But second, the good doctrinal sermon will usually have a rhetorical character, because it will be applied in the close to a practical result. It is the duty of the preacher so to establish the dogmas of the faith in the understandings of the people, that they shall not remain abstract dogmas, but shall reveal their close bearing upon the life. It was a golden maxim of the Protestant fathers, that "doctrines must be preached practically and duties doctrinally."

The reasons for doctrinal preaching thus defined, may be all traced to the principle that truth is in order to godliness. Sanctification is by the truth. Man is a reasoning creature, and the word and Spirit of God deal with him in conformity with this rational nature. All those emotions and volitions, which have right moral character, are prompted in man by intelligent motives. To say that one has no reason for his volitions, is to describe them as either criminal or merely animal. In the things of God man only feels as he sees, and because he sees with his mind. A moment's consideration of these obvious facts will convince you that there cannot be, in the nature of the case, any other instrumentality to be used by creatures for inculcating religion and procuring right feeling and action, than that which begins by informing the understanding. The truth, as seen in the light of evidence, is the only possible object of rational emotions. From this point of view, we easily understand how unreasonable are the notions and demands of those good people who decry didactic preaching. "Such discourses," they say, "are dry and repulsive. They give us merely theology in its bare bones. They inflate the head with conceit without warming the heart. The aim of Christianity is but to make men feel and act aright. Let the preacher then aim directly at the heart, producing right feeling, and all will be accomplished." Now, I might assent to the latter statements, and yet raise the question, How shall the heart be reached, except through the head? How can a rational creature be made to feel intelligently, unless we cause his reason to apprehend that which may be the object of rational feeling? If any affection is produced otherwise, it must be merely animal or else evil. Heat without light is blind, as light without heat is cold. The Sun of Righteousness, like the natural luminary, becomes the fountain of life in his appropriate realm by giving heat through light. To the objection that didactic preaching is dry, I answer, that if it ever seems to be so, this is the fault of the preacher and not of the truth. If his attempted development of doctrine be confused, illogical, iterative, tedious; if the didactic unfolding of truth be perversely severed from the practical results, he may not be surprised to find that he (not his subject) is dull. But so far is didactic instruction from being dry, I assert nothing else is interesting to a reasonable nature. My meaning is, that the skilful inculcation of truth enlists the attention without fail, for this is insured by the mind's instinctive appetite for knowledge. And, moreover, no rational emotion can excite the heart, except as its power is grounded in some express or implied truth seen by the mind. The truth which generates the feeling may be very plain or obvious; it may be implied, and not expressly obtruded. Yet, had there been no successful didactic agency, there would have been no influence upon the feelings. It may also be retorted that if many unskilful didactic attempts are dull, nothing is ever witnessed more drearily wearisome than many a hortatory appeal grounded in no intelligent display of truth, which professes to carry out the theory I have exposed.

Referring to the other part of that theory which professes to find the sole practical end of preaching in right action, I find another forcible argument for doctrinal preaching. Is it said, " Now are we Christ's friends, if we do whatsoever he commandeth"? I reply by the question, How can a rational creature so do, as to please a spiritual God, without comprehending a reason for his obedience? Man is a moral creature only as he is a rational one. The moral motive must be intelligent, or it is naught. Unless a ground of obligation is apprehended by the reason, conscience is untouched, and the action which man takes is either that of moral indifferency, or of animal instinct, or it is criminal. Hence it follows that doctrinal instruction is as rudimental to all right action as to right feeling.

The result of all this is, that no people can be formed into stable, consistent and righteous Christians without much doctrinal instruction. My argument is reinforced by the example of Christ and his apostles. These inspired preachers are eminently doctrinal; in other words, they are full of explanations of, and evidences for, the great truths and facts which make up the Christian system. They give us an illustrious example of the method of dealing with the human soul, by always grounding their appeals to the heart upon appeals to the mind. The preacher may amuse the curiosity of his hearers with human speculations; he may excite by the scintillations of his rhetoric, but if he has not instructed them in divine truth, he has done nothing. A permanent religious effect is impossible.

In concluding this subject, let me add a word touching the extent of this doctrinal instruction. Shall it embrace all the doctrines of the Scriptures, popular and unpopular? And what discretion shall the pastor allow himself in avoiding collisions with the prejudices of his hearers? He must not keep back any revealed truth. The Scriptures leave no room for question here. The preacher must be able to take his charge to witness with the apostle[1] that "he is pure from the blood of all men, for he has not shunned to declare unto them all the counsel of God." "All Scripture is given by inspiration of God, and is profitable for doctrine."[2] Indeed,

---

[1] Acts xx. 26, 27. [2] 2 Tim. iii. 16.

this conclusion follows directly from the nature of the preacher's commission. But, on the other hand, the pastor should be "a scribe instructed unto the kingdom of heaven, who is like unto a man that is a householder which bringeth forth out of his treasure things new and old."[1] The apostle, although the most faithful of men, "fed some with milk, and not with strong meat, for hitherto they were not able to bear it."[2] Candour will never permit the true minister to disclaim any doctrine taught by the Bible, when he is directly required either to avow it or to deny. Candour will ensure his inculcation of the whole circle of revealed truths in scriptural relations and proportions. Yet he will study so to connect the disputed with the admitted, and to proceed from the known to the unknown, as to obviate all unnecessary prejudice and secure the happiest ingress for the truth. For doing this, he can find no rule so safe as to follow the Scripture models in the space and prominence allotted to different truths, and the connections in which they are introduced. You will not expect here a more particular enumeration of the heads of divinity which require frequent and ample display. This you will be taught rather by your systematic and pastoral theology; the former shows you which are the cardinal doctrines of our faith, and the latter informs you of the peculiar need for their repetition arising from man's native perversity of mind.

The second class of sermons is the practical, or ethical. By this term are intended those discourses which discuss the duties of the Christian life toward God and

---

[1] Matt. xiii. 52.   [2] 1 Cor. iii. 2.

toward man; with their nature, limits, obligations, and motives. These topics should abound in the preaching of every pastor. You will not understand me as recommending, here, the inculcation of a religion of self-righteous works. I would have you preach the duties of the law, not that men may learn to expect their salvation from them, but that they may know they cannot be saved by them. It is because "the law is our schoolmaster to bring us unto Christ;"[1] because "I had not known sin but by the law."[2] "For without the law, sin is dead." Men are "alive without the law; but when the commandment comes, sin revives, and they die." The whole policy of the pastor's instructions is contained, in germ, in that saying of Christ: "They that be whole need not a physician; but they that be sick." That men may heartily embrace the gospel, the essential point is to make them know and feel their radical disease. This you will not teach them effectually by mere general announcements of depravity and the fall. When the claims of the law are brought to their souls, when they are made to see perspicuously what is their extent, and that they are reasonable, when they become conscious of their own innate and fundamental enmity to those just demands, and bondage to evil desires; and when they hear the wrath denounced by God against every transgression; then there is hope that they will find themselves truly lost, and will cry to the Deliverer for rescue.

But, second: the practical definition of Christianity has been fully accepted by us. Its end and aim is holy

---

[1] Gal. iii. 24.   [2] Rom. vii. 7.

living.[1] Of this holy life, the law of God is the rule.
The believer justified in Christ does not, indeed, look
to the law for his redeeming merit; but he receives it
as his guide to the obedience of faith and love, as fully
as though he were still under a covenant of works. He
therefore needs practical instruction, as really as the unbeliever. It must stimulate and direct him in the
Christian race, and make him a " peculiar person, zealous
of good works." The exclusive preaching of doctrine
to professed Christians tends to cultivate an Antinomian
Spirit. The exclusive inculcation of duties fosters self-
righteousness. The edification of the Church, then, demands the diligent intermixture of both kinds. This
precept may be confirmed by the remark, that, as the
motives and obligations of all duties are rooted in the
doctrines, so the best illustrations of the doctrines are
by their application to the duties. The two are inseparably connected as grounds and conclusions, as means
and end; and their systematic separation in your instructions would leave your hearers incapable of a correct understanding of either.

But the crowning argument is again the precedent set
us by Christ and his apostles. While they were, as has
been remarked, doctrinal, they were eminently practical
preachers. Nothing can be more instructive than the
manner in which the Epistles to the Romans, the Galatians, the Ephesians, the Colossians, and the Hebrews
proceed. In their introductory chapters, they lay a
solid foundation of argument and testimony for some
cardinal doctrines of·redemption; and from these, they

---

[1] Eph. i. 4; Titus ii. 14, *et passim.*

glide into the enforcement of duties by a beautiful transition. The pastor has here models given by inspiration, and obviously conformed to the nature of man as a reasonable and moral creature.

Some important observations remain, touching the mode in which the law should be preached. "We know that the law is spiritual, but we are carnal, sold under sin." [1] The apostle tells us that he had not been made aware of his own concupiscence, except the law had said, "Thou shalt not covet." It is imperative, therefore, that you so unfold the law of God, as to exhibit its searching requirements of right thoughts and feelings, as well as right actions of the bodily members "As a man thinketh in his heart, so is he." "From within, out of the heart of man, proceed evil thoughts, adulteries, fornications, murders." The disease of sin is never so probed as to lead the sufferer in earnest to the Great Physician, until the seat of the evil is revealed in the heart itself. And it is chiefly by disclosing the spirituality of the law, that we affect the convicted soul with a suitable apprehension of the breadth of the law, of his own enmity and inability, and of the infinite holiness of its Author, at once.

Next, let the claims of the law be always enforced, not as moral observances only, but as evangelical duties. If you suppose that, by calling this class of sermons the ethical, I designed to recommend your founding your appeals to men's consciences on the fitness of things, on the natural claims and advantages of virtue, I have been much misunderstood. It is only the morality of

---

[1] Rom. vii. 7, 14.

the cross which the Christian pastor should teach. It
will not be amiss, indeed, for him to show, transiently,
how completely the best teachings of natural morality
are at one with those of the gospel. But his chief
motives should always be drawn from the latter. Let
him inculcate virtue, not like a Seneca, but like a Paul.
He should trace every precept of the law to its connection with the redeeming love of Christ, and draw
thence his incitements to obey. Would he urge, for
instance, Christian fidelity on parents? He will not
content himself with appealing to the law of nature
expressed in the instinctive parental love, with arguing
from the feebleness, dependence or loveliness of our
offspring, or with promising the comforts which dutiful
children confer upon our old age. These will be the
least of his grounds, and most briefly despatched. He
will proceed to crown his argument, by directing the
hearts of parents chiefly to that Redeemer who claims
our children as of his kingdom, to the divine blood
with which he has purchased their immortal souls, and
to the future of glory and bliss which he offers, chiefly
through the means of parental fidelity, to confer on
them. Thus, every labour of the father for his child
is connected with the Christian's constraining principle—the love of Christ.

It is a precept of prime weight, that your enforce-
ments of evangelical duty and charges of shortcoming
be definite, and even specific. There is, I apprehend,
in the pulpits of our Church, no lack of general declara-
tions concerning man's depravity, transgression and
guilt. Nor do we find, among the ungodly, any back-
wardness in making the general confession that they

are sinners. But this vague sense of sin and guilt is manifestly without effect. They confess, and still transgress. They avow, in words, their need of cleansing and justification, and yet refuse the salvation offered, with all the supineness of conscious security. It is to be feared that a quickening of these dead hearts will never be effected by launching at them the commonplaces of theology. The mere statement of their responsibility and guilt, in general, will be inadequate. But if their own duties and delinquencies were brought home to them in their details, they would, with the blessing of the Holy Ghost, be made to feel wherein they were sinners indeed, and why under the curse. My meaning may be explained by the instance I employed above. Tell your unrenewed hearer that he is a parent, that he owes duty to his child, and he will readily admit it. Charge shortcoming on him in this duty: he will admit this also, and after the admission he will be as callous as before. But now let us suppose the parental duties defined, and enforced from their high, evangelical obligations, and the cruelty of that parental neglect, which usually destroys the soul of the child, justly painted in the lights of the eternal world. May we not hope that the delinquent parent will acquire some definite conviction of his sin, and especially that his eyes will begin to open to the enormity and malignity of that state of heart charged upon him by the Scriptures, and hitherto so firmly disbelieved by him? In this view of practical preaching, we have a powerful argument for its employment to lead sinners to the Saviour. It is only when we become specific, and apply the general principles of evangelical duty, with close discrimination, to the circumstances of our hearers, that we make the law their "schoolmaster to lead them unto Christ." While we are instructing God's people in the details of their duty, we may be teaching his enemies the number of their sins.

LECTURE IV.

THE SAME TOPICS CONTINUED.

I RESUME, young gentlemen, the remarks which the expiration of my hour arrested, upon the proper nature of the practical sermon. I was remonstrating against vagueness in the application of obligations to duty upon the conscience. But there is an error to be avoided on the other side. There are species of details which are unsuitable for the pulpit. I do not conceive that much of casuistry should be introduced into practical sermons. This belongs rather to the pastor's study than to the desk. The minute distinctions by which nice cases are to be adjusted, if they be addressed to a promiscuous company of persons not vitally interested in the particular problem, will be surely misunderstood by many. Thus they will minister to the morbid scruples of some consciences and to the license of others. And even in our private instructions love is the best casuist. Let the great principles of gospel love be presented with a breadth and warmth which, instead of dissecting, will dissipate the doubt.

Nor should the preacher, under pretence of definiteness, encumber his sermons with secular details of the means for executing a duty which has been established. He may be assured that the attempt to do this will lead

him at once out of his province. He will enjoin on
mechanics Christian honesty and fidelity to engage-
ments; he will urge the agriculturist to diligence for
the glory of God. But let him not then proceed to instruct the former of the materials and species of work-
manship to be employed for executing faithful work,
nor presume to dictate to the latter a rotation of crops.
He would thus cease to be a minister of religion, and
would be only a master among his apprentices.

In like manner I conclude that good habits or virtues
of very narrow extent, or of secular concernment, should
not be selected as prominent subjects of practical sermons. The preacher, for instance, who should fill his
hour with recommendations to the habit of neatness, or
of method in little things, would be but trifling. The
Sabbath time of candidates for immortality in this fleeting world should have a more momentous concern.
Let the grave truths and duties of the gospel be urged
to save these souls in Christ; the vital grace which will
then actuate them will, with very few words, set them
aright touching all these minor morals. Is it argued
that Christ has told us, " he that is faithful in the least
things is faithful also in the greater;" that the apostle
Paul requires us even when " we eat and drink to do
all to the glory of God," and that the Holy Ghost,
speaking by Solomon, did not disdain to teach that " he
that hateth suretyships is sure," and that " much increase is by the strength of the ox"? I reply: let the
preacher, like the sacred writers, inculcate these propositions as definite principles indeed, but not in beggarly
details, and let him give them that small relative space
in his sermons which the all-wise Spirit has given them

in the Bible. This will secure him against the error which I oppose.

The third class, of narrative or historical sermons, is not different in one aspect from the other two. Its peculiarity is that by employing the parables, biographies, and histories of the Scriptures, it teaches in the concrete. The truths taught may be either doctrinal or practical. It may be conceded that the practical is more frequent in these narratives, but doctrines are not excluded.

That this method of presenting truth should be often employed, might be inferred from the fact that more than half of the revealed Scriptures is narrative or biography. God, who knows what is in man, has evidently judged this a suitable way to instruct him. Experience shows that it is the way most intelligible and pleasing to the popular mind. Nor are the reasons of this obscure. A perspicuous narrative, with its lifelike personages and successive incidents leading to their catastrophe, presents the simplest food of curiosity, which is the appetite of the mind. The truths embodied thus are more vividly apprehended. Presented in the concrete, they relieve us in the labours of abstraction and generalization, which are so irksome to the common mind. This method has all the advantage of illustration over naked argument. As the picture of a human face is more intelligible than a verbal description, or as one derives a clearer view of a region from a map of its parts than from the reading of the field-notes of its survey, so is the narrative embodying a truth more perspicuous and pleasing than a didactic statement. Would the preacher define and recommend the virtue of constancy in the right? The history of Daniel does it better than all his definitions and arguments. Would he illustrate faith? He has Abraham. In Peter at the cock-crowing he finds true penitence painted. Christ weeping over reprobate Jerusalem shows us compassion more distinctly than any description can.

The fact that the preacher is merely the herald to deliver God's message is sufficient to answer the question whence the materials for narrative sermons are to be drawn. The reply is: primarily from the Bible. The main storehouse is the parables and histories deposited there. Nowhere else have we sufficient guarantee for the certainty of the events and the impartiality of the portraiture. But I am persuaded that authentic and instructive incidents in the history of the Church, and in the lives of the martyrs, and even of the saints of our age, might be used with excellent effect, as subordinate illustrations of truth. The preacher, in employing these, should see to it, first, that the events recited be of unquestioned authenticity, and next, that they be of congruous seriousness and dignity.

While the narrative method is so valuable to the preacher, its peculiar difficulties should not be concealed. One of these will be found in the recital itself, by which he places the events before his hearers. It must be specific, that it may be graphic; for unless there is defined outline, there is no picture. Yet it must be brief, lest it should weary. If he employs the very words of the sacred narrative, he seems to his audience not to be an orator, but the mere repeater of a familiar lesson. If he paraphrases it in his own language, then he is set in dangerous contrast with the inspired story, which the hearer has before him. For such is the life, compactness, expressiveness, eloquence of the scriptural histories, he must be no mean artist whose recital of the same events does not suffer by comparison with theirs. But, for the tyro, the chief difficulty of historical sermons is to catch correctly the precise didactic scope of the sacred narrative, and to limit himself to it. Certain schools, of even Protestant preachers, have given us deplorable examples of error here. They have used the plain histories of the Bible as though they were riddles for the exercise of an ingenious fancy. They have formed allegories where the Holy Ghost has warranted them in seeing none. They have interpreted these histories as though any analogy which a vagrant imagination could invent, between a Bible fact and a supposed moral, were a perfect demonstration that this was the truth which the Spirit intended to teach in that place. Your own good sense should show you that a mode of interpretation cannot be correct, which enables different men to extract the most variant meanings from the same words. It is utterly condemned by what has been established concerning the preacher's mission. He has naught to do save to deliver God's message out of the Scriptures; his only concern is with the intended meaning of the Holy Ghost in the place expounded. Hence, in a narrative sermon, the preacher's first task must be to ascertain faithfully, from the whole context, the precise scope of the Spirit in placing these events in the infallible record. What principles of truth or duty did He here illustrate to the Church ? This must be his topic; and nothing else. When Moses tells us how Jacob made for his darling son a coat of many colours, we are not authorized to teach our hearers that the righteousness of the saints was there presented in type. We have only an infallible portraiture of the mischiefs which parental partiality may work. When another prophet tells us how the priests of Dagon in Ekron, professing to desire the restoration of the ark of God to its sanctuary, shut up the calves at home from the unbroken kine which drew the cart, he does not give us an allegory to teach us the exclusion of infants from membership in Zion. He only intends to teach us the dishonesty of unbelief. The perverse taste for thus abusing the historical Scriptures may be accounted for, in part, by the influence of such books as Bunyan's "Temple of Solomon Spiritualized;" but more, by a guilty vanity in preachers, who desire to make the multitude gape with some mighty conceit of their wisdom.

To overcome these difficulties, no little good sense, taste and diligence in the preacher are required. A fine narrative sermon is perhaps the highest work of sacred oratory, and demands the greatest skill. But it is also the most attractive species of sermon.

Under this class comes what has been called, in the modern religious cant, the " occasional sermon." This is a discourse headed by some words of Scripture, which professes to employ some grave or startling event of the day to enforce the principle of religion suggested by the text. Thus, the death of a popular public man, the fatal wreck of a ship, a conflagration, or a flood, produces in some quarters a shower of these occasional sermons. The plea for their defence is drawn from the doctrine of divine providence directing these instructive occurrences, and from the utility of improving the impressions which they make on the sensibilities of men. But a sound taste will usually condemn the custom. Facts show that the apparent awe produced by these catastrophes is not directed by such sermons to a sacred end. The more usual result is the gratifying of curiosity and the unwholesome love for new sensations. The explanation of this is not difficult: it is found in the fact that these discourses are almost unavoidably social, instead of spiritual, in tone. The practical effect of the very selection of this event, as of sufficient gravity to displace God's own word and occupy the sermon, is of itself fulsome. It seems to say, "So important a people are we, the death of our public servant, the sinking of our ship, the burning of our town. rivals in moment the mighty events of Eden and Calvary." The pulpit-sycophant, usually, does not fail to reflect this overweening idea in all his style. His whole effort is to exalt and exaggerate the tremendous occurrence; whereas the real duty of the pulpit is to endeavour, both by act and word, to sink all human events into insignificance beside the sublime facts of redemption. The acute observer, accordingly, does not fail to perceive that the main effect of these commemorative sermons is to inflate the self-importance, instead of alarming the impenitence, of the hearers. If there is any force in the plea that these striking extemporaneous events may and should be employed to impress divine truth (as I freely admit), this good end may almost always be sufficiently gained, by introducing the incident, with suitable modesty and brevity, in the application of scriptural truth, during a customary sermon. By this means, all is made of such events which can be legitimately made of them, and good taste and propriety are saved.

The funereal discourse is also usually classed under narrative sermons. Upon this species of sacred eloquence I must pass the same verdict with that given against the occasional sermon. Against the custom of delivering a gospel sermon at a funeral I say nothing. But this is wholly distinct from the funereal sermons proper, where the preacher is expected to delineate the life and character of the deceased, to pronounce a pious eulogy upon them, and to determine the destiny of their souls for heaven. Such discourses are usually unmingled evils. There are a few of God's servants whose sanctity is so universally approved even by those who are without, and on whom the Redeemer has so manifestly set his divine image, that it may be the pastor's duty to urge their example upon the Church. But if he is wise, he will find exceedingly few instances of such; and in all other cases he will content himself with presenting at the funeral some appropriate gospel truth without encomium upon the dead. To commend this rule, the consideration of taste urged above will usually be sufficient. It is fulsome for us to set any human character, or career habitually in competition with the gospel in the claim upon men's attention. The preacher is often liable to the odious imputation of prostituting his holy office to gratify the social importance of survivors. If he is honest, he will, of course, only applaud those whom he honestly esteemed as true Christians. But when he is called to bury others, of whom he cannot but have an ill opinion, he must observe an absolute silence. This itself, standing in contrast with his customary eulogies of others, is a significant reproach, and is felt by the bereaved as such. It is better, therefore, to avoid the dilemma by a uniform silence. But chiefly, the tendency of funereal eulogies is to degrade, in the estimation of the hearers, the standard of that piety which is necessary to save the soul. The pastor should remember that he is probably more ignorant than any one else of the blemishes of the brethren. Before him they are always reserved. When he visits them, they array themselves in their Sunday clothing and their Sunday manners at once. If he has the dignity of bearing appropriate to a pastor, the tongue of the tattler is stilled in his presence, which elsewhere ventilates so freely the faults of his neighbours. Hence, there is usually danger lest the people should be possessed of a just suspicion against the deceased, of whom the good pastor knows and speaks only praise. If his error is glaring, his credit for good sense and discretion is fatally wounded; if the discrepancy is slighter, the tendency of his eulogy is to produce the impression that redemption is an easy task, and heaven may be lightly won. For has not the preacher seen this man enter that blessed place? "And yet," say the people to themselves, "we know how sorry a racer he was in the Christian course." I ask, emphatically, are they not the few in our churches, whose faith and hope are so approved and clear that they themselves judge any other sentiments appropriate, in view of death, than solemn awe and trembling doubts? Now, since good manners forbid the pastor to re-echo their own estimate of themselves, and since honesty forbids his uttering the contrary one, his wisdom will usually be to say nothing upon the subject.

You will observe that I have said nothing of hortatory sermons as a separate class. In strictness of speech there should be none such. Action is only produced by conviction. The only legitimate weapon of conviction is the truth. The well-ordered, warm, and logical argument is indirectly the best exhortation you can apply. Direct exhortation, which is not founded on argument, is meaningless. There are sermons, sometimes called hortatory, in which the appeals to the conscience and will are grounded on simple and obvious truths. Here the direct argumentation may be exceedingly brief. "Life is uncertain, therefore prepare to-day for its end." The ground of hortation is disputed by none, and so requires no argument; yet is the appeal based upon a reason, which is not the less a reason because it is very conclusive to every mind. But there is another just sense in which all sermons are hortatory; for have we not learned that the characteristic of the orator is to impel his hearers to some action?

This review of the three classes of sermons will assist the pastor in cultivating that variety, within scriptural limits, which is so useful to interest and instruct his people. By preaching doctrinally, practically, and historically, with judicious alternations, he will show himself "a workman that needeth not to be ashamed, rightly dividing the word of truth."[1] Not a few young pastors are harassed with the fear of exhausting their stores of instruction. They dread, with a species of terror,

---

[1] 2 Tim. ii. 15; see also Matt. xiii. 52.

the time when they will have discussed all the topics
of redemption, and will have nothing more to say, except they repeat. And unfortunately this fear is confirmed by the dulness of too many of their seniors.
They even argue a justification of their fear, saying:
"Is not the circle of revealed truths a definite one?
Are not the points which are of sufficient importance
to require or permit pulpit discussion limited in number? Then after a time that circle must be completed
by the pastor. And just in the degree that his treatment of the several parts has been what it ought to be,
thorough, perspicuous, impressive to the memory, will
he find himself precluded from a second discussion;
for if the right things were said by him at first, shall
he now say the same things? Or shall he say new
things which are less correct?" The answer to these
difficulties is, that while the truths which make up the
circle of gospel theology are limited in number, their
applications to the different phases of human experience
and character are infinite. The true pastor will find a
fountain of inexhaustible variety if he will become
acquainted with his own heart and the hearts of his
charge. Faithful communion with himself, under the
guidance of the Word, and an intimate inquiry into
the wants of the souls over whom he watches, with diligent study, will always furnish him out of his treasury
with things new and old. He will find his mind so
teeming with scriptural and timely topics of instruction that his only difficulty will be to find occasions
enough to present them.

LECTURE V.

THE TEXT.

THIS term is well understood as meaning the portion of the Scriptures upon which a sermon is founded. A preliminary question may deserve a brief inquiry before our discussion of that subject proceeds. It is, whether there is reason for the employment of texts by preachers. Some eminent critics, among whom may be mentioned Voltaire,[1] have denounced the usage as senseless. They have urged that no similar custom ever prevailed among the orators of classic antiquity; that it is artificial and unnatural; that it imposes a mischievous necessity upon the sacred orator of weaving his whole discourse out of the contents of a single sentence, which tempts him to artificial and strained divisions; and that it even occasions an abuse of the integrity of the scriptural meaning, because an apt text cannot be found, in words, for every religious or moral duty to be taught, and the preacher is thus tempted to wrest a passage to suit his special purpose.

In defending the uniform use of texts I wish to admit expressly that many abuses of them, by both the Romanist and Protestant clergy, justify a part of these

---

[1] "Remarks upon the Influence of *Père Bourdaloue* over the French Pulpit."

criticisms. Where pastors confine themselves, according to our unfortunate fashion, to texts of a single sentence, instead of explaining the Scriptures in their connection; where they wrest or accommodate the meaning to cover their human speculations; where they employ a fragment of the Word as a mere motto; these exceptions against their usage are justly taken. But when I defend the employment of texts, it is their legitimate use, which is to be unfolded anon.

In reply then to the condemnation of the usage, I urge that the posture of the preacher is essentially different from that of all other speakers. His only work is to expound and apply to the people an authoritative message from God. This is too extensive to be unfolded in one discourse; he must therefore present it in successive parts. What then more natural, yea necessary, than that he should preface the exposition of the day with the words of the divine message which he is then to expound? There must be a reference, either express or tacit, to that message. The whole authority of his addresses to the conscience depends upon the correspondence evinced between his explanations and inferences and the infallible Word. It appears, then, that the use of texts is not an artificial fashion, but a custom dictated by the very nature of the preacher's peculiar mission. Let us suppose an instance from secular oratory nearest akin to this: that there was in the commonwealth an order of ministerial officers whose chief duty was to instruct the citizens in the constitution of the state, presenting this fundamental law as the sole ground of authority for all other magistrates and laws. Obviously, we should expect to hear such a teacher reg-

ularly read the portion of the constitution he was about
to explain, if not at the beginning, yet at some cardinal
juncture of his discourse. This portion would be virtually his text. Such discourse could not proceed without it. It may be added that the use of the text is now
venerable by long custom, and that its formal announcement gives weight and authority to the instructions
thence derived. There is then no cause to omit, and
every reason to preserve, the usage.

The first and most important difference of texts (and
thence of sermons) is that between the long and the short.
If the text contains a number of verses of Scripture,
the whole of which are to be explained and applied in
their connection, the discussion is called an "expository" sermon. If the text contains only a single proposition, or at most a brief passage of the Word presenting one point, it is denominated by some a "textual" and by others a "topical" sermon. But both of
these terms are inaccurate here, for assuredly every expository sermon ought to be textual in the true sense,
and you will learn that many expository and narrative
sermons may be topical. I acknowledge that I am not
careful to invent a more exact name for this species of
discourse upon insulated fragments of Scripture, which
should never have had place in the Church at all. We
will call them, for convenience, sermons without context.

If you ask me to compare these several kinds of sermons, I shall reply that all should be virtually expository, else they are not true sermons. A prevalent exercise of the pulpit should be the delivery of those
explanations of connected passages of Scripture which
are called in our books of Church order, "popular lec-

tures," in modern phrase "expository preaching." And when the pastor discusses only a single sentence or proposition of Scripture, as he will often and legitimately do, it should yet be a true exposition, an evolution of the meaning of God in that sentence, with constant and faithful reference to its context. There are but two kinds of single propositions which can properly be made subjects of this species of sermons. One is, of those propositions which contain truths so cardinal to the whole system of redemption, that it is proper the preacher should give them particular and abundant attention, according that large space allotted to them in the Bible itself. Such are the fundamental doctrines of original sin, the new birth, justification by faith, repentance, satisfaction for guilt, divinity of Christ and of the Holy Spirit. Single sentences, or even clauses of the Scripture, setting forth transcendent truths like these, may well receive the exclusive treatment of a whole sermon. These I would call *capital texts*. To give them such prominence is but conforming to the "proportion of faith," for the Bible itself gives similar extent to its treatment of them. A sermon on such a text, if it is what it should be, is in the best sense expository, for it explains whole tracts of the Scripture teachings, which, whether standing in the sacred page near to, or remote from, the particular text discussed, have their fair representation in it. The other kind is that which I would call *epitome texts*, where a single proposition contains the point of a whole discussion, the moral of a whole parable or history summed up for us by the Holy Spirit himself. Thus, Rom. vi. 1 (" What shall we say then ? Shall we continue in sin that grace may abound)?" states the prevalent subject of discussion in the whole sixth chapter. The pastor may adopt this single verse as his text. But it is then his duty to unfold the argument of the Holy Ghost upon it, and not one of human device; so that his sermon is substantially an exposition of the whole passage. So Luke xviii. 7, 8 ("And shall not God avenge his own elect? . . . I tell you that he will avenge them speedily") gives us the intended "moral" of the parable of the importunate widow. In preaching from it correctly we expound the parable. The epitome text may also be used, although not in juxtaposition with the passages which it compresses. Thus, John xvii. 21 ("As thou, Father, art in me, and I in thee, that they also may be in us," etc.) states what is unfolded in John xv. 1–8, or in 1 Cor. xii. 11–17, or in Eph. iv. 16, etc. But still, if the preacher is faithful to his duty in preaching on the Saviour's petition, he will pursue only a scriptural exposition of it, so that his sermon will be expository of a part or all of these more expanded statements.[1] I repeat, that unless the single proposition is related to the Word in one of these ways, it is not suitable for a sermon; that a discussion without scriptural context is not true preaching, and that, in the sense above defined, there is no other species of preaching than the expository.

But I would urge that the expository method (understood as that which explains extended passages of Scripture in course) be restored to that equal place

---

[1] For other specimens of the epitome text, compare Gen. xv. 6 with Rom. iv.; Gen. vi. 3, first half, with Heb. x. 26–29; Tit. iii. 8 with Tit. ii. 11 to iii. 7; Luke xvi. 9 with vv. 1–8.

which it held in the primitive and Reformed Churches; for, first, this is obviously the only natural and efficient way to do that which is the sole legitimate end of preaching, convey the whole message of God to the people. I point to the fact that no one ever thinks of teaching the text-book of any other science in any other way. What would be thought of the master who professed to teach a system of geometry or mechanics by commenting in a brilliant way on one and another apothegm selected from the author? If you will recall the scriptural theory of preaching which was stated at the beginning, you will see that it gives us no other conception of the work than the expository. It is to unfold to the hearers the counsel of God for their salvation. To accomplish this it is not enough to dwell with disproportioned fulness on some fragments. A continuous exhibition must be made at least of those important books of the Scripture which present the system of redemption, with reference to the remainder for illustration. Let us recur to the just simile of the die impressing its image and superscription on a plastic substance. To produce a fair transcript, the artisan must press it down equably, and place the whole outline upon the wax. This is accomplished by the exposition in course of the chief parts of the Bible. But our fragmentary, modern method of preaching without context is as though the servant to whom the die is committed should divide it into small pieces, and then, selecting favourite letters of the legend or features of the carving, should force them into the wax at a high temperature and with extravagant pressure. But the remainder is scarcely brought into the faintest contact with the surface. What can one expect save a cluster of rude, shapeless indentations rather than the symmetrical imprint of the Redeemer's beauteous image on the soul? You may ask, "Will not this unconnected series of theological lessons yet form in the end a complete outline of scriptural doctrine?" I answer, nothing short of the regular expository method will give assurance of this. The same impulses which have caused us to prefer the fragmentary method will be very certain to limit our range of subjects. Does any one hear of an instance where one of these preachers has faithfully carried his charge through the Confession of Faith, or any similar didactic summary, in a series of doctrinal sermons? No. Our caprice, our fondness for some topics rather than others, our indolent reluctance to grapple with those heads of doctrine of which we are less informed beforehand, the exigencies of pastoral interruptions, always ensure a partial range of instruction. But the course of sermons on the Confession would still be inferior to the course of se mons on the Bible, because the latter gives us God's infallible arrangement, natural, historical and germinant, while the former gives us man's.

This remark suggests a second, not less important. The connections of truths among themselves are as essential to the system as the separate propositions. No man understands the system until he comprehends these relations. Now, however complete may be the circle of points presented by the faulty, modern mode, their scriptural relations are not taught to the people. Expository preaching is necessary to show them how truth affects truth, and how to connect the parts of their creed. We have found no better description of the preacher's work than that given by Nehemiah of Ezra's : he " read in the book of the law of the *Lord* distinctly, and gave the sense, and caused them to understand the reading." A prime object of pastoral teaching is to teach the people how to read the Bible for themselves. A sealed book cannot be interesting. If it be read without the key of comprehension, it cannot be instructive. Now, it is the preacher's business, in his public discourses, to give his people teaching by example, in the art of interpreting the Word : he should exhibit before them, in actual use, the methods by which the legitimate meaning is to be evolved. Fragmentary preaching, however brilliant, will never do this. The pastor must teach his flock how to expound for themselves, by frequent practice in company with them.

Do not these observations explain much that is imperfect in the Christian character of our day ? There is a profusion of preaching and public exercises ; yet there is far less scriptural intelligence among our church-goers than among our ruder forefathers. The religious opinions of the Church reflect· the narrow, partial and exaggerated traits of the pulpit. The people are not grounded in the Scriptures. There is little symmetry or stability in their religious character. Hence the facility with which they permit the thousand sects of the day to pervert the Word into a seeming support of their errours.

Third. The improvement of the pastor in biblical knowledge is closely connected with that of his people. He must profit in the Scriptures for their advantage. He who does not preach many expository sermons will seldom become an able and learned interpreter. So irregular and exacting are the duties of the pastor, it is practically inevitable that his studies must be chiefly shaped by the direct demands of his pulpit tasks. He will find himself compelled to study mainly those things which will prepare him for the next Sabbath's sermon. If this is to be a discussion on a single proposition without context, his inquiries may lead him to theological text-books, to literary sources, to human dialectics. These are the helps which furnish him with the artificial division and topics which he seeks. But he will be diverted from the direct study of the Word, which should be his chief labour. If, on the other hand, his preparation be expository, his studies must be of that kind. Thus he will become mighty in the Scriptures, and "his profiting will appear unto all."

Fourth. The expository method secures for the pastor sundry conveniences and advantages. One of these not to be disdained is, that he is thus relieved of the harassing doubt and hesitation which often attend the selection of a text. Instead of having his spirits consumed for a day by this question, he proceeds at once to attack the work of preparation which is laid out for him in advance. Another gain is, that it enables the preacher to embody and use many points which, separately, are too brief to offer a sufficient tract of thought for a whole sermon. Many such are presented to the modern preacher in his Bible-reading. They offer a few interesting and suggestive thoughts. At the first glance he thinks he has in them capital subjects for sermons; but when he proceeds to elaborate them, they are found incapable of farther extension. If ·sermons of ten

minutes' length were in vogue, they would be exactly
suited for them; but as they cannot be expanded, without platitude, to forty-five minutes, he must forego
them, or else trifle with his task.[1] Now, in expository
preaching all this material is employed; for these brief
tracts of thought being connected by the natural tie of
the context, are all interwoven into the discourse. Not
seldom, these minor subjects assume a temporary importance which, if their discussion has been neglected,
will cause the minister to regret his oversight. For
instance, one would scarcely deem it appropriate to
demand the whole morning hour of a large audience,
assembled to learn the way of salvation, for an explanation of the precept, "Swear not at all." Matt. v. 34.
His sensible hearers would say that he were better employed teaching lost souls how to escape hell. Yet it
may well happen that some day an intrusive Tunker or
Quaker may here embarrass the consciences of many
good people in his charge, if ignorant of the scriptural
solution. Now, had this pastor expounded the "Sermon on the Mount" in course, he would have found
the suitable and graceful occasion to say these few
paragraphs which are needed on this subject.

A more weighty advantage is, that the expository
method enables the pastor to introduce without offence
those delicate subjects of temptation and duty, and
those obnoxious doctrines and rebukes, which, on the

---

[1] For example, I once heard a minister occupy a large country
congregation with a refutation of the crotchet of Adam Clarke in
favour of Judas' salvation. The people were at first interested; but
at the end of fifteen minutes the subject was exhausted, and they were
left with the blankest appearance of surprise and discontent.

opposite method, always incur so much *odium*. The fragmentary preacher will find it a very difficult and delicate thing to request his charge to give him the Sabbath hour for the discussion of polygamy, of divorce, of the other sins against chastity. The taste of many will be disgusted. They will ask, "What foul taint does our pastor suspect in us, that he supposes these offensive subjects necessary?" Yet there may be good cause—if not now, hereafter. Some Mormon emissary may seduce some of the more ignorant and unstable to his abominable creed. Some better minds may be harassed with skeptical difficulties concerning the polygamy of the saints of the old dispensation. We know that the awkward silence of the pulpit concerning the seventh commandment has been the occasion of much of the shocking levity of opinion which prevails as to its breach. Now, if the pastor has engaged to preach an exposition of the whole book of Exodus, all is made easy. He did not introduce these subjects there: it is God who has done it; and if he would be faithful, he has no option to omit them. So, the doctrine of predestination is so obnoxious to some minds that to obtrude it voluntarily on them is, in their eyes, almost an assault. But if the pastor is expounding in course the Epistle to the Romans, he cannot be blamed by the most unreasonable for treating that point; for it is obviously there, and he has no choice. Once more, if the pastor introduces, of his own motion, denunciations against a sin which is prevalent among a particular class or with a few persons, there is danger of a violent outcry against his "personalities." He is charged with singling out the objects of his criticism in order to

inflict a malicious pain, by making their fault con-
spicuous; for no transgressor is impudent enough to
make open complaint because God rebukes him in His
word. But if the language of condemnation stands in
the passage which comes up regularly for exposition,
the cavil is silenced. It was not the choice of the
minister that the sin of these men is now denounced:
it was their own choice that they impinged against the
immutable law of God.

Fifth. The immemorial usage of the Church should
commend this method to us. The sketch which I gave
you of the history of preaching showed that this exercise among the Hebrews, the apostolic and the primitive
Christians, was expository. The opposite method was
traced by antiquaries to the Romish clergy of the dark
ages. The great Reformation was emphatically a reformation of the pulpit in this particular, and a revival
of expository preaching. The better Puritans still
honoured the custom; and it has been left for our century to imitate the error of the twelfth and to discard
the method again. But even our age has not been
wholly without instructive witnesses: some of the most
eminent and useful pastors who have adorned the
Church have continued to honour the ancient usage.
Among these may be mentioned Dr. John M. Mason.
It was his custom to occupy the morning hour with an
expository discourse, and the evening with the free
discussion of some scriptural principle or fact evolved
by the explanations of the morning. He has left his
emphatic testimony against the neglect of expositions
in the sermon preached to his people on resigning his
charge in New York. He here says (speaking of the

choice of his successor), "Do not choose a man who always preaches upon insulated texts. I care not how powerful or eloquent he may be in handling them. The effect of his power and eloquence will be to banish a taste for the word of God, and to substitute the preacher in its place. You have been accustomed to hear that word preached to you in its connection. Never permit that practice to drop. Foreign churches call it *lecturing*, and, when done with discretion, I can assure you that, while it is of all exercises the most difficult for the preacher, it is, in the same proportion, the most profitable for you. It has this peculiar advantage, that, in going through a book of Scripture, it spreads out before you all sorts of character and all forms of opinion, and gives the preacher an opportunity of striking every kind of evil and error, without subjecting himself to the invidious suspicion of aiming his discourses at individuals."

The real obstacles to the adoption of this mode of preaching are two: the fear that it will not interest the people, and the preacher's indolence. To the first I would reply, that the popular caprice is no safe rule to the gospel-minister in choosing his methods of pastoral instruction. If this sycophantic motive may cause him to give his charge sermons without context, while he knows that they are defective as means of edification, why may it not justify sacred theatricals also, or any other trick of the clerical mountebank? If expository preaching is necessary for the best interests of the people, then the faithful servant of Christ has no option to discard it: he is bound to employ it, rendering it as attractive as he innocently can. While it has less glitter and ostentation than the other method, if the preacher does his duty in it, he will not find it lacking in solid pleasure. Good expository preaching is always permanently attractive, and always most attractive to those whom it is most important to attract. It meets the great appetite of the human mind—the desire to know; it instructs. No man who has any intelligent sensibility toward sacred things can fail to make the reflection that, if the Bible is our authoritative rule of faith, then it is a matter of transcendent, of infinite concern to him to get the right meaning of that book. But all popular readers of the Scriptures have a strong consciousness of their own blindness of mind to much that they read there. They feel that in many places they have not the key of knowledge. Hence, he who proposes to open the meaning of the Scriptures meets the most serious desire of their religious nature. If this work is done successfully, without undue pedantry and prolixity, but with a plain and honest mastery of the task, which is obvious to the good sense of the hearer, if his judgment is convinced that the preacher has indeed given him the clue of correct understanding, nothing can be so attractive to him. He feels that this is precisely what he needed. The expository method is also naturally adapted to sustain the interest of common minds, in that it provides them with frequent and easy transitions of subject. To be held long to the contemplation of the same abstract thought is exceedingly irksome to them. Indeed, the ability to retain the same ideas fixed before the mind's inspection, for a long time continuously, is the last and highest result of severe philosophic training. It was this which made a Newton's mind as that of an arch-

angel among mortals in the walks of science. Shall
we expect this rare power in the common people? But
the ambitious preacher on insulated texts, if he is a
correct logician, holds up his one main proposition
throughout his sermon, and elaborates it with a perti-
nacity which is insufferable to the untrained mind.
(If he is not a correct logician, then the case is still
worse.) But when connected subject follows subject
with a pleasing variety, the attention is relieved and
the curiosity pleasantly stimulated.

The only real obstacle to the interest of the hearer is
one which may be removed by a simple expedient. It
is too great a tax to the memory and attention to comprehend a criticism and exposition of an extended passage which has been only heard once or twice. For the
comprehension of the exegetical argument requires a
distinct view of the very words, often, on which the
preacher remarks. Let, then, every worshipper bring
his Bible with him to Church, and keep it open before
him. This was always done by our forefathers, who
knew and valued expository preaching. The Church
is the school of Christ; a school without its text-books
is a sorry affair. If our conception of preaching were
correct, nothing could appear more preposterous than
that sight which is now usually witnessed among us—
a whole assemblage of pupils without a single Bible,
save that in the teacher's hands! If you will insist
when you become pastors that your people shall bring
their Bibles to Church, you will, in that simple measure, work a precious reform.

There is a yet higher reason, which guarantees the
power of good expository preaching over the souls of

the hearers. It presents divine truth in those aspects and relations in which it was placed by that God who knew what was in man. We, in our self-sufficiency, detach a cardinal truth from its context; we exactly define our proposition; we discard the argument by which the Holy Ghost has seen fit to sustain it; we construct another, recasting the elements of proof in forms dialectical or theological, according to the rules of our human science. The effects always disappoint us. Our discourses have far less power over the conscience than we hoped. The ignorant may gape after what they suppose our wondrous learning and logic; the educated may applaud the regularity and art of our discussion; yet souls are not awakened. But now let the preacher humbly take the same gospel proposition in its context. Let him make all his human learning ancillary to the simple work of ascertaining and explaining the argument of the Holy Spirit. Let him drink into the very meaning and temper of that inspired discussion. And let him do nothing else but place it, without change or addition, in contact with the souls of his hearers. He will find with delight that he has now opened a way to their hearts. God's sermons will tell upon them as men's sermons never do. Your conceit and ambition may persuade you that your human arrangement is more regular, more logical, more complete than his. He knows better, for he is omniscient. Have faith and humility to trust his truth in his own biblical forms, and you will find your sermons clothed with a true power and unction. If you thus honour his word, he will honour your ministry with success.

The second, and, I surmise, the decisive, obstacle to

expository preaching in our day is the indolence and incapacity of preachers. In truth, to get up a human oration upon some point of Christian doctrine or ethics, embodying a few commonplaces made ready to our hands by books, and concealing our platitudes under the forms of a regular discussion, is comparatively easy. To expound aright requires the highest taste, judgment, experience and learning. I avow, young gentlemen, that it is not easy to apprehend exactly the mental wants of those whom you would instruct, so as to give just the explanations which are german, to conceive correctly the precise scope of the Holy Ghost in the passage; to state this perspicuously to the common reason; to evince the correspondence of your statements with the very mind of the Spirit by a plain, homely, exegetical logic without pedantry, which shall be clear and convincing to common sense; to apply the truth to heart and conscience; to select the most appropriate and useful inferences; to preserve throughout the "analogy of the faith," and to superfuse the whole with evangelical warmth,—this is not easy. But if it be well done, it will prove "the power of God and the wisdom of God unto salvation."

By some an objection is raised against expository preaching, that it is less consistent with the purposes of oratory, because of its lack of unity. This virtue, we shall see, is a cardinal trait of the oration. But, it is urged, if the speaker passes over a large portion of Scripture, explaining the whole with its variety of subjects, unity is lost. Now this objection is founded on the assumption, which is untrue, that the Scriptures themselves lack rhetorical unity. They readily divide themselves into sections, each of which contains some one dominant scope. We find such a natural section sometimes in a narrative designed by the Holy Spirit to exemplify some virtue or cluster of virtues; sometimes in a parable or series of parables illustrating one main truth; sometimes in a doctrinal discussion. Why may not the "workman rightly dividing the word of truth" select one of these parts, bounded by its natural limits, as the text of his discourse? Then, inasmuch as the passage has its own unity, his exposition will be the more truly rhetorical as it is the more faithful. There are a few parts of the Scripture, as the one hundred and nineteenth Psalm and the Proverbs, which seem not to admit this division, because each verse introduces a separate maxim or sentiment. But even in these a more thorough consideration will detect a connecting clue. Of the one hundred and nineteenth Psalm, Dr. Thomas Scott has said, that it is not a golden chain, but a box of separate golden rings. Yet examine, for example, the first part, ALEPH; you will find that amidst the rapid transitions there is a prevalent subject, conformity to God's will. Verses first and second declare the blessedness and characteristics of this grace. Verse fourth refers to that divine authority from which the obligation to it flows. Verse fifth expresses that aspiration after it which is the response of the Christian heart to the announcement of this divine command. The sixth and seventh verses give a fuller expression to this sacred longing. And verse eighth concludes the thought of the section, with strict rhetorical propriety, by a practical vow of conformity to the divine will, and a prayer for the aid and forbearance of God in the imperfect endeavour.

But, in fine, is it proved that all the pastor's instructions must needs be rhetorical? True, the regular sermon is a sacred oration, and I define the oration as a discourse always converging to a practical end. But may not the pastor have public teaching functions, which are homiletical rather than rhetorical? In this humbler department of his work, then, there may be appropriate places for expositions which even resist reduction to a complete unity.[1]

---

[1] See, on this whole subject, "Thoughts on Preaching," by Dr. J. W. Alexander. It is gratifying to find nearly all the positions and arguments of this lecture, which I had regularly delivered to my classes several years before the death of this eminent and useful pastor, affirmed in his posthumous work.

LECTURE VI.

THE TEXT.

THE student will bear in mind that by "the Text" I intend that passage of Scripture which introduces and contains the sermon, whether it is a single proposition, or even clause of Scripture, or a portion of many verses to be expounded. When we proceed, therefore, to the rules for selecting texts, our matter divides itself naturally into two parts.

The selection of the text for an expository sermon has virtually been discussed in previous remarks. The reasons urged for this mode of preaching will usually dictate, that the pastor shall treat some important book of the Scripture "in course." What books he shall select must be determined by his pastoral experience and good judgment. They should obviously be such as are rich in evangelical facts and doctrines, and so chosen that, taken as a whole, they will form a complete outline of the system of revealed religion. But the book to be expounded being chosen, no farther question as to the choice of the text may be supposed to remain; the preacher's work is laid out ready to his hand. This is usually true, save that an important point remains—the fixing of the *termini* of the passage to be treated in the next sermon. The extent of Scripture to be embraced must be determined partly by its richness in matter. If the passage be very fruitful, a smaller compass can be taken. If it consist largely of perspicuous narrative, or such-like detail, not requiring explanation, the preacher may despatch a much longer portion. But the chief consideration to guide him here will be the unity of the topic. He will terminate his exposition for the occasion, where he finds such a natural change of subject as introduces independent matter. And in choosing this *terminus* he will pay little regard to those artificial divisions into chapters and verses which, as you know, have no inspired origin, and are often far from judicious or discriminating.

A few more detailed remarks may be necessary for the selection of single texts. I hardly need repeat the rule, that they should belong either to the class of capital texts or of epitome texts. And the theory of the preacher's function which I have asserted will show you, without many words of mine, that it is never proper to employ a text as a mere *motto* to introduce the sermon. This vicious usage degrades the Bible into a mere collection of literary apophthegms. Nor will the true minister select and mature his subject in his own mind, and then seek a text for it. The sermon should not dictate the choice of a text, but the text should determine the whole character of the sermon. But, affirmatively, I would impose the following rules:

1. The text should be God's word. This rule has not been to all preachers as self-evident as you may suppose. Nor will one be sure of its observance by seeking his texts always within the Bible. He will, of course, not take them from the Apocrypha. Nor

will he found a sermon on a faulty rendering of the
English version, nor on a false or questionable reading
of the original. For even though, in the case last mentioned, the preacher may honestly believe that he can
clear away the question as to the genuineness of the
reading, it will be better for him to leave the text unused, than to inflict upon an audience so little accustomed to critical discussion the arguments which will
make them think with him. But the chief danger of
violence to this rule is in the adoption of sentiments
uttered by mere men and recorded in the Scriptures, as
texts for sermons. The thoughtlessness of preachers in
this particular is illustrated by the divine mentioned
by Dr. George Campbell,[1] who took the words of Satan
to Eve (Gen. iii. 5), " Ye shall be as gods, knowing good
and evil," as a text to discuss the future glory of the
Christian. So another was betrayed into adopting the
words of Gamaliel (Acts v. 38), " If this counsel or this
work be of men, it will come to naught," as a scriptural
and infallible maxim. You will observe that the only
thing for which inspiration makes itself responsible in
such a passage is the truth that this man actually did
utter these words, and that they, with their attendant
circumstances, are recorded with perfect historical correctness. When the book of Acts tells us that Festus
exclaimed, " Paul, thou art beside thyself: much learning doth make thee mad," are we to understand the
inspired historian as vouching for the apostle's lunacy,
and for the still more false assertion that learning causes
madness? It is preposterous: all that the inspiration

---

[1] Sacred Eloquence, Lec. VII.

of Luke guarantees is the simple fact, that this scene
did occur, and that this wretched pagan, Festus, was a
sufficiently great fool to utter this slander and nonsense.
I need not point out to you how much more preposterous it would be for the Christian minister to
wrest the sacred narrative so as to make the Holy
Ghost teach either that learning produces lunacy, or
that St. Paul was a madman. I have selected an extreme instance in order to give you a plain caution
against this mistake. Yet there are two cases in which
the things done or spoken by uninspired men, but recorded by inspiration, may be made the foundations
of sermons, if they meet the other requirements. There
may be a sanction of the act or sentiment by the Holy
Ghost which is sufficiently intimated in the context or
in the other Scriptures. If this sanction is sufficiently
ascertained, then the words of man are covered by the
infallibility of God, and are therefore of authority to
us. The other case is that in which the sentiment or
act of the uninspired creature, although not sanctioned
as either right or true, may give an instructive example
of some scriptural truth. Thus, the preacher may not
take the falsehood of Satan (Gen. iii. 5) as authority for
teaching the future deification of the minds of believers : he might perhaps use it as an illustration of
the important fact, that those who tempt to sin, like
their father, usually employ some flattering lie. Or
the story may teach us, as Eve learned by her sore experience, that an overweening ambition leads in the end
to disaster instead of gain.

2. The text must be accepted and discussed only in
the very sense which it had in the mind of the Spirit

as he uttered it. The preacher has no concern with, and no right to, any other. It is nervously remarked by the Rev. Richard Cecil, that "the meaning of the Scripture is the Scripture." The propriety of my law is plain from the fact that the preacher is a herald, and that it is God's word which is committed to him as his instrument for the redemption of men. If his task is to deliver and commend God's message, what right has he to change it or to represent it as other than it is? Besides the risk of giving a fatal and specific wrong guidance to some soul in the very perversion of that particular proposition of Scripture, such a custom confuses the minds of hearers in their efforts to understand the word, and cultivates irreverent feelings toward its authority. The falsehood of that man is full of impiety, who, avowedly standing up in a sacred place to declare God's message to perishing souls, says that the Holy Spirit has said what he has not said. I would impress you with a solemn awe of taking any liberties in expounding the word. I would have you feel that every meaning of the text, other than that which God expressly intended it to bear, is forbidden fruit to you, however plausible and attractive—fruit which you dare not touch on peril of a fearful sin. One may ask, "Am I not justified, provided the meaning I give, although not actually placed in that text by the Holy Ghost, is still a scriptural truth taught elsewhere in the Word?" I answer, No; this is only a palliation. This secures you from positively destroying the souls of your hearers by giving them, then and there, false directions as to the way of life. But the license still does mischief; because it confuses and misleads them in reading the

Scriptures and undermines their reverence and confidence toward you and them.

The exact mind of the Spirit in the text must then be ascertained, before you presume to preach on it. The methods for doing this, by the grammatical study of the original with all accessible learned helps, and by meditation on the context and the connection of thought in which God has placed the passage, belong rather to the science of interpretation than to sacred rhetoric. I need only add that a proper apprehension of the preacher's mission will make him intensely honest and prayerful in his study. My second rule is violated when the text is discussed in a sense which it bears while disjoined from the context. Thus the words of Rom. xiv. 23, "Whatsoever is not of faith is sin," when read without any attention to the apostle's scope, have been wrested to teach the doctrine that the obedience of a sinner cannot be accepted by God until he is a justified believer. This is a scriptural truth; it might be correctly preached, for instance, from Heb. xi. 6: "But without faith it is impossible to please Him." But when we advert to the subject of Rom. xiv. 23, we find that the inspired author is speaking of the sin of disregarding positive precepts of the old ceremonial law, while the conscience and judgment were still in suspense concerning their obligation on Christians. So that the meaning of his concluding proposition is, every act is wrong which is not prompted by a full conviction of its lawfulness. A similar error was committed when a venerable prelate chose the words of Ezek. xxxvii. 3, "Son of man, can these bones live?" to preach at the funeral of a Christian the doctrine of the resurrection of the body. The death and the resurrection of that text are both symbolical, and God's question is, whether a people so obdurate and ruined as the Jews then were could be restored.

The rule is sometimes violated by taking the mere illustration for the truth illustrated; as when Blair founds a sermon touching "the Sentiments Appropriate to Middle Age" on the words of 1 Cor. xiii. 11, " But when I became a man, I put away childish things." The apostle merely borrows this fact from the history of his youth, to explain the difference between the spiritual knowledge of the Christian in his militant, and that of his glorified state.

The rule is also outraged by all those liberties in accommodating texts which are so common even in our own pulpits. I have heard more than one Presbyterian minister derive from the words of God to Moses (Ex. xiv. 15), "Speak unto the children of Israel that they go forward," the proposition, that it is the duty of the Church to make ecclesiastical and spiritual advancements. What is this more than a species of sober punning on the words, "Go forward"? All that the expositor is entitled to draw from this incident, for instruction of modern Christians, is the plain principle which finds example in this command to Israel, and its issue. And that principle is, that the people of God must "walk by faith and not by sight;" that they must regard the express command, and not the seeming obstacle. A very different thought, truly! These familiar instances have been detailed to guard you against violations of this imperative rule.

3. No passage of Scripture is suitable for a text

which does not contain a distinct and important point.
Because a sentence is a part of that Scripture which is
declared to be all inspired and all profitable, it does not
follow that it is a suitable proposition to furnish instruction for a sermon.   Every continuous composition
must contain many passages which are not cardinal,
but yet are necessary to connect those that are.   Let
the student compare Rom. i. 10, " Making request (if
by any means now at length I might have a prosperous
journey by the will of God) to come unto you," with
Rom. iii. 28, " Therefore we conclude that a man is
justified by faith, without the deeds of the law."   The
former is only incidental to the introduction of the
Epistle.   The latter is a great truth falling at once
under the classes of the capital and the epitome texts,
containing the designed summation of a most important
inspired argument, and a doctrine of prime rank in the
theology of redemption.   He who should attempt to
make a whole sermon of the former must needs trifle
or go out of his text.   The latter furnishes grave matter
for a volume.   That conceit of some of the Puritan
divines, which caused them to compose a separate sermon on each verse of a book of Scripture or of a Psalm
was therefore but a serious trifling.   Under an appearance of great reverence and value for the Scripture, it
really misrepresented and perverted its fair meaning.
The Holy Spirit did not mean a sermon in every sentence he uttered: it is incorrect for us to represent him so.

Under this rule I would also embrace the maxim of
Claude, in his celebrated treatise of the " Composition
of the Sermon," notwithstanding the opposition to it of
some respectable writers.   He requires that the text

shall be so taken as to contain not only a distinct, but
a complete, compass of inspired truth. We must not
take for discussion, he teaches, less of the passage than
will give us the whole thought of the author expressed
in that place upon the one point. For example, let the
passage under consideration be 2 Cor. i. 3, 4. The text
is not complete if we stop with the words, " Blessed be
God, the Father of our Lord Jesus Christ, the Father
of mercy and the God of all comfort." Nor does it become complete if we add only the words, " who com-
forteth us in all our afflictions." We must proceed
farther, and include also the design : " That we may be
able to comfort them who are in any trouble, by the
comfort wherewith we ourselves are comforted of God."
For the apostle's topic here being his own gospel consolation, we have not fairly represented his thought
until we cite all that he states on that point in that
sentence. The reason which requires this completeness
in the text is, that otherwise our presentation of the
truth is fragmentary, and therefore incorrect. The
objection to this requirement is not valid. It is argued
that the rule compels the preacher to include perhaps
more particulars concerning the topic than his time
permits him thoroughly to discuss. The objectors
claim that, if his discussion is faithful to the meaning
of inspiration as far as it goes, this is enough, though it
is fragmentary. I reply that our expository theory of
the sermon leads us to a different conclusion : the
preacher has no other task than to unfold the mind of
the Spirit. And the whole force of the objection is removed by the remark that it is always legitimate for
us, after having fairly stated, in paraphrase or sum-

mary, the whole meaning of the word, to inform our hearers that we limit ourselves, for the time, to the particular discussion of a part of the matter given us by the text.

4. The text should be perspicuous. The amount of our fourth rule is that the pastor will always prefer a passage of Scripture from which the meaning can be made plain to the people by a simple exposition, rather than one which would require an exegesis difficult and prolix. If the two passages compared contain substantially the same truth, let the simple one by all means be the preferred text. This rule will, of course, receive some modification from the facts that the preacher's business is to explain the Bible to his charge, and that there are a few truths of revelation not unworthy of occasional inculcation which are taught only in obscure passages. Must you wholly rob your people of this instruction because you can only introduce them to it by a somewhat laborious exposition? Surely not. And it may be wise sometimes to tax the powers of your spiritual pupils to their highest bent, in order to strengthen them. Should you push the principle so far as to forego every text which required your explanation, this would be a confession that the calling of the religious teacher is unnecessary—that the people understand all they need know without his help. You will, therefore, accept this rule as general only and not universal.

But I would urge, much more absolutely, that you should never indulge the affectation of choosing odd or curious texts. Some ministers are fond of selecting passages from which they may ingeniously deduce far-

fetched and unexpected propositions. Others perversely
prefer to found the discussion of some well-known doctrine which is expressly taught in many plain declara-
tions of the Bible, on some unusual text from which it
can only be drawn, if at all, as a remote corollary, or
obscure implication. These tricks are always attributed
by sensible hearers to the preacher's vanity and conceit.
They suspect that his prime motive is to cause people
to gaze and gape at his ingenuity and wondrous learning. When the strange text is announced, it is intended that each hearer shall say to himself, " Now how
on earth will he get anything from that?" But when
the preacher has solved the riddle they will applaud
him as a wondrous man! Only idle and shallow people can be pleased thus; to the well-instructed all such
artifices are odious.

The plea may be made that it is lawful and desirable
the preacher should evince the riches and harmony of
the Scripture, by thus disclosing the same cardinal truths
as taught by implication in the obscure, which are expressly set forth in the plain passages. True. It is
claimed also that the pastor should not be ever teaching
his people " which be the first principles of the oracles
of God," but should so exercise their discernment by
reason of use, as to solve for them the more difficult
parts. True again; but the reasonable and natural
order for each sermon is the same which governs the
whole course of instruction. We proceed from the simple to the complex. The perspicuous passage should
be the text, and the preacher should then apply this to
solve the more remote and obscure. The latter he may
skilfully introduce in the course of his discussion, after

the clearer text has prepared the way, that its light may be thrown upon them and thus facilitate their comprehension.

There are particular texts which are almost classical in the Protestant pulpit, and which in each generation have been made the foundations for great sermons upon capital topics of Christianity. Shall the young pastor attempt these? I reply, that his good taste will lead him to avoid such a treatment of them as will suggest to cultivated hearers the idea of either imitation or rivalry of the known master-pieces. But, on the other hand, it is both his duty and his wisdom to dwell most frequently on these grand. subjects. As they occupy the major place in revelation, so must they in his preaching. And he who never grapples with great subjects will never have great powers.

In conclusion, the pastor should study appropriateness in his selections of subjects and texts. A sermon to be followed by the sacrament of the Lord's Supper should present some central doctrine of the cross. When God's providences call the people to humiliation, some topic of divine truth should be urged which displays the holiness of the Law and the evil of sin. When the people are bowed in true repentance they need the consolations of the gospel. The minister preaching by invitation to another pastor's charge will be chary in employing topics of reprehension. The people will receive such correction, if it be timely, more suitably from their own spiritual guide.

LECTURE VII.

CARDINAL REQUISITES OF THE SERMON.

WE have now reached a subject which may be regarded as intermediate between the department of Invention and that of Disposition. This is the consideration of the general qualities which must characterize the structure of every sermon. These may be called the cardinal virtues of this species of discourse. Some of them are common to all orations; some are peculiar to the sermon. They are *Textual Fidelity, Unity, Instructiveness, Evangelical Tone, Movement, Point* and *Order*. I shall now proceed to explain and enforce each of them.

The quality of *textual fidelity* will be easily comprehended, if you recall the preacher's position as the deliverer of a message. The people roughly but accurately express it by the phrase "sticking to one's text." It is simply a strict fidelity throughout the discussion to the subject and teachings of the text. The best argument to enforce upon you this virtue is suggested by the same fact—that the preacher is a herald. The first quality of the good herald is the faithful delivery of the very mind of his king. Our conception of our office, and of the revealed word as an infinitely wise rule for man's salvation, permits us to discuss the text in no other spirit. Our business with it is to commend

105

God's own meaning in it—nothing more, nothing less, to every man's conscience in his sight. Our task is to impress God's own die, as he has engraved it, upon the plastic soul, that we may produce his image.

But textual fidelity also secures us important ends besides the high and sacred one of obedience to our charge. It is a means for securing unity, which, as we shall see anon, is also essential to good discourse; for if the text is discreetly chosen so as to contain one main subject, and if the discourse is faithful to the text, this is itself a sufficient guarantee that unity will not be fatally wounded. Textual fidelity will give you that of which the young pastor often feels so great need— fruitfulness and variety of matter. Those who are inexperienced in discourse imagine that they secure copiousness by allowing themselves to ramble. But they are mistaken. It is the steady contemplation of definite truth in its definite relations which enriches the mind with instructive thoughts. If your powers are relieved of this labour by the permission to rove, they will remain barren and unawakened, and will run the narrow round of your familiar commonplaces. This remark leads to another, that the habit of wandering from your text is in the end wasteful of your stores. You may have relieved the vacuity of your minds by introducing foreign matter, but you will find to your cost that you have thus anticipated and used important topics which should have furnished you other independent discussions. Thus, the tyro has a text which sets forth the great evangelical grace of repentance. Instead of studying it thoroughly, and pouring out some of the rich stores of instruction and appeal which this

Christian sentiment furnishes, he indolently attempts to supply his barrenness by some commonplaces upon the subject of faith, justifying his expedient upon the ground that the text-books tell him faith and repentance are twin graces. The consequence is that a few weeks after, when he would preach upon faith, he finds that he has forestalled himself; the fundamental propositions on that subject (because familiar) have been recently uttered by him, and his present discussion must either be repetitious or fragmentary.

It is usually wise to extend this fidelity to the text, not only to its abstract doctrine, but to its imagery. Let the sermon wear, in the main, the same figurative drapery with the passage on which it is founded. The reason for this is, that as we trust the infallibility of the divine doctrine, so we may always trust the appropriateness of the inspired rhetoric, except where a change of usage and habits of thought have reversed the ancient associations attached to the images. Besides, it will be the pastor's duty to present oftentimes the same capital truths. He will often find occasion to remind his charge, with the apostle, that "to teach the same things to him indeed is not burdensome, and for them it is safe." It will then be a great gain to the freshness of his preaching to throw over his subject, in imitation of his text, the new colouring of a new trope. And this is more than a mere advantage of style; for as every just metaphor suggests some true parallelisms of relations belonging to the thing represented, the new figurative dress will teach us some additional element of the truth. The great doctrine of the new birth, for instance, is represented as an opening of blind eyes also, and as a quickening of dead souls. Each of these tropes presents the truth in new aspects. Let the preacher avail himself of their variety and instructiveness. But in doing this he must carefully guard against excess, and see to it that he does not expand a metaphor into a vicious allegory. Let not the preacher, enforcing the admonition of Prov. xxix. 1, "He that, being often reproved, hardeneth his neck shall be suddenly destroyed, and that without remedy," make the impenitent sinner an ox throughout his discourse. Here a severe judgment and taste must be his guard.

Unity is necessary to every work of art—to the oration, the drama, the poem, the painting, the architectural structure, the statue. There is no canon of rhetoric more universally admitted than this, which demands unity in discourse. But what is this quality? It is not sameness or singleness of idea. It does not forbid variety, diversity, nor even contrast, in the subordinate parts. Nature's unity is full of variety. It is not that singleness which the dialectician expresses by unicity, but it is the combination of parts into one whole. It is a component individuality which gives unity to art. Hence, so far is it from being true that the aggregation of several parts destroys it, we may see that unless there be more than one part there will be no unity, but unicity only. Unity is what results from union. The requisition of this quality, then, in its severest form, does not exclude the widest range of variety in thought and illustration. Indeed, it is sometimes most strikingly displayed by combining things diverse, or even contrasted, to enhance one effect. Thus, in Hogarth's picture of a market scene, designed to produce the sentiment of the grotesque, amidst every angular and ungainly figure which his fancy could group together, he has introduced a greyhound. The graceful and flowing outlines of this animal enhance by contrast the main effect. The fable of Laocoön has been immortalized by two arts, the pen of the classic poet and the chisel of the sculptor. The resultant impression designed in the reader or spectator is that of sympathetic horror. The athletic frame of the father, with his herculean muscles strained with agony, is in the strongest contrast with the almost feminine softness of the limbs of his sons. But all are enfolded in the resistless coils of the dragons, against which manly vigour is as impotent as infantile grace. In like manner, should the preacher's aim be to dismiss his hearers with the most distinct and impressive feeling of the worth of the soul, he may enforce it by ideas as remote from each other as heaven from hell, by the preciousness of the joys of the saved and by the miseries of the lost.

Affirmatively, rhetorical unity requires these two things. The speaker must, first, have one main subject of discourse, to which he adheres with supreme reference throughout. But this is not enough. He must, second, propose to himself one definite impression on the hearer's soul, to the making of which everything in the sermon is bent.[1] You will remember that the

---

[1] Quum igitur . . . rem tractare cœpi, nihil prius constituo quam quid sit illud, quo mihi referenda sit omnis illa oratio, quæ sit propria quæstionis et judicii; deinde quorum alterum . . . est accommodatum ad eorum animos, apud quos dicimus, ad id quod volumus, commovendos.—*Cic. de Orat.*, b. ii., ch. 27. § 114.

distinguishing trait of the oration is that it is always practical, that it concludes by saying to the hearer, "Do this," that its *terminus* is in a volition, and that its aim is to pass through the understanding into the motives of the soul. Unity of discourse requires, then, not only singleness of a dominant subject, but also singleness of practical impression. To secure the former, see to it that the whole discussion may admit of reduction to a single proposition. To secure the latter, let the preacher hold before him, through the whole preparation of the sermon, the one practical effect intended to be produced upon the hearer's will.

You will now, I think, have little difficulty in determining with what this unity may or may not consist. All digressions, episodes and corollaries are not sins against it. If they lead the hearer's soul away from the one chief end of the discourse, if their result is to divide or abstract any power of attention or feeling from that end, they are excrescences. But if, while they seem to open side channels of thought or emotion, their current returns and debouches into the main one, so as to add volume and *momentum* to it, then they are legitimate. The discourse may have only the greater beauty and force because of an apparent diversion of the progress. On the other hand, unity is often violated by introducing too many explanatory topics. It is marred by a range of exposition wider or more protracted than is necessary for distinctly apprehending the main proposition. You have correctly inferred, from my assertion that all true preaching must be expository of the Word, that I give great weight to the context. But its discussion should be extended no farther than is needed to place the meaning of the Holy Spirit, in the text, in its proper connection of thought. This rule must be strictly observed; for otherwise, since all sacred truths are connected among themselves, there might be no limit to the trespasses committed upon the unity of the text. So it is vicious to intrude an illustration or an episode only for the sake of the piquancy of the thing introduced. What is this but to sacrifice the fruit to the foliage, the end to the means? Perhaps it is a more important caution to remind you, that unity is by no means secured by a series of remarks which are all upon the subject of the same proposition. Let it be, "Faith justifies us." A number of pious remarks about faith may be made, each one of which shall be scriptural. (A definition, for instance, of its nature; a reference to its source in the grace of the Holy Ghost; a discussion of its perpetuity; an examination of its warrant; a description of its effects on the heart and life.) The preacher imagines that he is very faithfully discoursing of faith all the time; and yet it is manifest that there is no convergency whatever in these several remarks. They may be all referred to the same subject, and yet point as diversely as the *radii* which issue in opposite directions from the same centre. The proper image of rhetorical unity is not found in the star, which scatters its rays on every side from one point of light, to be absorbed and lost in the darkness of space, but in the ·lens, which collects many parallel or even dissentient rays into one burning *focus*. But to return to the proposition cited in our instance: if all the remarks of the discourse had a true bearing upon the copula or affirmation, "Justification *is* by faith," then there would be a necessary unity. I need not detain you to show at length that the connection of truth with truth and doctrine with doctrine constitutes no plea for heaping one upon another in the same discourse. Regeneration implies original sin. He who should therefore claim that a full discussion of the new birth must include a discussion of our fall in Adam, has not the first conception of rhetorical unity. By the same argument it would follow that, since all truth is connected, each sermon must be a complete *syllabus* in theology. These two results would then be inevitable: that there could be but one sermon in substance, and that this one sermon must remain for ever a *bare syllabus*. The hearers would therefore never gain a full and impressive view of any one point of Christian theology; they could never receive more than a barren smattering of sacred knowledge.

There was a very pious and venerable class of ministers who insisted, more plausibly, upon a canon which violated unity in another way. Their rule was that no sermon was correct unless, whatever the text, it included a statement of the whole plan of salvation, sufficiently detailed to be understood and embraced, with the aid of the Spirit, by a soul which heard it then for the first and last time. Their reason for this requirement was, that the preacher could never know but that there was some ignorant soul present who was destined not to hear the gospel again. You will not understand me, in dissenting from this pious rule, as retracting anything I have urged upon the duty of continually holding up the cross. I will admit that a missionary, who preaches transiently to ignorant and destitute per-

sons to whom he will not soon return, should honour
the spirit of the precept by preferring uniformly texts
which contain the very marrow of the gospel. But
then, he will be able to expound the way of salvation
without violating unity, or taking liberties with the
meaning of God's word. Textual fidelity will then not
only permit, but require, the presentation of those cardinal truths which are suited to the soul enjoying its last
opportunity of salvation. But the ordinary pastor who
meets his people frequently should limit himself in
compliance with the demands of unity, lest, by attempting to make all his sermons comprehensive of the
whole system of redemption, he should make them all
meagre.

Having thus defined unity of discourse, I add that
it is demanded by the very nature of the mind. If
image follows image before our attention, without any
tie between them, the impression of the second obliter-
ates that made by the first. There can be no cumulative effect. But if the several topics are convergent
toward the same conviction of mind and purpose of
will, the second promotes the impression begun by the
first. The hearer's soul is consequently borne toward
the designed *terminus* by the accelerating force of the
whole, and a powerful effect is produced. Unity is as
essential to strength as to beauty. The sermon which
lacks this quality can only do good by accident. "The
words of the wise," saith Solomon, "are as nails fastened by the masters of assemblies, which are given from
one shepherd." The nail is only driven home by successive blows upon the same spot. The engineer who
would batter a breach in the enemy's wall does not

scatter his cannon-shot.   He makes all his guns converge upon a single spot.   Thus an irresistible force is
applied, before which no masonry can stand, while by
the opposite method he would only have scratched the
whole surface of the fortress, without breaking down
any part.

The next property of the good sermon I have named
evangelical tone.   This is a gracious character, appropriate to the proclamation of that gospel where "mercy
and truth meet together, and righteousness and peace
kiss each other."   It qualifies both the matter and manner of the sermon.   To superinduce upon matter not
evangelical the preacher's unction of style and delivery
would be unnatural and almost impossible; for it is a
fact worthy of notice that a purely secular oratory, like
that of the Pagan classics, presents of this quality no
trace.   To deliver evangelical matter in any other tone
is inappropriate to the preacher's attitude, as a ransomed sinner honoured to become the herald of the law
and of mercy to the lost.   First, then, this attitude dictates that the matter of the sermon shall be prevalently
evangelical.   We cannot better describe it than in the
words of the apostles, when they so frequently speak of
their work as "preaching Christ," or "preaching Christ
crucified."   We do not conceive that they mean to declare, the only facts they ever recited were those enacted
on Calvary, or that they limited themselves exclusively
to the one doctrine of vicarious satisfaction for sin.
The abstracts of their sermons, recorded in the New
Testament, show that this was not true.   But we find
that these facts and this doctrine were central to their
teachings.   They recurred perpetually with a prominence

suitable to their importance. More than this, they were ever near at hand, as the *focus* to which every beam of divine truth must converge. The whole revealed system, with its doctrines and duties, was ever presented in gospel aspects. The law, when preached as a rule of conviction, led to the cross. The law, as a rule of obedience, drew its noblest sanctions from the cross. Such being the method of the inspired men, I would willingly define evangelical preaching by the term scriptural. Let the preacher present all doctrines and duties, not in the lights of philosophy or of human ethics, but of the New Testament. And for enforcement of this quality I cannot do better than refer you to the apostle's declaration, that when he came to preach among the Corinthians (1 Eph. ii. 2) he " determined not to know anything among them, save Jesus Christ and him crucified."

The testimony of Church history and of man's spiritual instincts, to the superior and abiding power of evangelical matter over the soul, has been already briefly cited. All the great preachers, from the apostles to our day, whom God has honoured to revive and bless his Church, have been evangelical : Ambrose, Augustine, Chrysostom, the Reformers, the orthodox Puritans, Whitefield, the Wesleys, the Tennents, Davies, Chalmers, Summerfield, Nettleton. The pure gospel usually attracts the multitude of those who hunger after God, while the Ritualist and the moralizing pulpit philosophers, after the tinsel of novelty is lost, parade their wares before empty benches.

Evangelical tone includes also that quality which is happily denoted by the French divines, *unction*. This

term is suggested by that scriptural trope which so frequently represents the effusion of the Holy Ghost as an
anointing from God.[1] It expresses, therefore, as you
will easily apprehend, that temperature of thought and
elocution, which the Spirit of all grace sheds upon the
heart possessed by the blessed truths of the gospel. It
is not identical with animation. Every passion in the
preacher does not constitute unction. While it does not
expel intellectual activity, authority and will, it super-
fuses these elements of force with the love, the pity, the
tenderness, the pure zeal, the seriousness, which the
topics of redemption should shed upon the soul of a
ransomed and sanctified sinner. It is defined by *Vinet*
as " the general savour of Christianity, a gravity accompanied by tenderness, a severity tempered with sweetness, a majesty associated with intimacy." Blair calls
it " gravity and warmth united." Its necessity to the
happiest effect of preaching will be apprehended, without other argument, if you simply represent to yourselves the sentiments with which the soul eminently
pervaded by the grace of the Holy Ghost would undertake the sacred and merciful work of the gospel proclamation to guilty fellow-men. The most complete
conception of the quality is that ideal which you derive,
from the Evangelists, of the temper of the preaching of
Jesus Christ. To deliver such a message as his, without any tincture of his temper, must ever be felt as a
harsh solecism. To affect unction is manifestly impossible. It is, in short, a quality not merely intellectual or sentimental, but spiritual. Although not

---

[1] See, for instance, 1 John ii. 27.

identical with ardent piety, it is the effluence of ardent piety alone.   A correct taste alone cannot communicate it.   It cannot be taught by rhetoric alone.   It cannot be acquired from imitation of others.   But it is the Holy Spirit who communicates it to the cultivated mind and pure taste, by enduing the soul which is thus prepared with an ardent zeal for God's glory and a tender compassion for those who are perishing.   Thus we are led from another quarter to the same conclusion—that only the eminent Christian can be an eminent preacher of the gospel.

Continuing this subject, I remark that every good sermon is *instructive*.   This quality is not the same with that which distinguishes the doctrinal discourse; for it should pervade all practical and narrative sermons as well.   It is to enforce this obligation, especially as to these kinds of discourses, that I give place to instructiveness as one of the general virtues of the preacher.   It is not that quality described by the phrase "intellectual preaching," in the affected dialect of the day.   The odious thing intended by the latter is a sort of religioso-philosophic and human speculation, which is ambitious of profundity, and which a covert pedantry inflates.   But the instructive sermon is that which abounds in food for the understanding.   It is full of thought, and richly informs the mind of the hearer.   It is opposed, of course, to vapid and commonplace compositions; but it is opposed also to those which seek to reach the will through rhetorical ornament and passionate sentiment, without establishing rational conviction.   The instructive sermon will have an important subject; it will be rich in matter and will communicate solid knowledge. It will exhibit truth in its rational connections, so that the hearer shall feel himself advanced and established in a firm system. But this food for the mind must be none other than scriptural food. He would greatly abuse my meaning, who should make this requisition for instructiveness a pretext for intruding foreign and secular information into the pulpit. Thus the question recurs, whether he who limits himself strictly to the circle of revealed truths will find enough to make all his sermons rich in matter. Again I answer, with confidence, that he will. But I do not conceal the truth that, in order for this, he must be a man of diligent study and of ripe acquirements. He need not expect to possess this virtue who is not mighty in the Scriptures and thoroughly informed in their theology. He must have obeyed the injunction of the apostle to Timothy (1 Epis. iv. 13, etc.), " Give attendance to reading, to exhortation, to doctrine." . . . " Meditate on these things; give thyself wholly to them, that thy profiting may appear unto all." But such a pastor will always find, in the exposition of the Scriptures to his people, in the defence of the doctrines and order of his Church, in the application of these principles to the ·diversified exigencies of their consciences, abundant stores of thought to enrich all his sermons. If, after selecting his subject, he does not find this affluence of matter, let him accuse his own ignorance and set about informing it.

The necessity of instructiveness in all sermons appears from the same considerations by which I urged frequent doctrinal preaching. Religion is an intelligent concern, and deals with man as a reasoning creature.

Sanctification is by the truth. To move men we must instruct. No Christian can be stable and consistent save as he is intelligent. Instruction alone can prevent revivals from becoming mischievous excitements, and Christian zeal from degenerating into fanatical heat. Let it be considered, in addition, that the desire to know, or rational curiosity, is the natural appetite of the mind, and that knowledge is its proper food. Knowledge is the light of the soul, and as sweet as the light is to the eye so pleasant is truth to the mind. It is true that the understanding is conscious of a species of *vis inertiæ*, and that an effort is often necessary to rouse it to the labour of apprehension. But that effort is wholesome and cheerful. The desire to know is one of the most vivid sentiments of the soul, and its gratification is one of the purest and most uncloying pleasures of our nature. The apostle[1] enumerates it among the elements which compose the immortal bliss of heaven. Hence, you may securely rely upon instructiveness as an unfailing power to attract the people permanently to your ministry. If you would not wear out after you have ceased to be a novelty, give the minds of your people food. Young pastors not seldom yield to a timidity, lest the multitude should be repelled by the homeliness of the truth; and they imagine that they are catering better for the popular tastes, by relieving them of the labour of attention and amusing them with rhetorical pyrotechnics. I do not here remark upon the wickedness of such an expedient. Pastoral experience proves that it is not adapted to its end, low as

---

[1] 1 Cor. xiii. 12.

that end is. The men who draw the multitude are (if we except those who have more successfully satisfied the depravity of our race by positive error) the instructive pastors. The crowd flocks a few times to behold the empty show. But when it feels the necessity of being fed, it resorts to the place where solid food is provided for the mind, even if it be with plainer equipage. Make your people feel that they are gaining permanent acquisitions of knowledge from you, and they will not desert you.[1]

---

[1] I once asked a sensible, plain man, who was familiar with the popular oratory of Randolph, what was its charm with the common people. He did not mention, as I expected he would, his magic voice, his classic grace, the purity of his English, his intense passion, the energy of his will, his pungent wit, his sarcasm, or the inimitable aptitude of his illustration. But he answered: "It was because Mr. Randolph was so instructive; he taught the people so much which they had not known before."

LECTURE VIII.

CARDINAL REQUISITES OF THE SERMON.

MOVEMENT, saith Vinet, is the royal virtue of style. But it is a quality belonging both to structure and style, characterizing the oration as a whole. Indeed, it may be said, without exaggeration, that it is this which makes discourse eloquence. Cicero asks in one place, *Quid aliud est eloquentia, nisi motus animæ continuus?* This discriminating question suggests the true nature of the quality. The oration has movement, because the soul, whose progeny it is, has movement. The impression of eloquence is not merely a communication of conceptions, opinions, mental convictions, facts; but it is the communion of the speaker's soul, in all its powers, with the souls of his hearers. It is an impulse communicated from the one to the others. Have we not defined eloquence as the emission of the soul's energy through speech? There is no work of the mind which so nearly possesses the attributes of life as the oration, for the living soul pours its own energies directly into its discourse. Motion is the sign, the test of life. The form which moves not is dead; it may be beautiful, but it has only the beauty of the corpse. And when we remember that the practical object of the oration is to impel the hearers to some action of soul through the incitement of their

121

own rational emotions, we see the necessity of movement in such discourse.   If it does not succeed in trans-
ferring the hearer's soul to a new position or a new
practical conclusion, or, at least, in causing it to travel
afresh to a position once occupied before, it has failed
of its work.   Now, bodies pass from place to place by
motion.   The impelling body must move through this
interval in order that the body impelled may do so.

I have stated these thoughts in order to disclose both
the nature and necessity of movement.   Reflection will
show you that it is a broad and fundamental trait of
discourse, extending to the thought, the logic, the emotion and the language.   Continuity must manifestly
belong to it.   Movement is not a blow or shock, communicating only a single or instantaneous impulse, but
a sustained progress.   It is, in short, that force thrown
from the soul of the orator into his discourse, by which
the soul of the hearer is urged, with a constant and
accelerated progress, toward that practical impression
which is designed for the result.   If in any part the
discourse is narrative or descriptive, incident must follow incident as fast as they can be clearly exhibited to
the hearer's apprehension.   If it is explanatory or
didactic, the expansion of the idea, or the addition of
thought to thought, must be constant.   If it is demonstrative, a stronger proof must urge the mind, immediately after each preceding one, toward the goal of
conviction.   In its emotional character, the discourse
must sustain and perpetually raise the emotion inspired
to its proper culmination at the change or the end.
But every true oration, whether narrative or didactic
or argumentative, is also virtually emotional.   The

speaker must remember that man feels as he sees, and because he sees: mental conviction or apprehension is in order to emotion and volition. Hence movement will require that the two elements—the didactic or logical and the emotive—however interfused through the progress of the oration, shall always be related to each other in the order of their nature. The definition of a duty will precede the incentives to it. The appeal to the mental convictions will ground the application of the motives. The contrary order would be unnatural and would interrupt movement. Again, that the movement may be continuous, it is necessary not only that a thought, image or argument shall succeed a previous one without dallying, but that the successor shall be coherent with its predecessor; for otherwise, instead of furthering the impression begun, it would institute a movement in a new direction and give a shock to the mind. We are thus led back to the maxim which demands thorough unity. And in one sense the vigour or force of the incoherent thought which intruded itself would only render the sin against movement greater, because it would impel the hearer farther aside from the proper line of the progress. In style, movement requires a certain economy of words. Amplification will not be excluded from its proper place; but it will never be carried beyond the real expansion of the thought and addition of new ideas. Indeed, the best mark of legitimate amplification is, that it shall be a real progress of the ideas, and, in a certain sense, climactic. Nothing is more wearying to the hearer than that amplification which merely revolves the same thought, or which proceeds from the concrete back to the abstract, and from the definite to the general, in an anti-climactic order. The language of the orator must possess, in all its flow, a nervous brevity and a certain well-ordered haste, like that of the racer pressing to his goal.

Prolixity, therefore, is a sin against movement. Every epithet should be retrenched which adds nothing to the true rendering of the thought. This virtue is violated, of course, by all needless repetitions, by all digressions and episodes which lead away from the true path of the discussion, by tedious or superfluous explanation and definition. It is marred also by useless subdivisions, and by every formal appendage to the method of the discourse which is not necessary to make its order clear. This remark will explain to you the excessive dryness which you have doubtless felt in reading the multiplied subdivisions of some of the Puritan divines. It is as though the progress of the mind toward its goal were arrested at every third step for some useless formality. What can be more wearisome to the eager mind than such a journey? Once more, although the structure and the style may be free from these faults, a slow and hesitating enunciation may weaken the impression of movement in discourse. The speaker should utter his words, not indeed in a hurried or huddling manner, yet with such deliberate readiness as shows that his own soul is not halting for them in its career. But let me here caution you, that the attempt to escape the charge of prolixity or tediousness by means of undue haste of utterance always disappoints itself. Our estimate of duration is relative to our consciousness of the mental processes which have occupied us in the interval.   Hence a marked rapidity suggests the feeling of protracted time.   Moreover, the speaker, by this expedient, makes a public confession of the conviction that he is wearying his hearers by unreasonable length; and nothing is more natural than that they should regard him as guilty of that of which he so obviously feels guilty.   But if the movement is real and not merely mechanical, and the appropriate and pleasing utterance of the thoughts beguiles the consciousness away from its own labours, the discourse appears shorter than it is, and the hearer regrets that it is ended so soon.

The importance of movement in public speaking can scarcely be exaggerated.   Among those who really have matter to present, and who possess the fundamental quality of perspicuity, I am persuaded that the difference of impressiveness is chiefly due to their movement. Without it there is neither animation, force nor beauty. Horace mentions it first among the virtues of his great epic model, Homer: "*Semper ad eventum festinat.*"[1] Discourses should be like the river; sometimes it flows more rapidly than at others, but it is never stagnant. Now it glides quietly between grassy banks.   Anon, it ripples with cheerful music over its pebbly bed.   Again it rushes like an arrow, flashing sunlight down its straight channel.   Sometimes it clothes its mighty waves in foam as it dashes against opposing rocks.   At last, it sweeps with deep and silent force through its delta. But it flows onward always, never pausing, toward its destined ocean.   Should the voyager be anchored at the loveliest spot in all its course, it would soon become

---

[1] Ep. ad Pisones, line 149.

irksome. But he descends the current with an interest and pleasure ever new.

Of the virtue of *point* the remark must also be made that it is a quality both of structure and style. Unless the former be pointed, no art of language can make the latter so. Perhaps the single word, "point," conveys as distinct an idea of this excellence in discourse as any definition can. The thought must be incisive. There must be, in order to this, first, a chief truth, practical and important, distinctly apprehended by the speaker in its relation to the action of soul which he would excite. And the whole matter of the discourse must be so arranged as to make this proposition salient. Next, the speaker must have a clear comprehension of the relations between proposition and proof, and between knowledge and emotion, so that the means of conviction and incitement shall be properly subordinated to these ends. The result will be, that with the help of perspicuous language, this relation will be clearly apprehended and felt by the hearer. The cardinal thoughts and conclusions of the sermon will then impinge upon him with the aggregate force of the whole proofs and motives.

Let me here resort to an illustration very diverse from the one used of the last topic, but only in appearance inconsistent with it. The pointed or incisive discourse may be likened as to its framework to the ancient war-ship. Its weapon of offence was its beak. Let us suppose that the architect had left the ponderous mass of pointed metal which formed this beak lying in some accidental position amidst the timbers of the ship, and all those timbers a disorderly heap of rubbish merely thrown together and set adrift upon the sea as a raft. The impact of this shapeless pile, instead of piercing the opposing trireme, would only have dissolved itself into fragments; and the intended prow would probably have sunk out of sight without even coming into the feeblest contact with the enemy's hull. The architect, therefore, commits no such folly. He places the beak at the forefront of his structure. He causes the chief beams of his framework to converge to its base, and frames them into it. He adjusts the ribs and braces to support these in turn, so that there is not one piece of timber in the whole ship which does not lend its strength, either directly or remotely, to sustain the prow immovably in its place. And now, when the triple banks of rowers raise their chant and strain at their oars all in concert, they launch the pointed 'beak into the adversary's side with the *momentum* of the whole ship's weight. In like manner, the impression made by an oration depends upon its point, and this, in turn, depends upon the prominence of the cardinal thoughts and the perspicuous subordination of the rest to their support. The style which best seconds this structure is that which is lucid, compact and nervous, which individualizes the hearer and addresses him in the second person, which prefers the special statement to the general and the concrete to the abstract.

Many sermons are deficient in point. They either have no valuable and practical truths of cardinal weight, or these are not made to stand out to the apprehension of the hearers. No decided impression can be expected from such addresses. No lodgment is made in the conscience of the people; they go away with the vague feeling that they have been only listening to a strain of goodish but aimless talk. This failure of pointed effect is due sometimes to a sickly nicety of style, which shrinks from the directness of oral address and affects the delicacy of the essay. But more often it is the result of weakness and confusion of thought. And this, in turn, proceeds from indifference of heart. Earnest purpose and desire are always pointed. The distressed beggar needs no rhetoric to teach him how to make the point of his petition prominent. The children of this world never fail to press their points plainly when the objects of their natural desires are involved. Let the preacher, then, cultivate that faith which makes the ruin and the rescue of sinners dread realities to him; let him share the constraining love of Christ in its power; let him feel a consuming zeal to save souls. Then he will not go into the pulpit aimless, except with the grovelling object of satisfying decency and filling the allotted hour with the expected pious talk. He will have a definite and absorbing purpose, a message to deliver, and a result to effect, which he cannot leave unaccomplished without grief. This holy passion, and this alone, will give his sermon true point. The true cause of the vapid and aimless discourses, which are heard from so many pulpits, is that the preachers are not under the active influence of faith and love for souls. Thus we learn again that true and fervent piety is the prime qualification for sacred eloquence.

The last of the general attributes of good discourse is *Order*. This is the result of *Disposition*, and we are thus led to this department, which the text-books on rhetoric make the second division of their science. The order which disposition aims to produce is so important, and the subjects which claim our attention here are so numerous, that I must proceed more deliberately and fully than I have upon the previous kindred points.

Disposition includes both order and division. These are inseparably connected. Order is the proper arrangement of the parts among themselves; division discriminates the parts.[1] Division, therefore, bears to order the relation of means to ends. We divide in order that we may arrange. What right order is can scarcely be better defined than in the words of Horace.[2]

> "Ordinis hæc virtus erit et venus, aut ego fallor,
> Ut jam nunc dicat jam nunc debentia dici,
> Pleraque differat et præsens in tempus omittat."

It requires that each thing be said in its right place. This quality Vinet very properly declares to be "the character of true discourse." He declares that there is no discourse without it. Every one has heard the line of the English poet: "Order is heaven's first law." There is a truth contained in these words, and it has an important relation to this subject. The plan and work of our Creator are methodical in all their parts. Law rules everywhere; all the powers of nature are so constituted that they cannot customarily act at all, save in accordance with their law. This is true of the powers of the human spirit. And this fact points us at

---

[1] Quinctil., L. vii., § 1, preface: "Sit igitur (ut supra significavi) *divisio* rerum plurium in singulas; *partitio* singularum in partes discretus ordo . . . *dispositio* utilis rerum ac partium in locos distributio."

[2] Ep. ad Pisones, line 42, etc.

once to the general consequence, that if we wish a fellow-creature's soul to apprehend and feel a group of thoughts and motives, these must have their method, and that, a method conformed to the law by which his spirit acts. Accordingly, we find that it is a spontaneous demand of the human mind that there shall be order in what it views. Disarray is displeasing to it. A heap of stone and timber is not an architectural structure, but an unsightly mass of rubbish. A mixture of brilliant gems is not a mosaic picture, but a quantity of pebbles, and the richer their colours the more dark and confused is the mass. A mob of men is not an army. The atoms of this mighty universe, without an orderly connection, would be only a vast nebula of dust. Have not the poets, ancient and modern, found in *chaos* the strongest conception of that which is repulsive and abhorrent in matter?[1]

But, to be more specific, I would show that order promotes the recollection[2] of a discourse both by the preacher and hearer. That the preacher should be able to recall the parts of his sermon with ease while pronouncing it is of great importance; and to the extempore preacher it is absolutely necessary. To the hearer, recollection of the discourse is almost equally essential for edification. If he cannot recall what he has heard, he can receive no other benefit from it, than the slight accession made to his right habitudes of feeling by the evanescent impression of the moment. Now,

---

[1] Paradise Lost, book ii.

[2] Cicero de Orat., B. II. c. 86, § 353: " Hac tum se admonitus invenisse fertur (Simonides) ordinem esse maxime qui memoriæ lumen afferret."

what is called memory is one of the processes of suggestion. We only recollect what has passed out of our
conscious knowledge, for the time, in virtue of some tie
of association connecting it with some other idea in the
mind. But these ties connect things according to a
regular law. The bonds of association are such as
these : previous juxtaposition or proximity, or else
some relation of resemblance, contrast, causation, or the
connection of premise and proof. The tie established
by mere previous juxtaposition before the mind is far
the feeblest. Let one attempt, for instance, to commit
perfectly to memory a hundred names, having no other
previous relation than that they composed the same
muster-roll : he will find the task greatly harder than
that of learning a hundred words formed into sentences
expressive of a certain sequence of facts or thoughts.
He will even find that the drudgery of learning the list
of names is diminished by placing together those beginning with the same letters of the alphabet. Why is
this ? It is because the slight clue of a similarity in
one letter (with the well-known order of the alphabet
to aid) gives a stronger tie of association than mere
juxtapositions before the mind at a previous time. In
speaking, you address to your hearer a series of thoughts
which he is to remember. Now, do you not see that
every trait of natural order in the ranking of these
thoughts diminishes his labour ? The memory takes
them up with ease, because their connection with each
other presents them to her ready grasp. The more exactly they are arranged under their several proper heads,
and the more correctly their sequence is conformed to
the logical order of nature, which proceeds from premise

to proof and from conviction to action, the easier it is for your hearer to regain them.[1]

That discourse should be perspicuous is too plain to need words; for if it cannot be apprehended, why utter it? Horace has fixed the connection between order and perspicuity in a single phrase (*lucidus ordo*) so felicitous that it can never be forgotten. The reason why method aids perspicuity has been already given in part: it is because it aids memory. And it cannot but be, that the mind will grasp the materials of thought presented to it in those relations which are conformable to its own laws, better than if their order is deranged.

Correct method is essential to strength. "*Tantum series juncturaque pollet.*"[2] It is the orderly framing of the beams of the ship together which gives strength to its hull and impact to its beak. Without methodical juncture, all the timber and metal might be present, and yet have no more coherence than a mass of driftwood. The arch is firm only when the stones are placed in their order. The confused multitude of men

---

[1] See Cecil's homely but expressive instance, in his *Remains*. He says, "Send your maid into the streets to make a dozen separate purchases, and she will forget a third of them; but give her a clue of arrangement, and she will easily remember all. Thus, you say to her, 'Betty, remember that to-morrow is washing-day, and that this evening your mistress will entertain a few friends at tea; so we wish you to buy, for the first, soap, indigo and starch, and for the latter, tea, sugar, coffee, crackers, bread, cakes, this and the other fruits, and butter.' This principle of natural classification so relieves the difficulty of recollection that she easily performs all the commissions exactly."

[2] Horace, Ep. ad Pisones, line 242.

is helpless before a disciplined detachment of soldiers in battle-array, because the latter have the force of union. So, confused discourse can never make a forcible impression. When trains of thought are relinquished before they are pursued to their full results, and are then resumed and intruded into the midst of other thoughts; where those things are anticipated which should have been postponed until the hearer was prepared to apprehend them; where the order of time, dependence and inference is reversed, each incipient impression is neutralized by the succeeding, or else none is made, because the matter could not be apprehended. Order is the means of strength, because it is essential to unity and point. Let me ask you to recall what was said upon these topics. Unity consists in a methodical juncture of parts into one whole. The elements are many, perhaps diverse; the resultant effect is one. What except order can secure this? Again, we saw that it is the proper subordination of proofs to cardinal propositions which made these salient and incisive.

The mind intuitively apprehends beauty in method, while confusion is always unsightly to it. And let us not disdain this element as unworthy the gravity of sacred discourse. No innocent means are unworthy which assist even in a slight degree in commending saving truth. Moreover, I avow that when I observe how our Maker has framed our laws of taste, so that the sentiment of intellectual beauty always waits most instinctively on those sequences which are most true and just, I cannot depreciate it. It is a noble thing to make the TRUTH beautiful!

We have anticipated, in one particular, the good influence of sound method upon the preacher's own faculties when we showed how it promotes recollection. I can claim other excellent effects for it. It is greatly conducive to accuracy. In order to arrange we must analyze. Disposition requires careful inspection. Let a mingled mass of flowers be brought to the botanist, for example, to be classified. How does he proceed? He must examine their organs of reproduction minutely, that he may know to what species each belongs. Then he is prepared to group them according to their resemblances. And this botanist thus gains, in one morning, a more minute acquaintance with the parts of all these flowers, than the peasant who was accustomed to sweep them down together under his scythe has gained in a lifetime. It is thus of your thoughts: you find that as soon as you attempt to reduce them to a true order you are compelled to accuracy. The same labour also abbreviates and compacts your discourse by showing you what is superfluous. Vain repetitions are usually the result of confusion.

Just method is equally promotive of the fruitfulness of the mind. Men are usually better supplied with ideas than with distinct views of the relations between them. But a relation is often a new idea, and it may prove a very valuable one. When we would discuss any subject, our first glance at our own mental furniture usually gives us but few thoughts concerning our theme. On the one hand, it is impossible that the forgotten and absent conceptions can be called up by a direct act of our volition; for, in order to be made the objects of this act, they must be already present in conception. On the other hand, the impressions once made on the memory are not so thoroughly obliterated as they seem to be. This faithful guardian of knowledge preserves in her chambers many a treasure which we supposed to be lost, but she does not reveal them at her threshold without a summons. Your experience may furnish many instances in which ideas once learned, but withdrawn out of view in your memories, have been reproduced by yourselves without external aid. This proves that your minds still retained them in their memories, but not consciously. The question is, How may we regain our hold of these reserved stores of our own knowledge, when we wish to apply them to a given discussion? I answer, by proceeding, so far as we have any thoughts concerning it, to think systematically. Let the ideas which already present themselves be contemplated in their relations, and arranged in the mind according to them. Other connected ideas will speedily arise and rank themselves beside them, which, when they are subjected to the methodizing law of the mind, will, in turn, suggest others. The explanation is, that by ranking the thoughts you already have according to connections natural to the mind, while you do not, indeed, enable the will to make a thought absent from your conception the object of your volition, while it is still absent, you do direct the voluntary powers of the attention along those lines of association which call up the new matter by the force of suggestion. Thus the mind is placed in that posture in which memory can exert her fullest control over her unconscious stores. Thus the suggestive faculty is brought to its most fruitful state. And now the materials which these faculties present are ready for the endless combinations of imagination—comparison and judgment. If this explanation is true, it is obvious how much the fecundity of the mind must be increased for future efforts by the gradual formation of the habit of methodical thinking.

LECTURE IX.

WE find, then, that order in discourse is invaluable to the speaker himself, in giving accuracy and fruitfulness of mind, and in communicating clearness, strength, unity, point and beauty to his oration. It is equally important to the hearer to assist his remembrance of what is spoken. Now that we are agreed upon the value of the end, let us consider its means, *division*.

Vinet treats of this subject separately, under the two heads of logical disposition and rhetorical disposition. The former divides and arranges the matter of discourse according to the just logical connections of thought. It has reference only to the production of mental conviction. The latter divides and arranges with reference to persuasion of the heart, and aims at progress from the weaker to the stronger, from understanding to feeling, and from motive to action. Such is substantially his account of the distinction. I do not adopt it. No such separation is ever made in the actual structure of any oration, for we never have those which are exclusively logical or those which are exclusively emotional, but every true oration is both in one. Nor, as Vinet himself shows, can there ever be a discrepancy in the dictates of the two principles of division. Whatever is most truly logical is also most truly rhetorical. Nothing is really

137

rhetorical that is not based on right logic. The emotions to which the preacher appeals are only the rational. They can be incited only through the understanding. The warmth which characterizes them is but the temperature of the logical thought. Last, the remarks which need to be made upon the special management of the hearer's emotions can be properly made under the head of persuasion.

Approaching, then, the particular topic of *division*, we find, first, a question as to the *constituent parts* which should compose the regular discourse. These I account to be the *Exordium*, or introduction, the *Exposition*, the *Proposition*, the *Main Argument*, and the *Conclusion*.[1]

---

[1] Aristotle, b. iii., chap. 14, Rhetoric, says that discourse naturally divides itself into two parts, *proposition* and *demonstration*, because one naturally tells us first what he wishes to talk about, and then states what he has to confirm his assertion about it. But a subdivision of the matter will class them as *proem, proposition, demonstration* and *peroration*.

Cicero states the current teaching of the masters of his time thus (De Orat. L. ii., c. 19, § 80): "Jubent enim exordiri ita, ut eum, qui audiat, benevolum nobis faciamus et docilem et attentum; deinde rem narrare, ita ut verisimilis narratio sit, ut aperta, ut brevis; post autem dividere causam aut proponere; nostra confirmare argumentis et rationibus; deinde contraria refutare. Tum autem alii conclusionem orationis et quasi perorationem collocant: alii jubent, antequam peroretur, ornandi aut augendi causa digredi; deinde concludere ac perorare."

His own distribution is given (L. ii., c. 76, § 307): "Nam ut aliquid ante rem dicamus; deinde ut rem exponamus; post ut eam probemus nostris præsidiis confirmandis, contrariis refutandis; deinde ut concludamus atque ita peroremus, hoc dicendi genus natura ipsa præscribit."

Quinctilian, L. iv. Procœmium, § 6: "Sequitur enim, ut judicialium causarum (quæ sunt maxime variæ et multiplices) ordo explicetur; quod procœmii sit officum; quæ ratio narrandi; quæ probation-

I shall define each of these, give my reasons for regarding them as essential members of the sermon, and add some instructions for composing them. The argument, which after all is the body of the sermon, will then require us to return to it, that we may consider its divisions and rules. Many preachers demur against the uniform requirement of all these parts as necessary members of a sermon. They would claim a discretion to omit all of them except the argument, and perhaps the conclusion. They say our requirement is mischievously formal, and dictates a tiresome sameness. They depreciate such sermons as " casts all run in the same mould." Let me then, in advance, explain. Their sarcasm suggests an unjust analogy. Sermons are not dead casts run into any mould, changeable or fixed. Give a new mould for each attempt, to be demolished when once used ; I still reject and resent the illustration. Sermons should be living growths, like plants or trees ; none of them indeed monsters, none maimed, but each one modified within the bounds of the rudimental laws of its nature, by its own circumstances of growth ; so that they together present an endless and charming variety. Every natural tree must needs have certain constituent parts—its roots, its stem, its branches, its foliage, its fruit. But how end-

---

um sit fides, seu proposita confirmamus, seu, contra dicta dissolvimus ; quanta vis in perorando," etc. He thus, like Cicero, makes four instead of five parts, proem, narration, argument (including refutation of objections) and peroration.

The current of modern writers on sacred oratory concur in making the five constituent parts which I have given in the text of my lecture.

lessly diversified is the development of these members!
They cannot any of them be wholly absent, but the individuality of each tree determines their relative size;
so that we have every graceful difference of form and
stature, from the humble shrub to the tapering and
lofty pine. But this illustration I am willing somewhat to relax. I will admit that circumstances may
justify the preacher in reducing some of these constituent members to the extent of an apparent suppression.
When I assign them all to the regular sermon as essential parts, I intend that all will be present in the complete type, and that this is the model toward which
every sermon, even the most informal, must tend.

The *Exordium* is that prefatory matter which precedes the direct business of the discourse. The mind
seems naturally to demand such a preparation. Says
Cicero,[1] "There is, in fine, nothing in all nature which
pours itself wholly out and bursts forth on a sudden;
but Nature herself has prepared all things which are
effected, even those which are effected with the most
violence, by gentler beginnings." And again: "If
in that gladiatorial struggle of life, in which men
contend with the actual steel, many things are done
before they come hand to hand, which seem meant
not to wound but to make a show, how much more
is this to be looked for in the oration, where it is
not so much force as delectation which is required?"
Aristotle tells us[2] that the proem, like a prelude in

---

[1] Cicero de Orat., L. ii., c. 78, § 317.

[2] Aristotle, Rhet., b. iii., ch. 15. See also Quinctil., L. iv., c. 1., § 5.
"Causa principii nulla est alia, quam ut auditorem, quo sit nobis in
cæteris partibus accommodatior, præparemus. Id fieri tribus maxime

music or a prologue to a drama, introduces the main discourse, and that its ends or objects are to unfold the purpose of the main discourse, to produce attention, to secure the favour of the hearers to the speaker, as well disposed, well informed and honest, and last and least, to give elegance to the beginning. If the speaker has done his duty to himself and his subject, he has mastered it by previous study, and comes to the pulpit with his soul inspired and warmed with it. He cannot assume that his hearers are in this animated state. It may even be true that they are ignorant what his subject is to be. Now, this contrast between their state of feeling and his is unfavourable, at the beginning, to the institution of an active sympathy. When he is all fire and they as yet are ice, a sudden contact between his mind and theirs will produce rather a shock and revulsion than sympathetic harmony. His emotion is, to their quietude, extravagance. He must raise them first a part of the way toward his own level. Another reason for the *exordium* is, that some initial misconception, indifference or prejudice is usually to be expected in the hearer. While this continues, his hearty attention and favour will not be given. If the preacher then introduce his main proposition, and proceed immediately to deal with it, something at the beginning will be lost to the hearer. The loss of this must prejudice his comprehension of all the rest, and only the more, if the discourse is methodical throughout. The

---

rebus, inter auctores plurimos constat, si *benevolum, attentum, docilem* fecerimus: non quia ista non per totam actionem sint custodienda, sed quia initiis præcipue necessaria, per quæ in animum judicis, ut procedere ultra possimus, admittitur."

pupil who fails to attend while the alphabet is taught will be unable to go along with his class as they advance to words and sentences. Hence it is well that some preface shall precede the main subject, which will awaken attention and allay prejudice. The hearer should be approximated to the speaker's level of thought and emotion before the main subject is presented. But it is obvious that an *exordium* protracted beyond the attainment of this object would be an excrescence hostile to unity and to the purpose of the body of the discourse.

Our ordinary conversation does not usually introduce itself absolutely without preface; but often that introduction is virtually made for us before we begin to speak, by the remark of our interlocutor, by a question, by an event occurring in our presence, by a gesture, by an act. So if a similar circumstance has removed the supposed apathy or prejudice of your hearers and put them already in relation with your subject, the need of an *exordium* is already met. This may sometimes be done by the occasion itself, or by the devotional services preceding the sermon, or by the annunciation of the text. If any of these put you in possession of the attention of your audience, why may you not direct it at once to your main subject? A formal *exordium* is therefore not to be too much insisted on.

The *exordium*, as to its matter, must be, first, pertinent to the main subject of the sermon. It should be composed of an idea lying next thereto. If that idea is transferable to a different discourse and may introduce the second as well as the first, it is unfit to be the *exordium* of either. That which does not lead us up to our subject is, in fact, no introduction to it.[1] This member of discourse is the last in which the preacher should indulge in vague commonplaces; for it is now that he is seeking to make a good first impression and to stir the sluggish interest of his hearers. But indulgence in disconnected introductions will incline him to these trite generalities ; and the final issue will be, that he will be found commencing every discussion, however different the subjects, with the same stale ideas. Some preachers infringe the rule requiring a connected *exordium*, by affecting to begin with some topic which appears as remote as possible from the text, in order that they may exhibit their ingenuity by establishing an unexpected line of connection between them. While the audience are wondering how in the world he is to get around from his introduction to his text, he astonishes them by a gyration about the little circle of his knowledge, which leads him to the desired point. Every sensible hearer detects vanity as the motive of this display. Let the *exordium* never be far-fetched.[2]

---

[1] Cicero de Orat., L. ii. c. 79, § 325. "Connexum autem ita sit principium consequenti orationi, ut non tanquam citharœdi procemium affictum aliquod, sed cohærens cum omni corpore membrum esse videatur.   Nam nonnulli quum illud meditati ediderunt, sic ad reliqua transeunt, ut audientiam sibi fieri nolle videantur.   Atque eiusmodi illa prolusio debet esse, non ut Samnitum, qui vibrant hastas ante pugnam, quibus in pugnando nihil utuntur ; sed ut ipsis sententiis, quibus proluserunt, vel pugnare possint."

[2] Ep. ad Pisones, Horace, lines 146–150.   He says of Homer :

> " Nec reditum Diomedis ab interitu Mecleagri,
> Nec gemino bellum Trojamum Orditur ab ove,
> Semper ad eventum festinat, et in medias res,
> Non secus ac notas, auditorem rapit, et quæ
> Desperat tractata nitescere posse, relinquit."

The porch which leads into the house is in contact with it.

But, second, the introduction must not embody a thought which is essential to the main discussion. This is an error of structure to which the inexperienced and impulsive writer is prone. Approaching the work of composition with a mind fired by the subject, he finds those ideas which are cardinal to it prominent in his thoughts, and he can scarcely refrain from pouring out some one of them the moment he begins. The consequence is, that when he proceeds in earnest to deal with his proposition, he will find he has anticipated essential matter. He has now only the choice between a bald repetition of his first idea, or else a leaving of his argument fragmentary. A stone which is absolutely necessary to close his arch has been already laid in the threshold.

Third. An *exordium* should contain only one leading thought. If the first one introduced is related to the text, this leads us to it : why interpose another? If it is not, it should not enter the *exordium* at all : the second distinct thought which follows it does the real work, and the first was nugatory. There is no need of a porch to enter a porch : we desire to step at once from the porch into the house.

Fourth. While the thought of the *exordium* should by no means be trivial or uninteresting, neither should it be ambitious. It should not vie in splendour with all that are to succeed it, lest it should raise too much promise to the expectation of the hearers. The impression which they carry away from a sermon is usually that produced by its concluding parts. If you fail there to fulfil the promise of your outset, the pleasing surprise which you gave them in commencing will not cause them to pardon you the disappointment.[1]

From these rules you will easily infer that the introduction must be short, relatively to the whole sermon. A long and ambitious *exordium* is ruinous to all subsequent effect. It wastes time; it consumes the preacher's strength; it exhausts the sensibility of the people before the stage of the sermon for which it is needed. Young writers are usually inclined to dilate too much upon their preliminary topics. This is because they are zealous for thoroughness, and being inexperienced in the work of composition, they do not know how largely the whole discourse will grow upon their hands, when amplified in the same proportion. It is far better to abridge the introductory parts than to be compelled, by an ill-judged waste of time there, to mar the more important thoughts near the close. For this, as well as other reasons, it is well that the young preacher should not attempt to write his introduction until the discussion has been either written, or at least expanded in the mind.[2]

---

[1] Horace Ep. ad Pisones, lines 136–145 :

> " Nec si incipies ut scriptor cyclicus olim ;
> ' Fortunam Priami cantalo et nobile bellum.'
> Quid dignum tanto feret hic promissor hiatu ?
> Parturiunt monotes, nascetur ridiculus mus.
> Quanto rectius hic, qui nil molitur inepte :
> ' Dic mihi, Musa, virum captæ post tempora Trojæ,
> Qui mores hominum multorum vidit et urbes.'
> Non fumum ex fulgore, sed ex fumo dare lucem,
> Cogitat, ut speciosa dehinc miracula promat,
> Antiphatem, Scyllamque, et cum Cyclope Charybdin."

[2] Cicero de Or. L. ii., c. 77, § 315. " Hisce omnibus rebus conside-

I would point out the following classes of thoughts from which an appropriate *exordium* may be taken, without claiming that my enumeration it complete :

1. The text is often introduced in the happiest manner by unfolding the *nexus* of the thoughts amidst which it stands. Such an *exordium* is always german, and it makes a substantial approach to the evolution of the main subject. It promotes fidelity to the text, by placing it before the minds of speaker and hearer in the precise scope which it had in the mind of the inspired writer.

2. Akin to this is a form of introduction which may also be made exceedingly fresh and pleasing. It consists of a narration of the events, or. a description of the place and times amidst which the text was uttered by the sacred writer. Thus, should the preacher discuss the Saviour's compassion for reprobate Jerusalem (as described in Luke xix. 41–44), he may begin by describing the scenery of the city and its environs, as they appeared to our Lord from Mount Olivet the morning these memorable words were uttered. This picture should be rapid, truthful and graphic, but without the pedantries of topography. He may then superinduce upon this smiling landscape the vision of the Roman circumvallation and the ravages of the seige, as they doubtless appeared to the prophetic eye of Jesus. Thus he has both *exordium* and exposition. Or would he present for our imitation the forbearance of David toward

---

ratis, tum denique id quod primum est dicendum, postremum soleo cogitare, quo utar exordio. Nam si quando invenire id primum volui, nullum mihi occurrit, nisi aut exile aut nugatorium, aut vulgare atque commune."

King Saul, in 1 Sam. xxiv., let him relate briefly the history of the provocation the former had endured.

3. The text may be introduced by the recital of some incident or history from real life, which strikingly exemplifies the principles to be established. But such incident must have a dignity and gravity congruous with the sacred subject which it introduces. And this kind must be used under the restraints of a severe taste, lest the narrative should cause an interest too romantic for the didactic or argumentative sequel. A New Year's sermon on the text, "This year thou shalt die," was impressively introduced by the statement, that both Jonathan Edwards and Samuel Davies preached from this passage at the beginning of the years in which they were unexpectedly cut off by death.

4. A legitimate *exordium* may often be made by placing alongside of the text some related principle familiar and admitted among the hearers. If the text contains the general truth, some obvious application of it in a specific case or class may introduce it. If it contains the species, then it may be introduced by referring it to its more general principle. Thus the doctrine of the text has its *locus* given it in the thinking of the audience, which prepares them to consider it. Or else the principle cited for comparison may be related to the text by some agreement or difference, by examination of which it will be defined.

5. A striking introduction may also be made by citing some usage or opinion prevalent among the hearers, which is opposed to the doctrine or precept of the text. The Apostle Paul tells us (Acts xx. 35) that Christ taught: "It is more blessed to give than to receive."

The world regards the recipient as the more fortunate party. This beginning gives something of the vividness of paradox. It is, moreover, advantageous in making up the issue for discussion sharply. The affirmation of the opposite is then plain.

6. Sometimes the *exordium* is skilfully formed by a hypothesis, putting in a concrete form the unexpected doctrine to be proved. The preacher begins thus: "Let us represent to ourselves a man who in the following circumstances acted in the following way," etc. Such an introduction is not only graphic, but it gives the people, as it were, before they are aware, a concrete and distinct definition of that which is to be the subject of the discussion.

In style and manner the *exordium* should surpass all the remainder of the discourse by its correctness.[1] The preacher should remember that he is then making his first impression upon the hearers, and if this is untoward, it will be difficult afterward to repair it. But this accuracy aims rather at negative than at positive results in its first movement; it seeks to avoid offending the taste by errors of expression, rather than to make an immediate disclosure of the full powers and graces of the speaker. The latter should be progressive to the end.

Hence, second, the beginning should be unambitious, lest it should promise too much. It should embody no laboured argument, and make no display of learning or

---

[1] Cicero de Or. L. ii., c. 78, § 315. "Principia autem dicendi semper quum accurata et acuta et instructa sententiis, apta verbis, tum vero caussarum propria esse debent. Prima est enim quasi cognitio et commenadtio orationis in principio, quæ continuo eum qui audit permulcere atque allicere debet."

subtlety. Its matter should be clothed with a certain modesty of dress, excluding florid figures and chary of every ornament. The sentences should incline toward brevity, especially those which compose the first paragraph. The speaker should take care that he does not yield to the temptation to display his most brilliant stores in the *exòrdium*. That would be a most unfortunate impression, and fatal to the movement of his discourse, which should cause his audience to say, none of his subsequent ideas were as fine as the first.

Third. In warmth of tone the introduction should bear a due relation to the state of feeling which, at the beginning, prevails among the hearers. It should not be in strong contrast with theirs, so as to place the speaker out of sympathetic harmony with them, and yet it should suggest at once a progress toward a higher stage of emotion. The rule given by some rhetoricians, that the *exordium* must always be calm, needs modification. Sometimes the events which assemble the congregation give it, from the first, an elevated and excited tone. Why should the speaker causelessly forfeit this advantage? Why seek to lower that feeling which he must immediately endeavour again to raise? A cold beginning at such a time would be a sin against the sympathies of his audience. But usually they assemble in a quiet if not an indifferent temper. He who in such circumstances should begin in that strain of exalted animation which *Massilon* properly adopted in his funeral oration for the king of France, or *Fléchier* in his *eulogium* for Marshal Tureme, would so transcend the grade of emotion in his hearers that he would seem to them extravagant or fantastic. The law of movement in discourse has been strongly enforced by me already. According to this law, the animation of both speaker and hearers should tend continually toward its culmination in the *terminus* or change of the discussion. Now, exalted emotions cannot be long sustained at their height, neither can they be so easily excited a second time, after they have been once raised and allowed to decline. Hence the speaker should beware of appealing too prematurely to the powers of emotion in himself and in his audience. The happiest tone with which an *exordium* can be imbued is that of a latent or suppressed animation. The speaker does not too far outrun the interest of his hearers. But he is evidently curbing himself by an effort, and the partial flashes of heat which escape amidst the calmer progress of his introduction stimulate their expectation and awaken their sympathies.

Fourth. The *exordium* should disclose unaffected modesty.[1] Indeed, I should not be unwilling to require that degree of diffidence which produces at first a positive embarrassment. But it should be not only the *exordium*, but the orator himself, who is modest;

---

[1] Cicero de Orat., L. i., c. 26, §§ 119–121. "Mihi etiam, qui optime dicunt, quique id facillime atque ornatissime facere possunt, tamen, nisi timide ad dicendum accedunt, et in exordienda oratione perturbantur, pæne impudentes videntur; tametsi id accidere non potest. Ut enim quisque optime dicit, ita maxime dicendi difficultatem, variosque eventus orationis, expectationemque hominum pertimescit. . . . Quem vero non pudet (id quod in plerisque video) hunc ego non reprehensione solum, sed etiam pœna dignum puto. Equidem et in vobis animadvertere soleo, et in me ipso sæpissime experior, ut exalbescam in principiis dicendi, et tota mente atque omnibus artubus contremiscam."

and while he is diffident for himself, he should be bold for his cause.   This quality of diffidence should manifest itself to the hearer, but should never be the subject of the speaker's own remark; for whenever he begins to descant on his own modesty and embarrassment, every sensible hearer will conclude at once that they are assumed.   Indeed, preachers should never utter anything personally apologetic, and rarely should they make any allusion to their own circumstances.   If a minister begins by informing his audience that his preparation has been sadly abridged by events beyond his control, or that he is about to preach while suffering from sickness, he will be likely to make two impressions, each of which will be lamentable.   He will be suspected of a secret design to make the people, at the end, applaud him for speaking so brilliantly under circumstances so adverse.   It will appear also that, however this may be, he is more solicitous about his personal credit than about the glory of his divine Master and the success of his message.   An ostentatious avowal of diffidence is always understood as a betrayal of secret pride.   Again, the preacher should never attempt to play the sycophant to his audience.   He should not tell them how much he finds himself embarrassed by having to address so numerous or so respectable an assemblage.   Such professions are ever distasteful and deceitful in the eyes of intelligent persons: they see clearly that, if there is any real trepidation, it proceeds from the speaker's overweening self-esteem, and not from any respect for them or for God.

But a genuine diffidence, which is felt and not spoken of, is exceedingly favourable to the effect of the subsequent discourse. Its influence over the speaker himself is happy, not only by repressing those manifestations of conceit which outrage the hearers' taste and sense of devotion, but by arousing his own powers. The necessary effort to overcome his embarrassment gives warmth from the very friction, and *momentum* from the resistance subdued. Perfect self-possession is ever cold. This unaffected diffidence is a tribute to the audience more acceptable to them than any other, because it is spontaneous and honest. As a true woman feels more secret pleasure at the sight of a man of real merit and bravery abashed by her presence, than at the hearing of the neatest compliments ever turned by a *nonchalant* fopling, so every assembly is more gratified by this unwilling tribute of the speaker than by fluent professions of respect. It disarms criticism and opposition; it sets them at once in sympathy with the speaker; it assures them, better than any words, of his ingenuousness; it shows equally his profound sense of the gravity of his topic, and thus establishes, at the outset, appreciation and attention.

The remark already twice made, that this modesty must be real and not simulated, is self-evident. But the only source of such an emotion is God's grace, producing true and deep humility, reverence, faith and zeal for souls. Thus we are again led to the practical truth, that the prime qualification for the pulpit orator is eminent piety.

It has been much debated among teachers, at what stage of the preparation the *exordium* should be composed. I would recommend that it be done after the matter of the sermon has been selected and digested in the mind, but before the body of the discourse is actually written. The former part of this rule is necessary to secure in the introduction appropriateness of matter, the latter to secure harmony and movement in the composition of the whole.

LECTURE X.

CONSTITUENT MEMBERS OF THE SERMON.—CONTINUED.

EXPLICATION AND PROPOSITION.

UNLESS *explication* of the text has composed the *exordium* (which I have admitted to be sometimes proper), this will be the second constituent member of the regular sermon. The peculiar character of sacred eloquence gives us an explication in place of a *narration*, which the classic orators made their second member.[1] Indeed, in the sermon, this part will not seldom assume the form of narration, when the passage of Scripture to be explained presents us with an incident or a history. The reason which requires a narration before the main argument of the advocate is very plain and conclusive; the hearer must be put in possession of the facts of the case before he is ready to comprehend the discussion of that issue. Teachers of forensic eloquence have often remarked, that the issue may be virtually decided by the skilful advocate through the structure of his narration. He so states the events, with perspicuous brevity

---

[1] See citations on p. 146. *Vinet* (Skinner's translation, p. 154) says: "A sermon, whatever may be its kind, resolves itself always into a demonstration, and a demonstration never has place without a formal or indirect explanation. I mean to say, that every demonstration rests upon a foregoing explanation." ˙

and graphic force, as to charm the interest of the listener.   He connects facts so as to place in a strong light
those which are favourable to his claim, and to with-
draw into the shade those which are adverse.   Like the
consummate general, he secures his victory in advance
of the actual shock of arms by the method in which he
takes his positions.   Thus the narrative often becomes
the most important member of his discourse.

The same general reason demands an explication in
the sermon before the main argument.   The hearer
should be clearly possessed of the point to be proven
before he advances to the proof.   But there is a more
imperative reason, growing out of the posture and function of the Protestant teacher.   It is the boast of our
Christianity that it recognizes in the laity the right of
private judgment.   The minister is not a hierarch to
dictate dogmas to the implicit faith of subject souls
whose "ignorance is the mother of their devotion."
We "have not dominion over their faith, but are help-
ers of their joy, for by faith they stand."[1]   Unless their
faith is intelligent, it is nothing worth.   Unless they
see evidence to command assent in the light of their
own understandings, they do not really see at all; their
souls are still in darkness.   A second truth equally
plain is, that the meaning which they place upon the
word is to them the substance of the word.   The laity,
therefore, are entitled to have something more than the
mere assertion of their teacher to connect the meaning
which they are required to accept from a given passage

---

[1] See 2 Cor. i. 24; also, Matt. xxiii. 10, 11; 1 John iv. 1, 2, 3;
John viii. 32.

of Scripture with its terms. You have seen that it is
the peculiarity of the sermon that it impels the hearer's
will with the direct authority of God, and not merely
with human reasons and inducements. That your discourse may be a true sermon, then, its proposition must
be deduced from the language of its text by an exegesis,
which shall give your hearer's mind convincing evidence the meaning you propound is indeed God's intended meaning. It thus appears that the sermon cannot usually exist without explication of the text. There
may be cases where its words are so plain and unam-
biguous that your view of their meaning, without any
reasoning, appears conclusive. In these cases the explication contracts itself into a self-evident statement,
but it is still present in rudiment, and it is the necessary tie between the hearer's conscience and the authority
of the divine word in the text.

It also results from these considerations that the
object of the explication is both to define and to evince:
it must not only make plain what you apprehend the
meaning of the text to be, but it must also show why
you apprehend it to be such. It will often include,
therefore, *definition*[1] and *discussion*.

Your knowledge of logic will furnish you with the
technical meaning of definition, as a description of an

---

[1] Thus, if the text were Ps. lxxxiv. 11, "*No good thing* will he
withhold from them that walk uprightly," the nature of the good
here promised must be defined, or else the proposition cannot be sustained that God bestows all good upon his true servants. If, for
instance, it were natural good which was intended, the proposition
would not be true. The other branch of the explication of this text
will then be to show exegetical reasons that your definition is indeed
the one intended by the sacred writer.

object by *genus* and *differentia*. The more comprehensive and popular notion of a definition, as a set of
terms which so describe an object as to distinguish it
from all others, is more suitable to the use of the
rhetorician. The preacher should be chary of technical
definitions :[1] they suppose in the hearer a power of abstraction which is seldom cultivated, and they are more
likely to confuse than to enlighten the common people.
But when it is necessary to define, he should give a
truly essential definition, and should not delude the
hearer's mind by one merely nominal, substituting a
phrase for a phrase, while the one is no more discriminative than the other. Thus, it is no adequate definition
of "atonement" to say that it is "satisfaction," or that
satisfaction is atonement, unless the hearer is instructed
of the nature of the compensation intended by the word,
as that of penal obligation. But when you say that
"atonement" is compensation of our penal debt to God,
by the actual punishment of our Substitute, you give us
an essential definition : the idea of atonement is thenceforward distinctly separated in our minds. A nominal
definition (the explanation of a term by a term) is only
useful when the second term is better known by usage
than the former, and that in a defined sense. Thus,

---

[1] Cicero de Orat., L. ii. c. 25, §§ 108, 109. "Atque in hoc genere
causarum nonnulli præcipiunt, ut verbum illud, quod causam facit,
lucide, absolute, breviter uterque definiat. Quod mihi quidem per-
quam puerile videri solet. . . . Etenim definitio primum reprehenso
verbo uno, aut addito, aut dempto, sæpe extorquetur e manibus :
deinde genere ipso doctrinam redolet exercitationemque pæne
puerilem : tum et in sensum et in mentem judicis intrare non potest.
Ante enim præterlabitur, quam percepta est."

the "Decalogue" may be defined as the "Ten Commandments," because popular usage has given the latter phrase a particular meaning. I add a further precept, that the preacher should never attempt to define things already known or ideas absolutely simple. The natural relation of father and child, for instance, is already better known by experience than it can be by definition; and the idea of "truth," being simple and incapable of further analysis into other elements, cannot be better expressed than by the word "truth." To define in these cases is to waste words and to mar the movement of the discourse. Again, definition in discourse must always be brief; if protracted, it disappoints its own object, by overloading the attention and memory of the hearer. I remark again: sentiments and moral ideas are often better defined by a concrete illustration than by abstract terms. They may be represented in historical events selected from the Scriptures, or painted in a parable of our Lord, or suggested by some past or some possible experience of the hearer, in which the idea in question was exactly reproduced. Thus, when the lawyer of Luke x. 29 required of our Saviour to define who was his neighbour, his answer was the parable of the "Good Samaritan." He thus gave his questioner what was far more vivid, more interesting, and even more exact, than an abstract conception of the relation—a realization of it to himself in his own consciousness. It is the duty of the minister to study the means and cultivate the faculty of concrete definition after this beautiful model; for it is thus the people are to be successfully taught. Once more: the

business of definition should always be so completed
during the explication of the topic that, when the proposition of the sermon is finally announced, every term in
it shall be plain. No further explanation should be
needed or admitted, but the preacher should be ready
to advance at once to his argument.

The other branch of the explication is that which
evinces the correctness of the definition or interpretation assigned to the text. In ascertaining and establishing this, the preacher must faithfully employ all the
critical and exegetical aids within his reach. It is not
proper that I should here usurp the place of the teacher
of interpretation, but supposing you to have profited by
his instructions, I would give you some rhetorical guidance in their use before the people.

And, first: a strict integrity of mind should guide
you in the selection and use of a passage of the Scriptures as a text. Never venture to expound it to the
people, unless you are sure that you have the meaning
intended by the Spirit, and offer to them no other than
that. You should feel that in your sermon you have
no concern with any other meaning than that which
God has placed in the words, and if this does not suit
your purpose do not dare to employ them as a text. It
is never lawful for you first to select a topic and a
method for discussion, and then to warp or strain a
passage by accommodation, or any other exegetical expedient to cover it. The guilt of thus thrusting words
upon God is that of presumption, if not of profanity.
The detection of your license in the treatment of the
Scriptures would teach your hearers to regard you, or
the word of God, or both, with mistrust. Would you

teach them to revere the authority of that word? Show them that you yourself revere it.

Second. The explication of the passage on which you preach should be plain and convincing. In this part of his task it behooves the preacher to show the hand of a master workman. He should so establish the view of the meaning which he has adopted after careful deliberation, as to extinguish doubt and cavil in every attentive mind, and to commend his opinion conclusively to his hearers. And this should be done with an air of solid good sense rather than of scholastic nicety. The Bible should be approached as a popular book, and not as a learned riddle; a book given by God to the common people; a book which, while it contains unfathomable depths of wisdom and knowledge, yields its instructions, on all truth fundamental to salvation, to every honest and earnest searcher. The manner of the expounder should seem to say to his hearers: "These Scriptures do not indeed disclose their treasures to heedless indolence and shallow inattention, but they offer them to the faithful inquiry of every plain mind. Come with me, and we shall by prayer and carefulness find the undoubted meaning of the Spirit." But, on the other hand, the preacher should not flatter his people by intimating to them that they are as competent as he to expound the Word, nor should he permit them to depreciate learning and ability as valuable helps in the task. If your people were indeed as able as you are to explain it, this would only prove that you are not fit for your place. The spiritual teacher should in this matter "magnify his office," not by pretentious displays, but by solid ability and mastery of the Scriptures.

Third. Avoid especially in this exercise every trait of pedantry and of literary coxcombry. You should not readily choose a text which requires a learned and laboured exegesis to evince its meaning, but should rather resort to some plainer declaration of the same truth in another part of the Scriptures. The judicious expositor, while he will not be servile in his adherence to established interpretations, will never hunt for novel and startling senses in his text. He is more likely, by such crotchets, to establish a character for conceit than for originality or true learning. The sensible hearer will justly regard the unnecessary reference to learned authors, the citation of the original languages, the employment of the technicalities of hermeneutics, the quoting of erroneous explanations for the purpose of refuting them, as designed to display yourselves rather than the truth; for his good sense will remind him that none of these are really necessary to the unfolding of the meaning of the Word. The able expounder exhibits not the processes, but the results, of his learning. He employs indeed every aid of literature to ascertain the exact mind of the Spirit. But when he presents his view of that meaning to the people, he relies not so much on these minute rays of evidence as on the broad light of its consistency as a whole, and its harmony with the sacred writer's scope, and with the analogy of faith, to evince its justice to the people. The processes of learned criticism are the scaffoldings which assist in building the house; when it is completed these may be pulled away, for the structure will stand upon its own foundations and disclose the justness of its own proportions. Let me here commend to you, as of prime value for the popular exposition of the Word, those historical explanations which place the hearers in the precise point of view occupied by the sacred writer and his first readers, and which thus enable them to appreciate his scope. Introduce your explanations by a brief, lucid, archæological statement in popular form, and substantiated as far as possible by facts given in the Scriptures themselves; you will find this shed a flood of self-evidencing light over the whole passage, which will supersede the necessity for a dissecting verbal criticism. Is it your task, for instance, to expound the doctrinal parts of the Epistle to the Colossians? Explain to the people that the apostle was moved to write it by the following facts: He had just learned in his prison at Rome, that the Colossian church was infested with a type of pharisaic Gnosticism, which proposed a combination of Jewish asceticism with a reliance on the mediation and teaching of supposed super-angelic spirits, as the way of salvation. You may prove that this statement is historically true by the very words of St. Paul himself (chap. ii. 16, 18), without the seeming pedantry of citing uninspired antiquaries. This cause of the apostle's writing at once manifests the scope of his reasoning, and gives us the key to his masterly argument against the attempt to add any creature mediation to Christ's headship and intercession, and any will-worship or asceticism to his righteousness. A plain, historical disclosure of the author's scope is always the best popular exposition.

The most reprehensible pedantry of all is that which delights in criticising and amending the received English version. Instead of seeking for opportunities to point out errors in this precious work of our ancestors, its credit should be carefully sustained before the people, whenever this can be done without an actual sacrifice of our integrity and of the truth of the text. The general excellence of the translation merits this treatment. Such were the learning and labour of its authors, that he who is most deeply acquainted with sacred criticism will be found most modest in assailing their accuracy in any point. But it is far more important to remark, that this version is practically the Bible of the common people— the only one to which they can have familiar access. If their confidence in its fidelity is overthrown, they are virtually robbed of the written word of God. Hence, if to bring out the truth of your text, a correction must needs be made in the phraseology of this version, let it be made in such a way as not to impair its credit. If there be actual error, let it not be causelessly paraded. In most cases, the seeming inaccuracy may be explained by the fact, that in the transition of our own tongue, the English phrase has undergone a change since the translators (correctly) employed it. Thus when they say, as the translation of Μη μεριμνᾶτε, etc. (Matt. vi. 25), "Take no thought for your life," they are entitled to be delivered from their seeming contradiction of the other Scriptures, which command rational forecast, by this explanation, that the word "thought" then bore, as one of its common senses, the meaning of "morbid anxiety," which has since become obsolete. Let them have all the advantage of such just explanations. Thus let the confidence of your hearers in their English Bibles be preserved and fortified.

In conclusion : the explication will usually demand

the best exertion of the preacher's skill, because it is
necessary that the qualities above claimed for it be combined with brevity. It must not be protracted, because,
important as it is, it is not usually the body of the sermon, but is introductory thereto. If you allow this
preliminary to detain you from the main argument, the
hearer will feel that you are dallying with your work.
The grace and *momentum* of the discourse will be lost,
and weariness will supervene. There are, however,
many expository sermons, where a continuous explication, interspersed with reflections and applications, may
properly form the body of the discourse; in other cases
the explication should be short.

The third member of the regular sermon is the *proposition*. To this the preacher will be immediately led
by his explication. It states explicitly what is the precise subject or assertion which the preacher designs to
discuss. This is a very short, but a very essential member of the structure. It should be expressed, if possible,
in a single sentence, and that of the simplest possible
syntax, with the most definite terms. The statement
should be such as to leave no necessity, after the explication which has preceded it, for any further definitions or limitations. Every word and every connexion
of the words in this statement must be pondered with
care; and whatever other parts of the sermon may be
left to find their expression at the moment of utterance,
this should be enunciated in the very words prepared
beforehand. Such a propounding of the main subject
of discourse at the outset of the main argument is demanded by this plain reason, that if you wish the people

to understand what you say, you must inform them in advance about what you purpose to talk. Such an announcement is at once the necessary key to comprehension, and the clue of connexion for all that follows. The rule is therefore uniform and imperative.

Touching the manner of propounding, I have already said that the terms must be brief and absolutely perspicuous. We sometimes hear preachers announce their topics in sentences so tedious and involved, so overloaded with explanations and repetitions, so varied into forms of expression supposed to be equivalent, that at the end, the hearers are more in the dark concerning the subject of the coming discussion, than when the text was announced. If the text is itself a single proposition, and is perspicuous, it may be recited as the announcement. A second observation which I would commend to you is, that some simple means should be used to arrest the attention of all the hearers when you are about to announce your proposition, and to advertise them that you are now proceeding to this cardinal step. This may be effected by a significant pause, by an emphatic repetition of the propounding sentence, or by a cautionary preface, following the end of the explication, in some such words as these: "The following, then, my brethren, appears to be the doctrine of the text;" or, "This explication of the text shows, that it asserts the following proposition, viz." In a word, the preacher, upon pronouncing his proposition, should examine the countenances of his hearers, and be sure that he has their understandings as well as their eyes. If he perceives that a part of them are either inattentive or confused and doubtful of his real intent, he should not proceed until, by suitable repetitions, he has possessed every mind of his purposed object.

My third remark is, that the topic of discussion may be propounded either as a subject or as a logical proposition. I here use the last word in its technical sense, as a sentence which, by means of the copula, affirms or denies some predicate of some subject. Let us suppose that the text is a single verse, 1 John iii. 3 : " And every man that hath this hope in him purifieth himself, even as he is pure." After the explication, which by the help of the context, will plainly and convincingly show that the " hope" intended is that of redemption through Christ, that the " purifying" is that of spiritual sanctification, and that the person who is its pattern is the Redeemer, you may then deduce your topic either as a subject of didactic and illustrative remarks, " The sanctifying effect of the true believer's hope," or as a proposition to be demonstrated, " The believer's hope sanctifies all who are entitled to it." Let us suppose, again, that the sermon is an expository one, and discusses a longer passage of Scripture, in which a kindred truth is taught. Titus ii. 9 to chap. iii. 8. After such preliminary explanation of the scope and language as introduces the hearer to the leading idea of the passage, this may be deduced either as a subject, " The connection of the faith and the life," which will then be exemplified by a detailed examination of the verses ; or it may be stated as a proposition, " The true believer will be careful to maintain good works," which will then be proved by the arguments the apostle furnishes, and will be applied to his instances. The logical proposition is usually the safer form for the young preacher, because it is more exact, and compels him to a convergent discussion. When defining and urging unity in discourse, I reminded you that a series of remarks might be seemingly connected by their reference to one subject, which were each one true and edifying, and yet might' be as divergent as the radii issuing from a common centre. The preacher who is in danger of thus sinning against unity will protect himself by throwing his topic into the form of a proposition, and his discussion into that of a demonstration; for if he argues the affirmation of his predicate, all the parts of his proof must converge on the one copula. Some preachers, however, have the faculty of instructive didactic remark. They discuss their point, not so much in the form of a set demonstration, as of a series of explanations and instances. Their skill avoids the perversion of their flexibility of method into a real breach of unity. They are less formal, but not really less argumentative, than the avowed logician. And before some audiences there is even an advantage in the absence of technical forms of argumentation; for the display of these provokes some tempers to assume a mental attitude of resistance.

LECTURE XI.

ARGUMENT AND CONCLUSION.

THE fourth and most extended member of the regular sermon is the *Argument.* This indeed constitutes the main body of the discourse. I have already said, more than once, that it may often consist of a didactic discussion, which is not a formal demonstration. It may be a convergent series of illustrative or explanatory remarks. It may be a series of historical instances. Yet, as the intent is always demonstrative, and as the affirmation of resemblance in each illustration or instance is usually a brief tract of demonstration, the name of "Argument" is not inappropriate to this *main* discussion, in any case. As this is what constitutes the body of the sermon, the consideration of it must be extended and important. The larger part of all that falls under the head of *"Disposition"* will obviously pertain to this topic. I therefore postpone the farther treatment of it until our synoptic view of the constituent members of discourse is completed, lest I should be led to separate the remaining one too widely from the first four.

This last member is, of course, the *"Conclusion."* The reasons for its introduction correspond to those

168

which required an *exordium*. As the approach to the
main subject without any preparation would be abrupt
and unskilful, so to relinquish it without conclusion
would be awkward and incomplete. As a transition
stage of sentiment was found necessary to raise the
hearer, from his ordinary apathy, to the tone of the
sacred truth to be discussed, so a transition is desirable,
to consign him to the state of sacred meditation and
conviction in which the sermon is designed to result.
Again : the aim of all rhetorical discourse is to produce
a practical determination of the hearer's will. To this
end, the truths discussed should be so applied, after
they have been explained and demonstrated, as to connect the force of the whole in one effect. " A threefold
cord is not quickly broken." Each several head of discussion may be likened to one strand. It is the conclusion which twines them all together, combining their
strength and drawing the convinced hearer irresistibly
to his duty. The separate branches of argument are
the parallel rays of the sun of truth ; the conclusion is
the lens which refracts them into one burning focus.
Once more : these several parts of the argument must
be presented by the speaker, and considered by the
hearers, singly in detail; for to mingle the discussion
of them together could result only in confusion and
obscurity. The preacher must lay aside the first in
order to take up the second head ; he dismisses the
second in order to introduce the third. He must, in a
certain degree, call his hearers away from the previous
point to attend to the one in hand : he must require
them temporarily to exclude it, in order to give full
attention to the next. If, then, there were no con-

clusion, the branch of argument treated last would occupy an undue place before the mind of the hearer, and the force of the previous ones would be partly lost. Hence the necessity of going back, either by a formal or a virtual recapitulation, to suggest again all the heads of discussion which had been temporarily dismissed, and to deliver their cumulative weight upon the souls of the people. In a word, it is by means of the conclusion that the unity of the discourse evinces itself.

There may indeed be, especially in expository sermons, a continuous application where each topic is addressed to the conscience as soon as the exposition develops it. In such cases the final conclusion will be shorter, because the work of application has been already in part done. But even here a general conclusion will usually be best, to gather up the collective effect of the whole; because the partial applications made in the current of the discourse will be of special parts of the truth to special ends.

The conclusion may be one of five kinds. The first is formed by introducing the more general truth under which the proposition of the sermon is comprehended. This particular truth is thus made a stepping-stone for ascending to some higher and wider point of view, whence a more impressive prospect is seen of the importance and the relations of the duty to which the text tends. The subject of discourse may be, for instance, God's special providence. This will be defined, and then, in the main discussion, demonstrated. The preacher may then, in his conclusion, show that the denial of this doctrine is practically equivalent to atheism, since it seeks to exclude God from all actual, effective concern with his creatures, and makes such duties as those of reverence, faith, prayer, as unreasonable as would the actual demonstration that there is no God. Thus, any appeal to the conscience, which the preacher might desire to ground upon his proof of the doctrine of providence, would derive more solemnity and weight, since he could justly urge that disobedience in that particular was connected, by implication, with the enormity of the crime of atheism.

There may be a second form of conclusion, where an idea is introduced which, while single and particular, bears to all the heads of the sermon the relation of a representative epitome or summary. This is not identical with the first. The concluding thought may be a proposition into which the proposition of the text may be transmuted (as the detailed discussion will have evinced), and which will set the text in a more striking and practical light. Or else it may be a final head of argument, which, while most definite and pungent of all, will be seen to contain the previous ones by implication in itself. For example, let the text be John v. 40: " And ye will not come unto me that ye might have life;" the doctrine of which is, that the sinner's own perverse will is the practical obstacle to his salvation. This may be argued in detail by such points as these: The sufficiency of Christ's satisfaction and renewing grace for all men, and the sincerity of the gospel offer to all: The fact that no sinful being can effectually obstruct the sinner's coming, if he is himself willing, and that no holy being desires to do so: The nature of the sinner's inability as having its roots in a perverted will. The conclusion may then urge, as a final and most practical argument, virtually inclusive of all the preceding, that such is the nature of true faith and repentance, he who truly wishes to exercise them (his rudimental knowledge of the gospel being supposed) does in that wish begin to exercise them. Thence the preacher may urge upon each sinner's will the direct and immediate issue of consenting to a present salvation or rejecting it.

A third kind of conclusion may be found appropriate in doctrinal and didactic discourses, which consists of inferences or corollaries. The fruit of a discussion is thus well gleaned. There is an indirect but most pleasing confirmation of the proposition of the text, when its harmony with other truths is thus evinced. But these concluding corollaries should be chosen under the guidance of a severe taste and judgment. Since the theology of redemption is a system connected throughout, and every truth is related directly or remotely to every other, if full license were taken to introduce all possible corollaries, one might begin from one head of divinity and infer all the rest. The inferences deduced should, therefore, be near and conclusive, they should be grave and practical, and they should be such as will not forsake, but preserve and promote, the dominant scope of the sermon.

The fourth kind of conclusion is the recapitulation. This was the favourite form of the peroration or epilogue among the classical orators. It consists in a brief and weighty recital of the points already argued, terminating in the emphatic announcement of the main proposition first asserted. This recapitulation must be brief, lest it should weary the hearer as an idle repetition. It must be, while the same in logical *substance*, new in statement, or in the phase of presentation; for the orator should not sensibly repeat even himself.[1] It should surpass the previous discourse (not necessarily in loudness, but) in movement, force and animation. Thus the weight of the arguments is gathered up and delivered with cumulative effect. A good recapitulation is also the best expedient for fixing in the hearer's memory the plan of the discussion. If this is presented to him at the beginning of the argument, he will apprehend it as dry, vague and burdensome. Such a recital of heads to be discussed is indeed a "skeleton" of the coming discourse; it gives only the meagre bones, sapless and undeveloped. But the repetition, even if it be brief, following a full discussion, will suggest the several members of the discourse as the hearer has just seen them in the plastic hand of the orator, defined in their full dimensions, clothed with flesh and colouring, and instinct with vital warmth.

---

[1] Quinctilian, L. vi., c. i., § 2. "Rerum repetitio et congregatio, quæ Græce dicitur *ανακεφαλαιωσις*, a quibusdam Latinorum *enumeratio*, et memoriam judicis reficit, et totam simul causam ponit ante oculos; et, etiamsi per singula minus movebant, turba valet. In hac, quæ repetimus quam brevissime dicenda sunt, et quod Græco verbo patet, decurrenda per capita. Nam si morabimur, non jam enumeratio, sed quasi altera fiet oratio. Quæ autem enumeranda videntur, et cum pondere aliquo dicenda sunt, et aptis excitanda sententiis, et figuris utique varianda; alioqui nihil est odiosius recta illa repetitione, velut memoriæ judicum diffidentis."

A comparison of any of Cicero's perorations with the main argument will show how skilfully he complies with the last maxim. While he recapitulates the same points, it is always in new lights.

The fifth species of conclusion is the practical application. This is the most appropriate termination for the ethical or practical sermon ; but it is not unsuitable for the doctrinal, as is clear from the maxim, that doctrines should be preached practically as well as duties doctrinally. The object of the application is to bring the truth which has been established in the discussion to bear immediately upon the conscience and will. Since every rhetorical discourse aims at a practical determination of the hearer's will, it is obvious that this species of conclusion is in the strictest accordance with the design of eloquence.

The application may be either general or special. The former is one which urges a principle of duty concerning all classes of hearers alike. Thus, the truth that we "know neither the day nor the hour when the Son of man cometh" results in the application, "Watch therefore"—an injunction suitable alike to believer and unbeliever. The special application is that which separates the hearers into classes and directs the truth to their several consciences, in the particular phase appropriate to each. The advantage of this method is, that it singles out the hearer more closely, and brings the truth into more immediate contact with his heart. Definiteness is the necessary condition of pungent effect. Yet the subdivision of your audience into classes must not be carried too far, lest the multiplicity of your heads of application should render the discourse technical, tedious and dry, just where the unction and movement should be greatest.

Having mentioned the different kinds of conclusions, I would add some remarks applicable to them all.

When I grouped them, as to their matter, in five classes, I did not intend to be understood as forbidding the employment of a conclusion which might belong to two of these at once. For example, the peroration may be both a summary and an application. Indeed, whatever may be the matter of the epilogue, it should always be a virtual application. I would urge that the conclusion be always the subject of careful preparation. It is no less important that our last impression be a good one than our first. The practical sense which the hearer entertains of the effect and force of the sermon is that which is left upon his soul at its termination. " He is the conqueror who remains master of the battle-field."[1] Nothing can be more faulty than to leave the conclusion to the accidental suggestions of the moment. The speaker is then exhausted; he has expended his store of thoughts; he feels that while he is not willing to sit down he virtually has nothing more to say; he beats the air with empty declamation; he wears away the impression of the truths already unfolded, by their bald repetition; he endeavours to cover his retreat by noise. But the peroration, of all the parts of the discourse, should be the most sharply defined, the most trenchant, the most perspicuous, the most convergent. It would be a far smaller fault to break off, leaving the sermon a fragment, than to mar the impression already made by vague commonplaces or useless repetitions. Let not this critical part of discourse be left to the inspiration of chance.

But while an idle repetition, which gives nothing

---

[1] *Vinet*, Homiletics.

new to the expression of the thought, should be avoided, it would be a flagrant sin against unity to introduce foreign matter in the conclusion. The leading scope of the discourse must still prevail to the very close, even more strictly than in the midst of the discussion. The thoughts and images which compose the termination, while not identical with those already uttered, must be such as will carry forward both the same subject and the same impression.

All writers on eloquence, ancient and modern, seem to have concurred in the opinion that the peroration should excel in persuasion. You will be hereafter more distinctly instructed in the nature and means of this part of rhetoric, but you doubtless already comprehend that we mean by persuasion, as distinguished from argument, those appeals which are aimed directly at the heart. In the conclusion, if anywhere, the religious affections should be touched. The power of moral painting must now be invoked. The preacher's soul should here show itself fired with the force of the truth which has been developed, and glowing both with light and heat. The quality of unction should suffuse the end of your discourse, and bathe the truth in evangelical emotion. But this emotion must be genuine and not assumed; it must be spiritual, the zeal of heavenly love, and not the carnal heat of the mental gymnastic and *gaudium certaminis*. It must disclose itself spontaneously and unannounced, as the gushing of a fountain which will not be suppressed. What can give this glow except the indwelling of the Holy Ghost? You are thus led again to that great, ever-recurring deduction, the first qualification of the sacred orator, the grace of Christ. This demand for progressive animation and unction cannot be met by a mechanical and calculated increase of voice and gesticulation. When the preacher, who is not really penetrated in his own soul by the light and heat of the divine truth which he wields, begins to foreshadow the approaching end by the stale artifice of buffeting the cushion of his pulpit and the ears of his audience, every sensible person is wearied and repelled instead of being impressed.[1] He instinctively sets himself to resist being taken by storm by so deceitful an assault, instead of being swept along a willing captive to the preacher's light and love. Nor is a true fervour necessarily expressed always by increased loudness and force of gesture. The peroration may sometimes be less vehement than the previous discussion. A calm, solemn and earnest strain may impress the heart and conscience more than that which is animated and bold. The most profound convictions are often too deep to show an agitated surface. The discourse must be like a river which never ceases its motion toward the sea. But the stream which, where it is a rivulet amidst its native mountains, brawls and foams against the immovable rocks, at last disembogues itself calmly with its mighty volume of waters into the ocean. At the end it does not move with less force, but it moves without agitation, because its resistless current has swept every obstacle from its channel.

The last and perhaps the most important maxim for the peroration is that so tersely expressed by the words, *Ne nimis*. The preacher should restrict the length of

---

[1] The youths of the university described this by the coarse but **ex**pressive phrase, " Piling on the agony at the close."

his conclusion with a severe and jealous hand. Its object is only to place the truth which has been explained or proved in contact with the heart and conscience. Every word which exceeds this is an excrescence. When once the truth has found full access to the hearer's soul, the best possible thing to be done is to leave it there performing its own work. Protracting the discourse beyond this point only undoes what has been already effected. One object of the conclusion is to awaken emotion. Remember that vehement affections are never long sustained.[1] When the conviction has once invested itself with strong feeling in the soul of the auditor, that is the propitious moment to dismiss him to his own meditations. If he is then detained, the emotion will speedily subside, and with it the impression. The most important thing, therefore, is that you know when to stop, and that you be sure to stop when you have done.[2]

---

[1] Quinctil., L. vi., c. i., § 27, 28. "Nec sine causa dictum est; *'Nihil facilius quam lacrimas inarescere.'* Nam, quum etiam veros dolores mitiget tempus, citius evanescat necesse est illa, quam dicendo effinximus, imago; in qua si moramur, lacrimis fatigatur auditor, et requiescit, et ab illo quem ceperat impetu, ad rationem redit. 29. Non patiamur igitur frigescere hoc opus, et affectum quum ad summum perduximus, relinquamus; nec speremus fore, ut aliena quisquam diu ploret. Ideoque quum in aliis, tum maxime in hac parte, debet crescere oratio; quia quicquid non adjicit prioribus, etiam detrahere videtur; *et facile deficit affectus qui descendit.*"

[2] A shrewd and caustic Frenchman once uttered the following criticism upon the vice against which I warn you. If the image is homely, the sarcasm is not more biting than the folly deserves: "Your American orator is very ingenious and fluent, but his conclusion is too much like that of the pointer dog, who when he wishes to sleep turns around and around, following his own tail, and at last lies down just where he began."

LECTURE XII.

SOURCES OF ARGUMENT.

OUR subject now leads us back, young gentlemen, to the fourth, the main constituent part of the sermon. This, as we have seen, is termed the "Argument." Under this name is classed all evidence, everything, whether it be reasoning or testimony, which produces conviction of the understanding concerning the proposition or subject discussed. The speaker's ultimate object is always practical; but since man can only feel as his mind sees, and since his rational volitions follow the stronger present dictate of his own understanding, it is plain that the presentation of evidence must, in every discourse, be the foundation of all true effect.

Our treatment of this member of discourse naturally divides itself into two branches. Of these, one considers the matter, the other the form, of the argument. The former branch obviously falls into the department of "Invention," and the latter into that of "Disposition," if the old arrangement is regarded. But you will remember that I partially emancipated myself from the bonds of that distribution at the outset. The matter of the argument, or the sources from which it may be drawn, is to be considered first, because, as you will see, this decides concerning the form or arrangement. The nature of the matter to be organized largely determines the form of the organism.

Each scientific writer upon rhetorical reasoning has presented us with a classification of the sources of argument.[1] You will find them various. None of them,

---

[1] Thus, Aristotle, the father of logical science, in his *Rhetoric*, Bk. II., chs. 21–25, presents us the following classification:

The sources of arguments are *Enthymemes, Examples* and *Maxims.*

I. *Examples,* include
- a. Real occurrences.
- b. Imaginary analogous occurrences, as fables, etc.

II. *Maxims* (γνωμαι).
- 1. Class. Not argued.
  - The self-evident, or universally admitted.
  - The generally admitted.
- 2. Class. Deduced.
  - a. Those which are major premises of enthymemes.
  - b. Those which imply such premises.

III. *Enthymemes.*
- a. *Ostensive,* inferring propositions from admitted truths.
- b. *Refutative,* rebutting false propositions.

Aristotle then proceeds to enumerate fourteen sources or topics of ostensive enthymemes and five of refutative enthymemes, many of his distinctions between them being shadowy. Such a classification is manifestly much better adapted to entangle the public speaker in a thorny wilderness of distinctions, than to show him how to grasp the convictions of a popular audience.

Archb. Whateley (who is largely a modern Aristotelian), in his *Rhetoric,* p. 33, Amer. ed., ranks the sources of arguments under two grand divisions: I. The *A priori;* II. The *A posteriori.* Thus:

I. *A priori.*
- Argument from Cause to Effect, not only evincing the το ότι (the effect *is*), but the το πως (*how* it is).

II. *A posteriori.* Arguing from Effect back to Cause.
- 1. By Sign (σημειον).
  - a. From Result.
  - b. Consequence.
  - c. Effect.
  - d. Testimony.
- 2. By Example (τεκμήειον).
  - a. Experience.
  - b. Induction.
  - c. Analogy.

Dr. George Campbell (*Philosophy of Rhetoric,* p. 57, Amer. ed.)

however, are wholly erroneous, and several of them are instructive; but I do not regard the best of them as sufficient for our purpose. Some are inaccurate, in that they do not separate the elements of proof according to the generic and real differences in the modes of the action of the human reason. Others of them are in-

---

gives a classification which approaches nearer completeness, accuracy and practical utility, at once, than any other which I have seen. Says he: Evidence proceeds—

I. *From Intuitions*, including	*a.* Axiomatic beliefs.
	b. Dicta of self-consciousness.
	c. Primitive moral judgments.
II. *From Common Sense*,	*i.e.,* Conclusions so immediately near intuitions that they are uniformly admitted.
III. *From Deductions*,	*a.* Deductions of positive or mathematical force.
	b. Deductions of moral or probable force.

Dr. Porter, of Andover, *Homiletics*, recommends the following arrangement, which is neither exhaustive nor correct in any point of view. He says proofs may be drawn either, I. From the *Bible;* II. From *Consciousness;* III. From *Common Sense;* IV. From *Facts or Experience.*

Vinet's Homiletics, as translated by Skinner, p. 171, groups the sources of evidence as, I. Arguments from *Experience;* II. Arguments from *Testimony;* III. Arguments from *Reasoning.*

Aristotle, as a pagan, naturally omits that which must ever be the right arm of pulpit argument, the testimony of Revelation. Dr. George Campbell, writing chiefly for the secular orator, not unnaturally makes the same omission. Dr. Porter seems to recognize neither our intuitive judgments, mental or moral, nor our deductions from premises, as valid sources of conviction. *Vinet* appears to omit all appeal to consciousness and intuitions. Even Whateley fails to recognize that most important branch of popular argument, which consists in placing the proposition to be proved under the self-evidencing light of its equivalent intuition or self-consciousness.

complete, being rather fragments of a classification than exhaustive arrangements of the whole matter of argument. The objection which lies, in common, against the best of them is, that they are not practical; they do not group the kinds of evidence under classes truly convenient for instructing and aiding us in the rhetorical work; they state rather dialectical than practical grounds of distinction. It must, of course, be admitted that a correct knowledge of logic is useful and necessary for constructing an argument. But it is not my office here to teach this science. You are presumed to have learned its rudiments (which are sufficient for our purpose) while students of colleges, and my duty is to teach you how to apply this knowledge to rhetorical uses. This I shall attempt to do by seeking a simple and natural principle in the recognized laws of the mind itself, which will give us the guidance we need in constructing a system of practical rules for popular argument.

When we analyze the sources of our mental convictions, we trace all our beliefs ultimately to two fountains, self-consciousness and intuitive judgments. By consciousness we mean that knowledge which the soul has immediately of all its states as states or affections of itself. Of these informations of consciousness it is impossible to doubt, and for the truth of them it is absurd to demand premises. The evidence of that of which we are conscious in ourselves is as immediate and authoritative as the evidence to us of our own existence. Our intuitions are those primitive and necessary judgments whose truth is self-evident. They depend on no premises, because they, with the *dicta* of consciousness, are the first premises of all our deduced conclusions. They are necessary truths. The mind apprehends that the admission of them is inevitable, immediately upon an intelligent inspection of the statement of them, because it sees that to deny them immediately contradicts its own laws. They are, consequently, universally admitted truths; every fair mind, the world over, believes them the moment it thoroughly understands the terms of their enunciation. Of these intuitions, some are logical and some are moral. It is an equally original judgment of the reason that the whole of a body must be larger than either of its parts; that no effect can arise without adequate cause, and that virtuous conduct is meritorious of reward, as sin deserves punishment. When I call the last two moral intuitions, I do not mean that they are not strictly rational; I only signify that they belong to that peculiar and highest class of the judgments of the reason with which conscience concerns itself.

The most careful inspection of our elements of thought will show that our self-consciousness and our mental and moral intuitions include all our primary convictions. But that all other judgments must derive their convictive force, directly or remotely, from some óne or more of our primary judgments, is admitted by the reflecting minds of every age. Every dependent truth must have some other from which it depends, and the first truth of the series must be a primary judgment[1]

---

[1] Aristotle. See previous note. Basil, on Psalm cxv. Ανάγκη ε'καστης μαθήσεως ἀλεξετάστους εἶναι τας ἀρχάς. Turrettin, Loc. ii., Qu. 6, § 11. Prima principia nota sunt in seipsis, et sunt αναπόδεικτα

dependent on no premise, or else the ultimate source of every conviction is infinitely removed backward.

I believe, young gentlemen, that a correct view of the logical powers will show that self-consciousness and intuitions are even more immediately concerned in every deduction than the last consideration would indicate. A deduction is seen to be true by a syllogism—that is to say, by the comparison of a major and a minor premise where such a relation is perceived by the mind between the two as evinces the conclusion to be really contained in them. Now, first, it is the authority of self-consciousness which assures us, when we thus syllogize, that it is the same perceiving mind self, *ego*, by which both the premises are apprehended. Without this assurance, if it were not evident but that the major premise were entertained by one intelligent agent, and the minor premise by another, having no proper identity with the first mind, no validity of relation could be seen by the understanding, and no inference could be drawn. We learn thus that the testimony of our self-consciousness is the immediate condition precedent of every judgment of relation which we form. But second : By what power of the soul is it that the inference is seen to be really included in the premises of a correct syllogism ? I answer that it is (our self-consciousness co-operating) by an inspection of the reason. The act which the mind here performs is also an act of intuition, different indeed in its circumstances, but not in its kind, from the rational perception of a first truth. It is said that

(quæ aliunde demonstrari non possunt) alioqui res abiret in infinitum. Citation of moderns is needless, as all true logicians (*i. e.*, all except Positivists) are agreed.

the truth of an inference is only seen by relation to its premises. I answer, so, many axiomatic judgments are judgments of relation. Why then must the former action of the reason be less an act of direct inspection than the latter? Is it said that the primitive judgment of an axiomatic truth is inevitable when the terms are understood which announce the axiom? I reply, the judgment of the inference in a conclusive syllogism is equally inevitable, if its terms are all understood; the only difference is, that there are more terms to be correctly apprehended and more relations, and thus more intricacy and risk of fallacy in the inspection. The reason is the soul's eyesight, the power by which it sees truth and right. If one sees with his bodily eyes, he sees only by looking. Whether he uses a mirror or not, to see directly, or by reflection, it is still true that he sees only by looking. His act is still the same—an act of immediate inspection; it differs from any other case of eyesight only in its outward circumstances. So this eyesight of the soul, the reason, sees the true and the right only by its own immediate looking; all its correct acts are intuitions; every valid judgment resumes virtually the force of a primary judgment, and hence only its real validity.[1] But I would remind you that your acceptance of my opinion in this particular is not at all necessary to establish my maxim, that self-consciousness and intuition are the ultimate sources of all our mental convictions.

As I have attempted to resolve our deductive conclusions into these sources (and a parallel process would resolve our inductions into the same) let us illustrate the

---

[1] See Locke, Essay, b. iv., ch. ii., § 7.

truth by applying it to the cases of some other kinds of evidence. What is the nature of the evidence brought to the mind by its bodily senses? Self-consciousness convinces us of the rise of perception within us, and an intuitive judgment compels us to refer that effect to a real object without us as its cause. The evidence of my experience is, first, remembered perception brought from the past. (Self-consciousness tells me infallibly that the self which now recalls, is the same which before experienced, the same set of perceptions.) I then apply the remembered experience to the present analogous case by appealing to an intuitive judgment, that like causes produce like effects. The evidence of testimony is, in its first stage, that of our senses; we hear or read the words in which our fellow-creature affirms his statement. The same intuitive judgment, that effect must flow from adequate cause, then taking his utterance of that testimony as an effect, infers necessarily that something caused it. That cause must be either the actuality of what he asserts, or else some delusive or dishonest motive for asserting what has no truth, either existing in him or in his informant. The reason, in order to select the one or the other as the true cause of the utterance of the testimony, then considers the question of the witness' competency and credibility (unless these are already self-evident). In considering them the mind still refers to some primitive judgments.

You will observe, if you examine the lists of the sources of argument which I recited from other authorities, that they are all virtually included in the seven which I have now explained—*self-consciousness, intuition, deduction, sensation, experience, induction* and *testi-*

mony. And the last five all owe their authority to the
first two. Conviction of the understanding is always
to be traced ultimately to self-consciousness, or to some
intuition, or to some union of the two. But while these
are the primary sources, any truths of which the mind
has, through them, become convinced, may in turn become secondary sources. Of these, some will be found
more proximate and some more remote. Their practical value as sources of argument in preaching may not
be according to their nearness to primitive judgments,
but will rather be decided by their nature and their
range of application.

Now, for the preacher, the chief of these secondary
sources is the testimony of the sacred Scriptures. Their
authority as our rule of faith is inferred immediately
from their inspired character; for if God is perfect
truth, as must be assumed, or else all search for truth
anywhere is preposterous, and if the Bible is God's
word, then it is infallible, and of course authoritative
over the soul. But is the inspiration of the Bible self-
evident to its readers? I answer, it is not immediately self-evident—that is to say, the proposition, " The
Bible is inspired," is not axiomatic—but it is readily
found to be true upon bringing the internal and external evidences of it under the light of our self-consciousness, our mental and our moral intuitions. This is but
saying that God, in revealing himself to man, has clothed
his revelation with an amount of reasonable and moral
evidence adapted to the creature's nature, and sufficient,
when inspected, to produce a perfect conviction. There-
upon the word of God assumes its place as of plenary
authority over the soul in the department of which it

professes to teach, that of our religious beliefs, duties and redemption.

Let me here request your attention to two vital remarks. One is, that the fullest and most submissive faith is supremely reasonable. This is demonstrated by the fact that the postulate from which the authority of the Word over the soul inevitably arises (this, namely, that the Bible is inspired) has been irresistibly commended to the reason itself. Hence it is simply impossible there should be any competition between right reason and true faith. This is the Protestant, or, in other words, the Bible system. It does not demand the reception of the Scriptures as God's word in advance of rational evidence that it is such, upon the pretended authority of the Church, or on any such illogical pretext. But it presents to the reason and conscience credentials which triumphantly establish the claims of revelation, and then it places the Bible on the throne of the soul as authoritative witness for God—authoritative because proved true. The enlightened reason now delights to bow implicitly to it, and in doing so it finds the highest consistency with its own nature.

The other statement is this : Intelligent faith is still not rationalistic, in the vicious sense of that term. The basis of faith is not human speculation, but God's infallibility. It may be asked, " Did we not just now require the Scriptures to submit its claims of infallibility to our reason ? Is not the authority which the Scriptures exercise, then, only that which reason has conferred upon them ?" I answer, No ; the point is only a verbal fallacy. If a trope must be suggested, it would be far more correct to say that the Scriptures impose their irresistible evidences upon the reason. The Scriptures exercise all that authority which their own intrinsic truth confers; this reason does not confer, but receives. Here, then, is the radical difference between intelligent faith and rationalism. Faith makes reason the recipient of revealed light; rationalism makes it the source. Faith begins by recognizing, on reasonable grounds, the infallibility of the Word, and thenceforward bows to it implicitly. Rationalism denies that infallibility, and calls the Word in question at every step, making reason the source and measure of authority in every doctrine. In the true believer the reason receives the teachings of the Word as the eye receives the light of the sun. There are certain actions of the eye with reference to the light, the raising of the lid, the direction of the axis, the refraction of the rays. But these actions are merely receptive. The light is from the sun, not from the eye. So the light in the soul is from the Word; the actions of the reason touching it are only receptive, not productive; the authority which the reason recognizes is that of God, and not its own.

You now perceive that when once the inspiration of the Scriptures is established, they become practically the great storehouse of proofs for pulpit argument. Their teachings, though not so primary in the order of analysis as those of the self-consciousness and the intuitions, are far more extensive and useful; for even these primitive faculties are not always infallible: the Word is always so. They, unaided, can discern but a very few religious facts and verities, and none of these few are saving truths. Revelation discloses all those secrets of the divine mind which are necessary for salvation.   When we begin to reason from first truths to moral and theological conclusions, such are the darkness of mind and conscience and the perversion of will produced by sin, our deductions have but little value, save as they are confirmed by revelation.   The Bible is, therefore, for the preacher, the great armoury of weapons of conviction.

This examination of the sources of mental conviction has now led us to two principles, which need no further proof after their enunciation.   These I give you as the foundation of all rules for pulpit argument:

I. *In every resort to reasoning, recur as closely as possible to the primary sources of conviction, self-consciousness and intuitions.*

II. *Rely mainly on the testimony of the Word.*

You will see hereafter, how naturally these two principles include all that is valuable in the books concerning the sources and rules of argument.   I will proceed to inculcate, in the next lecture, some precepts in detail, deducing them from the two guiding maxims just announced.

LECTURE XIII.

RULES OF ARGUMENT.

THE first precept which I shall state, in fulfilment of the promise of the last lecture, is little more than a repetition of our second maxim. Sermons should ever be rich in Scripture. The testimony of the Word should be cited with a certain boldness and authority expressive of the preacher's confidence, not in himself, but in God, who there speaks. The manner in which this supreme umpire is ushered in should seem to say, "This is necessarily the end of controversy." Some preachers were accustomed to speak disdainfully of the human reason, as though it were the enemy of faith, and to resist the application of its powers to examine religious truth, in a manner which suggested fear and jealousy. Others, on the contrary, were perpetually taking so much pains to make revealed truth appear reasonable to the hearers, that they gradually taught them to feel they were under no obligation to believe, unless they could comprehend the reasonableness of what God declared. Both these errors are to be avoided. Let the preacher apprehend the proper functions of reason in revealed theology, and the harmony between this faculty and faith. Let him show his confidence in revelation by cheerfully inviting Reason to apply its severest examinations, provided it be fairly done. Let him so challenge the willing obedience of the mind for the Word as to show that the most humble and implicit submission is the highest wisdom.

The proof-texts cited should be pertinent, and they should be applied only in the precise sense which the Holy Spirit intended them to bear. What that sense is, the preacher must ascertain by a diligent and faithful study of them, before he ventures to use them. I would enjoin the same sacred integrity here which I urged when speaking of the use and exposition of the text. He who quotes the Scriptures in a sophistical spirit will gradually produce this impious result: the people will be taught to regard them as a sophistical book. Some will always be observant and acute enough to note and remember your inconsistencies of logic. You will find that you have taught them at once, to despise your arguments, to use the same weapons against you, and to treat the word of God with diminished reverence. But the highest reason against a disingenuous use of Scripture evidence is, that it offends God. How can we dare to pretend that we shall promote his holy ends by unholy means?—that we shall advance truths by falsehood?

When an important statement is made, other proof-texts may be well added to the first. While one word of God should be enough to silence doubt for ever, yet the concurrence of several satisfies the mind, by evincing a wider harmony between the proposition advanced and the sacred Scriptures, and by extinguishing any lingerings of doubt whether the first testimony was fairly applied. But proof-texts should not be multi-

plied to weariness; this would weaken instead of strength-
ening the impression, and would arrest the movement
of the discourse. The relevancy of these testimonies
may not be obvious without some exposition, or their
bearing, while valid, may be inferential only, or they
may suggest some interesting side-view of truth kindred to the main subject of the sermon. Shall the
preacher pause upon citing such texts to expound, to
apply, to deduce? I reply, he may pause, but it must
be under the restraints of a severe judgment. He must
see to it, that he turns aside no more than is absolutely
necessary to cause his proof-texts to yield a full support
to his text. Otherwise, the unity and movement of
discourse will be fatally marred; his sermon will be a
crude bundle of little sermons.[1]

2. My second rule is little more than an application
of the principle, that all reasoning should recur as closely
as possible to the original sources of conviction in self-
consciousness and intuitions. When you have occasion
to argue, in addition to your appeal to proof-texts, endeavour so to put your propositions, as to bring their
truth directly to the test of these original powers of
the mind. Where there is really but one step of deduction from first truths, this may always be done, and
often where the steps are more than one. It is effected

---

[1] Dr. Conrad Speece once compared this kind of preaching to a
Christmas-hunt in Virginia, where the boys took a rabble of untrained hound-whelps into the old fields to chase hares. A warm
trail was soon found, and hotly pursued until another scent happened
to cross it. The pups were sure to take this and run upon it until a
third was met a little fresher. Thus there was a mighty cry and race
all the day, and not a single hare caught at night.

by putting the case in a concrete instance, so stated as to present the true point of the argument palpably for the intuitive verdict of the mind. For example, let the proposition to be established be this : " The sinner's inability is no excuse for his irreligion." This might be argued metaphysically by defining inability, analyzing its elements, and showing that they are such as do not supersede our responsibility. I do not say that such analysis is never proper in the pulpit, but you will gain your point much more effectively and plainly by appealing at once to the sinner's consciousness, and compelling him to testify against himself that in each act of impenitency, omission and transgression (the aggregate of which makes up his irreligion) he acts his own preference. In every one he exercises his conscious free-agency. But now he also has a moral intuition, which tells him that there is responsibility wherever there is free-agency. This argument is self-evident to him. And, besides, it really defines to him the nature of his inability more clearly than any analysis.

We have all read an excellent illustration of the argument, from our intuition of cause and effect, for the existence of God, in the supposition that one should propose to account for the production of the *Paradise Lost* by the accidental falling together of a multitude of printers' types. We feel intuitively that this cannot be, because accident cannot be the adequate cause of all the varied order and beauty of that poem, in orthography, grammar, metre, euphony, invention, imagination and reasoning. How, then, can anything less than God have been the adequate cause of this wondrous universe ?

Take one more instance. The proposition, "Con-cupiscence is sin," may be argued theologically. But the convincing argument is to appeal to the hearer's self-consciousness, and to the impartial and intuitive verdict of his conscience. Let it be supposed that he is harbouring an inclination or entertaining a temptation to do an unrighteous act against his neighbour, or even that a feeling of unjust resentment against him is allowed to brood in his heart. He can truly say that no matured volition exists in his soul to do the wrong; no definite purpose has been formed. Why has he an instinctive unwillingness to have his neighbour know the adverse feeling? Why does he blush at the thought that others divine it? This proves that the feeling is not innocent; the immediate judgment of the reason is disclosed, condemning it as sin.

Under my second precept I may correctly place the commendation of experimental reasoning. For this, as we have seen, brings the proposition which you assert under the purview of the intuition, that like causes must produce like effects. The popular mind loves the experimental argument. It is to this kind of intelligence, practical and plain: it seems to bring the truths you advance within its own actual and even its sensible knowledge. It should therefore be much used in the pulpit.

3. If deductive processes are used, let the steps be few. The object of this rule is to bring the conclusion as near the first truth as possible. Some one has well said that if a chain of argument consists of more than two or three links, it is worthless for the public speaker. The people have a just suspicion of ratiocina-

tion in long-drawn trains. However carefully you
may conduct it from the beginning to the end, they remain doubtful of the result. They desire to be able to
look back after the journey is completed, and to comprehend all the steps at one view; they wish to see, not
only that they have passed over from first premise to
last conclusion, but also how they passed over. Now,
where the steps are numerous, the recollection of them
all is fatiguing: none but thoroughly-trained minds are
capable of it. When we remember also whence logical
fallacies usually arise, we shall appreciate the justice of
the popular dislike for long trains. The source of these
sophisms is commonly in some misapprehension or
transition in the meaning of terms. Now, each syllogism presents us with four separate terms, each of
which must be distinguished and remembered, as well
as their relations. As we multiply syllogisms, we
multiply the chances of fallacy in at least a quadruple
ratio. If we suppress a member of a syllogism for the
sake of brevity and of diminishing the number of
terms, we only increase the intricacy of the reasoning,
by thus compelling the mind to supply the missing
link.

You can now understand the popular prejudice
against "reasoning preachers." They are regarded as
dry and fatiguing. But, in truth, he who does not
reason is no preacher: he establishes no conviction.
The dry preacher is one who should be called just the
opposite of a "reasoning preacher," for he reasons
unskilfully, and therefore tediously. The attractive
preacher is the true reasoner, for he argues skilfully
and tersely. He is interesting, not because he gives

the understanding no logical grounds, but because he gives them aright : he who should do the former would make no impression whatever and would be supremely uninteresting.

4. Use many illustrations of your arguments. A brief caution, I trust, will be enough to remind you that mere illustration is not argument, and that he who substitutes the one for the other is a dishonest logician. When I say this, I except those obvious cases, where the illustration is expressed and the argument implied ; because the latter is made, by the help of the former, perfectly obvious, and does not now need an express statement to set it forth. The mind of the hearer grasps it validly without further words. Such are some of the illustrated arguments of our Saviour. But in these instances illustration is not made a substitute for argument : it is well understood by the hearer, that its only value is to lead to the reasoning which it suggests, and, in suggesting, explains. It must also be conceded that there are illustrations which are at the same time true analogies : they present a real parallelism of relations to those of the argument illustrated, in that respect wherein the force of the deduction resides. In such a case there is more than the force of mere illustration : there is analogical argument—a species of experimental evidence which is conclusive in proportion to the perfectness of the parallelism. I may cite, for example, the Christian grace of "adoption," the name of which suggests a beautiful illustration from the usage, as it prevailed in the civic life of the ancients. The adopted child of the Roman patrician was held of patrician rank, however vile his actual birth. This fact not only assists

us to comprehend the proposition, that the justified believer is made co-heir with the Son, but, because we must believe that the employment of the word " adoption" suggests a true analogy, it gives us also some probable evidence that the proposition is true. But it behooves the preacher to remember that in other cases illustration is not argument, and to be jealous of himself, lest he should cheat the understandings of his hearers or his own by the exchange. The use of plausible, ingenious, pretty but not truly analogical illustrations is one of the most refined arts of the sophist, seductive to the indolence of men's minds, and exceedingly hard to expose; for while the apparent analogy is obvious and broad enough for the lazy thinker, the discrimination which proves the appearance false and the analogy deceptive is nice and laborious, requiring perhaps a more careful abstraction than the original abstract logic would have demanded without the aid of any illustration. This is therefore a weapon as dangerous as effective, and its right use demands your highest Christian integrity.

The legitimate use of illustration, then, is to assist in the right apprehension of terms and relations, in order that the logic may be really brought under the inspection of the reason. If a proposition contains a first truth, as soon as its terms are perfectly apprehended, the truth which is in the copula becomes readily obvious to the mind's intuition. We no longer need any aid to see it; we cannot help seeing it. So, if a relation between propositions includes a sound deduction, as soon as all the terms and the intended relation are rightly apprehended, the inference is seen by the mind's inspection. We again find that aid is no longer wanted to see it; we cannot avoid it if we would. The difficulty of receiving the force of such logic as has just force is only in the precise apprehension of terms and relations, as they are meant by the reasoner. This requires fixed attention, correct abstraction, clear conceptions and faithful memory, as well as competent knowledge of words and syntax. Now attention and abstraction are most irksome to ill-trained minds, and such are those of the major part of mankind. Illustration happily relieves that pain, by assisting abstraction and alluring attention. It leads the hearer's mind easily to the designed conception of terms and relations, by setting them in a concrete form. It gives an indirect, but an exact and happy, definition of that relation of propositions in which the inference resides. It thus assists in getting the argument within the purview of the mind's inspection. The use of illustrations is, therefore, sanctioned by our first principle, which traced the elements of all mental conviction to self-consciousness and intuitions.

Another advantage is that derived from the wit of the illustration. When I mention the word *wit*, I suppose you too well informed to think that I intend something jocular. Wit is defined to be a sudden view of unforeseen but apt relations with the pleasure arising therefrom. This pleasure, while always vivid, may be elevated and altogether serious. Now a second gain of the good illustration is its serious wit,[1] the sudden and

---

[1] Many of our Saviour's illustrations, as well as those of the great uninspired masters of rhetoric, are rich in this element. See that of the two debtors, Luke vii. 41. The children playing in the market-

pleasing suggestion of a novel but truly apt relation between the concrete idea introduced and the reasoning step which is pending. The pleasure which this produces is easily reflected by association upon the reasoning itself. The hearer mingles it with the intellectual gratification derived from the intuition of the truth he has reached, and he carries away the argument and conclusion with an impression of delight.

There is still a third element of power in some illustrations—their influence over the emotions. This will be more successfully explained when I speak of the work of persuasion.

Illustration is, therefore, a potent aid to the orator. All masters of the rhetorical art have excelled in it. Our Saviour surpassed all others in the copiousness, terseness, aptitude, beauty, ingenuity, simplicity and wit of his illustrations. Hence, in part, it was that men said, "Never man spake like this man." You should humbly imitate him. You should study apt illustration and store up the materials for it from your observation and reading. The narratives of the Bible are your appropriate treasury. Another may be found in the store of known and moving contemporaneous events which an active mind collects. But in selecting an illustration you must observe two rules: one is, that it should be more simple and familiar than the thing to

---

place, Luke vii. 32. The good Samaritan, Luke x. 33. The wolf in sheep's clothing, Matt. vii. 15, etc. Some of them indeed are instinct with wit in its more biting aspects. What can be more stinging, and even humorous, than "the blind guides straining at a gnat and swallowing a camel?" Matt. xxiii. 24. Only our familiarity with them prevents our feeling the pungent wit.

be illustrated, otherwise it gives the hearer no aid ; the other is, that it must not only be apt and logically fair, but of a dignity and seriousness coherent with the topics of the pupit. An illustration which should degrade a solemn and elevated subject by its ludicrous triviality, or which should divert the emotions from their sacred channel by suggesting the unhallowed passions of the world and its strifes, would be a grievous blemish. In one sense, it would be a greater rhetorical sin, in proportion as it was more striking and ingenious.[1]

Although mental conviction, the subject we now have in hand, is reached through the reason, yet the speaker cannot overlook the fact that his hearers are creatures of affection and prejudice, as well as of understanding. These powerfully affect and obstruct the operations of the reason. We must, therefore, not only deal directly with the emotions in the work of persuasion, but in

---

[1] I trust that I shall not be charged with this vice, for the following illustration of it.

One moist, sunny afternoon, as I was coming from my house to this place, to give one of these lectures on Sacred Rhetoric, I saw the pertest possible little dog making most intent and anxious efforts to catch something, which seemed to be flitting before him upon the ground. I found, upon watching him, that the object was the *shadow* of an ephemeral, yellow butterfly, which was fluttering a yard above his head unseen by him ! He was fatiguing himself to catch the shadow of an insect which was itself too unsubstantial to satiate his hunger if eaten by the hour. What an illustration, said I to myself, of the sinner " who walketh in a vain show and is disquieted in vain," living for the deceitful hopes of sinful joys which, if won, would be empty !

But would this incident be fit for the pulpit ? No; the scene was too petty and too farcical, although startlingly analogous, to paint an error so momentous and tragical as that of the worldly soul.

our argument we must endeavour so to use logic as to evade these obstructions and obtain for evidence its best light. One great end of judicious arrangement is here indicated. Arrangement is also determined by a clear perception of the conditions of the question to be debated and the attitude of the parties. As the success of the military commander depends on the disposition of the several arms, so that each shall be brought into action where it will be most efficient, so the triumph of the reasoner results often from the skilful ranking of his arguments. These thoughts show the propriety of the following remarks :

5. Determine correctly on which side the "burden of proof" justly lies. If the preliminary presumption is in your favour, claim it, and throw the burden of proof upon your antagonist, that you may have to stand only on the defensive. This discreet position may make the difference between overthrow and victory. Sir Walter Scott in the "Crusaders" represents Count Raymond Berenger as refusing to stand on the defensive within his castle, which he might easily have made impregnable against the whole Welsh host. By rashly attacking them in the open field he incurred defeat and destruction, despite his skill and heroism ; he fatally threw away his vantage-ground. The law allows every accused person the presumption of his innocence until he is convicted. It is, therefore, the duty of his advocate to assume the defensive, and throw upon the prosecutor the burden of proving guilt. If the defence should undertake to show that the accused did not commit the act charged, it would find itself committed to the arduous and perhaps impossible task of proving a negative. This neg-

ative might be true, and the man really innocent, and yet its demonstration in that form might be impossible. Here the folly of assuming a logical obligation which did not belong to them would convert a triumphant defence into an abortive attack. Let an instance be also taken from our own science, theology. In a theodicy, or vindication of the divine attributes as concerned in the evils prevalent among creatures, those who assert that the perfections of God are consistent with these adverse appearances are entitled to the presumption; for "the earth is full of the goodness of the Lord." The initial probabilities are in our favour. Let those who assert the opposite assume the burden of proof, as is fair. Our defensive task then becomes comparatively easy; for the arduous thesis which our assailants have to maintain is this: that there can be no good reason, known to an infinite mind, why God should permit these evils, and be still omniscient, benevolent and almighty. This presumptuous assertion rebutted, our victory is won, and the fact that, within the limited circle where we comprehend God's providence, we see him regularly bringing good out of these evils is sufficient for that result. But if we undertook the *onus* of explaining fully how God is benevolent in the permission of all these evils, which his omniscience foresaw, and which his omnipotence might have excluded, we should find ourselves overwhelmed with difficulties; the task is beyond human ken. These examples may exhibit the usefulness of our rule.

6. The prejudices of hearers must be consulted in the order of introducing your proposition and proofs. If the truth to be established is not repugnant to your

hearers, you may consult other considerations exclusively; but if it is obnoxious to misunderstandings and prejudices, the form of proposition chosen should be one which, while perspicuous and not uncandid, shall state the truth in its* least offensive phase. The aspects of it which especially assail their previous ideas may be better asserted in the conclusion, after those adverse conceptions have been removed by explanation and argument. Further, I would recommend that the discussion begin, in such cases, with *a priori* arguments; for these, proceeding from cause to effect, both show that your proposition is true, and how it comes to be true, thus removing the incredulity and appearance of paradox; afterward, the other evidences may be introduced with better effect.

LECTURE XIV.

RESUMING the same subject, I remark, in the seventh place, that the arguments should follow each other in a natural and progressive order. They must be so arranged that the mind of the hearer will pass from the first to the second and thence to the third with ease, and that the effect of the whole shall be cumulative. The maxim which you will find in most books of rhetoric is, that we begin with the weakest argument and proceed thence to the strongest, in order to secure a climax. Whateley objects to this, that it is injudicious to advance the least impressive point first, because by so doing we risk making a bad first impression. The hearer, he thinks, will be likely to conclude that it is a trivial cause which is introduced by a trivial reason. He therefore advises that the discussion be opened with some obvious and forcible argument, that the weaker pleas be thrown into the middle, and that the remaining strong points be introduced last, to prevent anti-climax. There is, it must be admitted, some force in the objection which Whateley advances.[1]

---

[1] Cicero de Orat., L. ii., c. 77, §§ 313, 314. "Atque etiam in illo reprehendo eos, qui, quæ minime firma sunt, ea prima collocant. In quo illos quoque errare arbitror, qui, si quando (id quod mihi nun-

But if the old rule be modified in the following respects, I think it may be retained. Let no point of argument be elevated into a separate head of the discussion, at any stage of it, which is feeble enough to incur the risk of a trivial first impression. Such proofs, if noticed at all, should be compressed into a subordinate position. The impressiveness of respective heads of argument should be estimated relatively, not to the speaker's, but to the hearer's mind, as it apprehends them after they have been expanded. The professional man's habitudes of thought are likely to differ from those of the common people; whence a view that seems most weighty to the preacher may be felt by them as less impressive, even after his presentation of it. If now he places this last, he will depreciate instead of enhancing the final impressions, for it is in the people's minds that impression is sought to be made: he is not speaking to convince himself.

Some have urged that the right solution of these questions of order would be to select your strongest argument and stake the issue on that alone. They say that one good evidence is convincing, and the preacher of Christianity should never use a bad one. They ob-

---

quam placuit) plures adhibent patronos, ut in quoque eorum minimum putant esse, ita eum primum volunt dicere. Res enim hoc postulat, ut eorum expectationi qui audiunt, quam celerrime occurratur; cui si initio non satisfactum sit, multo plus sit in reliqua caussa laborandum. Male enim se res habet, quæ non statim ut dici cœptum est, melior fieri videtur. Ergo ut in oratore optimus quisque, sic et in oratione firmissimum quodque sit primum; dum illud tamen in quoque teneatur, ut ea quæ excellant serventur etiam ad perorandum. Si quæ erunt mediocra (nam vitiosis nusquam oportet esse locum) in mediam turbam atque in gregem conjiciantur."

ject that the solicitude to add a second and a third betrays a consciousness of the unsoundness of the first. This plan would have more plausibility if your audience consisted of a single man; but you preach to many at once. You know that the constitutions of different minds are various; so that a point which is effective with one may be powerless with another. The engineer who fires at a crowd loads his artillery with a number of grape-shot, not with a single ball. But I claim also that a second argument is not felt by any mind to be useless because a first has been found convincing. It confirms the evidence already seen, and guarantees us that its seeming force is not sophistical : it instructs us in the most pleasing manner in the harmonies and relationships of truths.

The testimony of Scripture is our most weighty evidence. Where, then, should the proof-texts be ranked? In many cases you will find that the declaration of a particular citation is related to some one head of your argument: this text should then be cited at the conclusion of this head. In other cases it would appear proper to place the chief array of texts at the close of the discussion, that they may have the honour of terminating debate. It seems inconsistent to continue human arguments after God's final verdict is announced.

8. Last, the preacher should see to it that his proof is unanswerable. Nothing should be advanced which is not solid, and all should be so perspicuously and forcibly put as to silence every mind which is not perverse. While every public speaker must be prompted to speak convincingly by whatever motive causes him to speak at all, this force is demanded of the preacher

by a more solemn obligation. It is God's truth which he advocates. It is a system which claims infallible certainty. Common hearers are apt to suspect that an inconclusive argument betrays an inconclusive proposition; for this, although not a just, is a most natural, inference. The result of sophistical preaching is to make Christianity seem sophistical. He is no small criminal who, by his indolence or heedlessness, occasions this profane deduction. Hence the preacher should be, as a logician, intensely honest. It is his sacred duty to practice the most painstaking care in constructing his arguments, and to be sure that he sees all around his points before he ventures them. You find here an additional reason against logical novelties and long-drawn ratiocination in the pulpit. No man can safely risk their multiplied occasions of fallacy. We should restrain ourselves within those solid grounds where we can be certain of our correctness; we should rely upon those broad and strong views of truth which are grasped firmly by the common mind. To secure this honesty, your study should be accompanied with much prayer, that the infirmities and uncertainties of the human understanding may be guided from on high.

Polemic argumentation is somewhat peculiar in its circumstances. All logical discussion may be regarded as indirectly polemical, for whenever we establish a true proposition we thereby virtually refute the opposite error. This method is called indeed indirect refutation. And this, let me say once for all, is usually the wisest, safest and most effectual mode of pastoral opposition against heresy. The minds of your people should be so filled in advance with the truth, that there will be no room for an enemy to inject an error. A controversial tone in the pulpit is usually to be avoided, and the habit of throwing your arguments into the form of a logical combat with an imaginary opponent is most unfortunate. The tone of the pastoral instructor should usually be didactic; his attitude is that of the father instructing docile children. But there are occasions when he must refute error directly. In his doctrinal sermons he must often meet known and aggressive objections which place themselves across the path of the truths he is asserting. There may be instances (of the occurrence of which your pastoral theology will decide rather than your rhetoric) when it will be your duty to make a formal warfare against some heresy. Since all reasoning is but reasoning, the principles of polemical argument are, of course, not different from any other. But there are some peculiar questions touching it which need to be answered.

1. The first is the question of arrangement. In what part of a discourse affirming truth shall objections be considered? On the one hand, it is urged that if you advance your own propositions and proofs before the objections are cleared away, you may find that these have totally obstructed the minds of your hearers. The fortress must be breached before the storming-party is sent in. On the other hand, Whateley well replies, that if you begin with the consideration of the whole group of objections, you prejudice your own cause in advance by showing the people how much can be said against it. He therefore recommends that the discussion be opened with some obvious and effective affirmative arguments, that the objections be considered in the mid-

dle, and the progress then resumed and closed with other direct and climatic proofs. A better rule is the following: Introduce objections along with those affirmative heads of your own argument where their solution is most natural and ready. You will nearly always find that there is special relation between a particular objection and some particular support of the true proposition. The latter presents the immediate point of view for exposing the former. The advantages of my rule are, that a formidable array of objections in any one place of your discourse is thus avoided by their distribution throughout it; that time is economized by taking up each objection just where your affirmative argument has prepared the way for a speedy and facile dealing with it; and, above all, that this method leaves upon the hearer's mind a strong impression of the satisfying harmony and beautiful consistency of truth.

2. Time should never be wasted by citing trivial or unknown objections. Give your hearers credit for good sense enough to apply your demonstration to the shallow ones, without words on your part. Indeed, a masterly affirmative argument is always the best refutation. To inform your hearers of an objection about which they were in happy ignorance, that you may have the glory of refuting it, is pedantry. It is as though a physician should give his patient a poison in order to exhibit his skill with antidotes. It may be that in consequence of some peculiarity or infirmity of constitution your antidote will fail to act, and then you will have killed your man for naught. But when you feel that an objection is so known and influential that it must be formally noticed, make thorough work with it. Let

your refutation be unanswerable. Nothing makes a more damaging impression of feebleness than to grapple with the objector without clearly overthrowing him. Your hearer is thus taught by yourself to suspect the justice of your arguments.

3. Opposers should always be treated with fairness and courtesy, except where their own insolence or wickedness demands chastisement.

One application of this maxim is to teach us abstinence from the use of controversial phrases, party names and all the old war-cries of polemic discussion. The preacher should rarely assault, by name, a rival denomination of Christians. If, for instance, a Presbyterian pastor begins: "*Methodists* teach that a true believer may totally and finally fall away from a state of grace : this I shall now refute," every person of that persuasion in the house will naturally feel as though he were personally assailed. But had this pastor advanced the opposite doctrine, so explained as to free it from odious misconceptions, in a didactic mode and temper, making only a respectful general reference to an honest difference of judgment upon it among the recognized followers of Christ, every fair-minded adherent of Wesley would have listened without offence, and would have come away with the pleasing impression that Christians were not so far asunder upon this vexed question as he had supposed. It is very much due to the observance of this simple rule that wise pastors (without infidelity to truth) preserve pleasant relations with other communions, hold their own ground triumphantly against encroachments, and even win accessions, without awakening denominational strife. And it is usually the rash contempt of this easy caution which plunges others into unseemly and mischievous rivalries.

Another lesson of my third maxim is, that objections, if stated at all, be stated fairly. Give them any weight which they may deserve. It is well that you should set your opponents' arguments in even stronger lights than they were able to throw upon them; for manifest candour is the best plea on your own side. The people will see that you have no fear of the objection, and this alone will almost reassure them as to your ability to annihilate it; but if they detect you dodging its real point, they will regard this as a confession of virtual defeat. By placing both the objection and its refutation in a clearer light than your antagonist, you make your hearers feel that you have that superior mastery of the whole subject, which entitles you to correct him and to instruct them. There are also objections which have real difficulty to the human mind, and yet the propositions against which they lie are true. The only solution of such cases is in acknowledging the limitation of our faculties. Let the admission be then freely made, and let the mystery, after being defined and explained as far as established truths enable us to do it, be left to the candour of the hearer.

Once more: see to it that, whatever may be the superiority or weakness of your logical ability, you surpass your antagonist in Christian charity and self-control. The people are very apt to associate a good man with a good cause. Your reasonings may not be appreciated; but the argument of a forbearing temper will be understood by the most ignorant.

4. My last precept may be expressed in the words

of that injunction which *Talleyrand* is said to have urged upon his diplomatic agents: "*Pas trop zélé.*" By this I do not recommend that you shall defend the truth of God against his assailants with a cold indifference: he deserves an ardent, loving zeal; but I mean that you shall be satisfied with a substantial victory for him. It is enough to convince the objector that he was mistaken: it is not well to attempt to convict him also of absurdity, of virtual idiocy and of malignity, except in those cases where such depravity has been so obtruded as to outrage the proprieties of truth and righteousness. If your auditors know your opponent as a well-meaning man, as a decent Christian, as a sensible person in other things, as entitled in the judgment of charity to the claim of sincerity, then they may be willing to go along with you in the conclusion that he has been obviously in error, provided the superior mastery of the subject which you display warrants such a claim. But when you demand of them that they shall also vote him a fool, a rascal, a deceitful traitor to truth, they will demur; for they will say, "Do not we know this person as, in the main, a good man?" By such an extreme use of your victory you will forfeit it, and restore to error a sympathy to which it is not entitled.

DIVISION OF THE ARGUMENT.

HAVING examined the nature of argument and given some specific rules for constructing it, we are now prepared to adopt a principle of *division*. The five constituent members of the regular discourse—exordium, explication, proposition, argument and conclusion—are, in one sense, divisions of the sermon. But among these the argument is the main body of the discourse, and it is the division of this of which I now speak.

.You have seen that method, which is an orderly arrangement of parts, implies discrimination. We must divide in order to dispose. The architect must assort and separate his materials before he can rear his building. The naturalist dissects his animals and plants, that he may classify. A few high authorities, *Fénélon* and Bishop Burnett, renounce division as a sin against unity.[1] The former objects that " divisions

---

[1] Fénélon, Dialogue ii., Concerning Eloquence. Burnett's " Pastoral Care," p. 249. But Fénélon really explains away his sweeping renunciation of divisions, argues the importance of distinct method, and gives a beautiful outline of what it should be. His objection, therefore, is no more than a repudiating of the scholastic formality, and of the habit of pre-announcing the heads.

I find Dr. J. W. Alexander, "Thoughts on Preaching," pp. 42, 52,

really clog and mangle a discourse," that "there remains no true unity after such divisions, seeing they
make two or three different discourses, which are joined
into one only by an arbitrary connection." This objection may be valid against divisions which are merely
formal, but not against those which are natural. There
cannot be a discourse without parts. Unity itself implies parts, and it does not consist in the amalgama-
tion, but the orderly juncture of the various materials
into one component whole. If the idea of this objection were pushed to its full extent, it would require not
only one head, but one single thought, so that the discourse must either be shortened to a paragraph, or else
expanded by mere repetition into a wearisome platitude.
In the landscape, unity of impression is not gained by
flattening the whole scene into a uniform, horizontal
plane, but by the happy combination of the swelling
hills, the smiling and undulating champaign, the field,
the wood, the mansion and the water. The historical
painting produces one effect, but it is by the grouping
of several distinct and perhaps contrasted figures. A
uniformity of colour would be no picture whatever, but

---

under the name of "free writing," recommending composition without a plan and objecting to it as cramping and impoverishing discourse. This language might well prove very mischievous to the
learner. The reason that Dr. Alexander could succeed without previous method was that through mental culture and long experience,
both in composition and *extempore* speaking, he had so thoroughly
trained his powers that he was able to excogitate a true method easily
and without conscious pause. Use had made the labour of arrangement so perfectly facile that it went on along with that of expression. Of course he no longer needed the previous skeleton. Let
not the tyro conclude thence that he can do the same.

a dingy, neutral expanse of canvas.   The preacher
must, then, at least divide his matter in his own mind
in order to have method.

All divisions of the main argument may be classed as
Scholastic, Textual or Topical.   The first is a legacy to
us from the dialectics of the Middle Ages, and it is
justly obnoxious to the accusations of the more rational
and natural moderns like *Fénélon*.   With an appearance of great naturalness and scripturalness, it is often .
really unnatural and unscriptural.   To the dominion
of this method many of the blemishes of the Puritan
preaching were due.   It consists in first deducing from
the text, by a suitable exposition, a strict proposition,
and, second, in treating first the subject of this, then
the predicate, and then the copula or affirmation.   Every
sermon must therefore have three heads—neither more
nor less; for, urged the scholastics, do not these three
things compose every proposition?

Such a procrustean bed must, of course, cramp or
mangle nearly every subject which was stretched upon
it.   To explain it, let us take an instance as favourable
to the method as can perhaps be found among important texts.   Eph. ii. 8 : " For by grace are ye saved."
The proposition deduced must be this : " Salvation is
gratuitous."   The first head must discuss the question,
What is salvation ? the second, the notion of gratuity
as predicated of God's salvation, and the third, the
affirmation.   Now, if one desired really to preach the
proposition of the text (which is the text) the first and
second heads should have been dispatched in the explication, and the assertion of the copula should have occupied all the argument, its heads consisting of the sev-

eral evidences which demonstrate the free grace of redemption. Another example may be found in 1 Tim. i.
15. The proposition derived will be: "The gospel
saying deserves universal acceptance." On the scholastic plan of division, the first head should treat of the
gospel saying, viz.: "That Christ Jesus came into the
world to save sinners." Here must be introduced the
doctrine of Christ's incarnation and person, the legal
and moral position of man as a sinner, and the nature
of salvation. Will this be a division of the sermon, or
a volume of theology? The second head will explain
the predicate, which is also complex, including the species of faith which Christ claims, and the nature and
universality of that claim on the conscience. Thus,
before the preacher can possibly arrive at the third
head, the actual assertion of this claim, which properly
is his only task in the main discussion, he is made to
range over the commonplaces of nearly the whole of
revealed theology! Once more: 1 John iv. 8 presents
us in its form an exact proposition: "God is love."
The first head under the scholastic method would answer the question, What is the subject, God? Can
there be a juster answer than that of the Catechism?
"God is a spirit, infinite, eternal and unchangeable in
his being, wisdom, power, holiness, justice, goodness, and
truth." The second head treats of love as simple benevolence, or the love of kindness, distinguished from
the love of moral complacency, and defined by the different postures and conditions of its objects, as grace,
pity or mercy. What a vast range of topics, scriptural
indeed and of sacred importance, yet irrelevant to that
truth which should have been the delightful burden

of the whole discussion, God's benevolence, to lead us away from it!

The Scholastic Division is, we thus see, faulty in its nature. Its usual error is to thrust into the third head what should be the real sermon, the main argument, and to degrade the chief heads of that body into subdivisions of a division. If this old method (of which you will now seldom hear an example) is to be employed at all, it is only when the whole sermon is designed to be explanatory, and the affirmation of its proposition is intentionally compressed into a subordinate space.

The Textual Division is simple, scriptural and beautiful in that class of texts and passages to which it fairly applies. It simply makes the distribution of the matter of discussion as the phrases or commas of the text stand in the Scriptures, changing nothing except perhaps the order of the clauses among themselves. I explain it in the following instance : 1 Cor. i. 30, " Who (Christ) of God is made unto us *wisdom,* and *righteousness,* and *sanctification,* and *redemption.*" The proposition is, " Christ is made of God our salvation." The heads are, because he is the source (1) of our sufficient illumination, (2) of our justification, (3) of our purification, and (4) (conclusion by summary) thus, of our complete redemption. Other instances, for which the textual division is suitable, may be seen in John xiv. 6 : "I am the way, the truth, and the life." In Rom. viii. 30; in 2 Cor. vii. 11 and in 2 Pet. i. 5–7. Wherever it is applicable it should be preferred as doing honour to the Word, and as fixing it most prominently in the hearer's mind.

But there are many texts where it cannot be fairly applied, because the several clauses or phrases into which the sacred writer has distributed his words were not intended by him to be logical distributions of matter, but rhetorical amplifications or emphatic repetitions, and such like. Let us suppose that we were required to discuss Rom. ii. 8, 9 : God " will render . . . indignation and wrath, tribulation and anguish, to every soul of man that doeth evil." If we should adopt a textual division here according to the four words, and represent "indignation" as one species of the recompense of sin, " wrath" as a second and distinct one, " tribulation" as a third, and " anguish" as a fourth, we should outrageously pervert the apostle's meaning. The passage is intensely animated : he uses, in the glow of his rhetoric, an amplification of each of the pair of ideas (God's righteous anger, and the misery it visits on the guilty) which he would evolve. Many other verses are incapable of a textual division, because the words, whether few or many, really present but a single, undivided point. Such are these (John iii. 7), where the sole predication is the necessity of regeneration, and the words, by themselves, suggest nothing whatever, as to the heads of the evidence, which demonstrate that necessity. Such is Heb. iv. 13 : " Neither is there any creature that is not manifest in his sight ; but all things are naked and opened unto the eyes of Him with whom we have to do." The only proposition for the preacher here is the assertion of God's omniscience of our spirits. In the explication you might briefly and appropriately touch the questions, What is meant by " manifest in his sight" ? How are creatures' spirits " naked and opened to him"? What are God's eyes? What is it which we "have to do" with him? But if these should be made the heads of the main discussion, there would be a mischievous breach of unity and a real violation of the apostle's scope. That intent is to impress us with God's perfect knowledge of all the acts and affections of our spirits. This result must be gained either by exemplifying or proving the truths asserted, under heads to be suggested, not by the phrases, but by the grounds of this truth itself.

This, then, is the idea of the topical division. Assuming that the author of the text did not design to indicate the true divisions of his thought by his distribution of words, the preacher seeks them for himself in the logic of his subject. He does not indeed seek them in unscriptural sources, nor even in unscriptural forms of expression; for the logic to which he goes for his divisions will be Bible-logic only. Having gathered these members of argument from the whole Scriptures, he will divide it according to its real discriminations of thought.

Topical divisions will usually fall under two general classes. First, where the form of discussion is strictly demonstrative, the design being to prove a proposition asserted, each distinct branch of the argument will form a head of the discourse. The division in this case is obvious, as soon as the several evidences are collected and arranged. Second, in explanatory sermons the subject will be decomposed by descending from *genus* to *species*. The truth unfolded will be set forth either in the parts which compose it, or in a series of different relations or aspects. For example,

let the text be, " Honour thy father and thy mother,"
and let us suppose that the task undertaken in the sermon is the didactic explanation of filial duty. This is
composed of—1. Respect; 2. Maintenance; 3. Obedience; 4. Affection. Or, as an example of the second
subdivision, let the text be Rom. xii. 11 : Be " not
slothful in business," and the task of the preacher is the
commendation of diligence. Its advantages may be set
forth—1. To one's self; 2. To one's family ; 3. To society ; 4. To the Church. Or else the practical sermon may seek to enforce a duty : its several grounds or
motives will in this case furnish the several heads, as
in the class of demonstrative sermons.

I would now announce a few rules of the most practical nature, which, as I conceive, should always guide
you in the forming of divisions, whether they be textual or topical.

1. Divisions should not be numerous. Although the
sermon is a composition very different from the drama,
the limit affixed to the number of acts by Horace[1] is a
safe one, at least on the major side. He prohibits more
than five. Multiplied divisions are every way objec-
tionable. They overburden the memory, whereas a
real object of method is to aid memory. While they
wear an appearance of great exactness, they are really
inaccurate, because the necessities of an artificial symmetry often constrain those who employ them to make
a distinction which is not according to a true difference.

---

[1] Ep. ad Pisones, line 189 :

" Neve minor, neu sit quinto productior actu
    Fabula."

They confuse and embarrass the hearer's mind. They destroy movement. They cast an air of insufferable dryness over a discourse. It is as though the tree, beautiful in the proportions of its stem, its branches, its twigs and its foliage, the natural constituent parts, were reduced to an unsightly heap of chips.

2. Whenever the topic of a head or division is announced or defined, the same precept should govern which was given for the statement of the proposition, and for the same reasons. The language must be carefully chosen for brevity, perspicuity and accuracy of meaning. The words must be discriminative, and they must not be numerous. To overload the mind of your hearer, in these critical sentences of your discussion, with obscure and involved expressions, is an unpardonable fault. As I enjoined it on you to study the choice of words for announcing your subject until your phrase is as terse, brief and true as possible, so I repeat this injunction as to the statement of these divisions. If you judge it admissible in any case to set out all your heads together at the beginning of the discussion, the terms ought to have that happy appropriateness and expressive brevity which will make it positively difficult for the hearer to forget them, and which will render them, after your subject is expanded, a correct miniature of the sermon. I recall just here a happy instance of such announcement in the sermon of an English divine on Matt. xxvii. 4. He announces as his subject the "Sorrow of Judas," and promises to treat, 1. Of its Origin; 2. Its Object; 3. Its Extent; and 4. Its Result. Its origin is then shown to be self-love. Its object is only the shame and penalty of his crime. Its

extent is only a flagrant secular transgression.   And its result is damnation.   Here are four simple but masterly strokes of·the pencil, giving a suggestive outline of the whole picture.   They are also discriminative and scriptural, as well as natural and easy, for they delineate the essential difference between spurious and genuine repentance.

3. The heads must, each one, present a branch of the discussion distinct from the others, and co-ordinate with them in relation to the main subject.   Never make a "division without a difference."   The inevitable result is confusion and error; for the lines of thought in the two divisions being virtually the same, the preacher will be guilty of anticipation and repetition.   It is not enough that the heads be truly distinct; they must also be co-ordinate.   If the real relation of a thought is subordinate to that which you propose to make your second head, it is a vicious arrangement to exalt it into a first, or a third head, and to give it a separate treatment.   It should be reduced to a subdivision of the head under which it belongs, that it may be promptly and correctly treated under its own class.   A moment's reflection will show you that the attempt to expand it independently must introduce repetition or obscurity.

4. The division should be thorough.   My meaning is, that it should comprehend the full strength of the proposition which you undertake.   In topical sermons that proposition may not be exhaustive of the whole meaning of the text; for I have expressly allowed the preacher, after fairly indicating in his explication the whole meaning of the text, to tell his hearers that there is too much in it for one discussion, and to undertake

the argument of only a part. In textual divisions the rule of thoroughness also applies in this sense, that no member of the text must be omitted in the division. The preacher must urge all that the sacred writer has urged in that place which is chosen for a text. This precept is grounded on the obvious reason that you are bound to do justice to God's truth: you are not permitted, after undertaking its presentation, to make a partial betrayal of its strength by the omission of a constituent ground of its force. It is not the part of a faithful herald to emasculate his king's message of any part of its authority. For example, the preacher who undertakes to present the scriptural evidences that Christ's sufferings were punishment, and made a vicarious satisfaction for guilt, has no right to intimate that he has done, before he has given the important argument for this truth, drawn from the nature of the Levitical sacrifices and the Redeemer's relation to them as an antitype. This would be to maim God's truth.

Such a rule implies, obviously, that the preacher is not to be guided by mere originality in selecting his materials. He must "bring forth from his treasury things new and old;" he must be willing to act, not as an inventor, but an expounder; he is humbly and faithfully to teach the people all those known but fundamental truths which other generations of ministers have taught to their contemporaries. Two objections may present themselves to your minds. The one is, that my rule may compel you to prolong your sermon inordinately, if you must not stop until you have exhibited the whole force of the Scripture argument. I reply, license must always be left to every reasoner, as to the extent to which he shall expand his arguments. If time forbids more. remaining heads may at least be named, with an advertisement to your hearers of the force you claim for them; or the people may be expressly told that you have not done, and that another sermon must follow to complete the truth. The other objection is, that I seem to require every minister, however humble his natural gifts, to equal the force of the greatest masters. I answer, that I do require of every minister, however humble his natural endowments, competency for his sacred work. I do not expect him, indeed, to rival the animation, felicity, imagination or splendour of the great genius; but I demand of him that he shall be substantially master of his subject, that he shall use the diligence required for declaring the whole counsel of God concerning it, in his own plain and homely way. This he can do, if he is faithful, without genius.

5. The parts must be ranked, *inter se*, in an order which is convenient and germinant. The requirements of movement and climax have already been enforced in my remarks on the structure of argument. The heads must also follow each other in such order that this consideration, which prepares the way for the facile comprehension of that other, shall precede. We thus gain the greatest economy of words, time and effort. It is also most desirable that the divisions be ranked in a germinant order, so that the first shall lead to the second, and the second to the third, by an easy and graceful transition. This is necessary to maintain the continuity of discourse, and to avoid the feeling of a shock or jolt in the movement. Nothing adds more to the grace of

discourse than pleasing transitions. When the matter
of the divisions does not furnish these obviously, they
should be carefully sought out. An apt illustration,
an episode, an incident, a contrast, briefly introduced,
may furnish the stepping-stone which is needed, for
a happy passage from one part of the discussion to
another. [1]

---

[1] The young preacher may, at first, find the application of these
principles touching method and division intricate and arduous. Let
me advise you, then, to concede all that can be allowed to the infirmity of our understandings, and by doing one thing at a time, to lighten
this labour as much as may be. Explore the field and collect the
materials first, without troubling yourselves at that stage with questions
of arrangement. After satisfying yourselves that you have substantially the whole ground before you, inspect each part, so as to become
well acquainted with it. Then proceed to the important question of
arrangement after these labours of discovery are completed. Do not
hesitate to use, in your private preparation, every convenience, such
as written *memoranda* of heads, which may assist the labours of recollection and comparison. Then, at length, after your method is
digested, begin the actual composition (if the sermon is to be written).
Let me exemplify my advice. We will suppose, for instance, that
the task I have set myself is to prepare for preaching on the next
Sabbath on Rom. iii. 20: "Therefore by the deeds of the law there
shall no flesh be justified in his sight," and that I propose to
treat it doctrinally, under a topical division, as a "capital text," or
important point in divinity. Such a sermon presents us the plainest
instance of the questions of arrangement. The proposition is quickly
and certainly deduced: "Justification is not because of the merit of
the believer's works."

I proceed to study authorities, as time allows: first the Holy Scriptures, and then the soundest treatises, such as those of Turrettin and
Owen. As I read I keep pencil and paper by me, and jot down everything which strikes me as possibly a point for the argument. I read
on until I find from the recurrence of ideas already gathered, that I
have apparently explored the whole field of discussion, at least in all

There remains one more question touching division on which modern authorities are divided. It is whether all the heads of a sermon must be pre-announced to-

---

its important outlines. The result, we will suppose, is the following immethodical list:

The merit of the believer's works does not justify:

Because by the law is the knowledge of sin.

Because all works are imperfect, while the law is absolute in its claims.

Because St. Paul excludes moral and ceremonial works.

Because the Bible says justification is gratuitous.

Because remission (a cardinal part of justification) implies no payment.

Because the Bible says, "justification not of law."

Because this would derogate from Christ's honour and inflate pride.

Because future obedience does not pay past debts.

Because true good works are only effects of, and so consequent on, justification.

Because justification is "by faith," but faith is receptive in its acting.

Because of Scripture testimonies, such as Rom. iv. 5; xi. 6; Gal. ii. 16; Tit. iii. 5, etc., declaring the same doctrine.

You will observe that my list has no marks or numbers as yet to indicate any order. It apparently contains eleven separate points—a number entirely too large for a sermon. Let us carefully inspect them. One thing which we soon perceive is, that the third, sixth and eleventh points are substantially similar, being all scriptural testimonies directly to the proposition. Let us reduce them to one head by grouping them together. The fourth and tenth are also so cognate, that they can without error be fused into one argument; for the purely receptive nature of faith in its actings about justification shows that this is gratuitous—faith being confessedly its instrument. The seventh point also is manifestly so near akin to these, that its force can be saved by making it a sequel or consequence under them. Boasting is excluded, and Christ claims all the glory, only because the work is gratuitous and man's agency in it simply receptive. The first, fifth and eighth points are also cognate. The function of the law, now that we have broken it, is to ascertain our debt of guilt; subsequent

gether, before the discussion of any is begun. The
scholastic and many of the Puritan preachers require
this ; and Doddridge even urges their repetition a second

---

obedience, however meritorious, cannot pay this off, and remission,
the petition of every believing sinner, is release of the debt without
payment from him.   After these unions, there remain five independent points, which, written again in their chance order, are the following :

All works are imperfect ; but the claims of the law are absolute.

St. Paul and other Scripture authorities expressly exclude the law
and the merit of works.

Justification is declared gratuitous, faith's only agency in it is receptive, no boasting is left to man, and Christ claims all.

Remission (a leading part of justification) requires no payment ;
and this, future obedience, when once the law ascertains our
debt, cannot do.

True good works are effects, and so cannot be causes, of justification.

In this list no heterogeneous arguments are grouped together. .The
number of heads is no longer too large, yet all the points are intel-
ligibly introduced in such connections that they support each other
better than when separated.   It now only remains that we inspect
our five heads again, to determine an order of sequence for them,
inter se, which shall be germinant, logical and progressive.   I
promptly perceive that the head which stands second above, consisting
of a group of express proof-texts, should come last, as making an end
of debate by the authority of God.   I therefore assign it in my mind
to the fifth place, thus disembarrassing further questions of order by
one element, at least.   I also perceive that the point of argument
which stands fourth in the list is nearest akin to the first ; for, in unfolding the senses in which God's law is absolute, I must show that
it demands perpetual as well as perfect obedience ; in failure of
which, it puts in an inexorable penal claim.   Here, then, is the
logical and natural transition from the one head to the other, in the
idea of debt, which works cannot pay.   I determine, therefore, that
the fourth must immediately follow the first.   I also see that these
must be (in the order last named) the first two heads of the sermon,
because neither of the remaining two is introductory to the others.
The head last in the list is most proper to close the reasoning, both
because the fact which is its premise (that good works are fruits of

time. They claim that this assists the memory of the
hearer to retain the sermon ; that it is necessary to his
comprehension of its method and plan ; that it defines
to him more clearly the precise point of the main proposition, which otherwise he is apt to misconceive; that
it enables him to relieve his restlessness, by marking
off the stages of the discourse, and thus calculating how
much is still coming ; and that if momentary inattention
supervenes, the hearer can still, by his recollection of
the heads, regain the thread of discourse.

But it is objected by many others that the precepts
and examples of the classic orators are against this
usage, for they did not proclaim their intended divisions
in advance ; and Cicero advises that they be studiously

---

justification) is evinced by the previous, and because it has a sharp,
demonstrative force which fits it for the climax. I resolve, therefore, that it shall be my fourth head. It only remains to assign the
head not yet numbered to the third place, where it coheres well with
what precedes. The work of arrangement is now complete as to the
main heads of the discussion, and gives us this result:

The merit of our works does not justify ; because,

1. All works are *imperfect ;* but the claims of the divine law are
   absolute.
2. *Remission* excludes *payment,* and *this* a *condemned* man's obedience cannot make.
3. Hence justification gratuitous, faith's agency in it receptive, and
   boasting excluded.
4. True good works are effects, and so cannot be causes, of justification.
5. Paul and others confirm—Cite and apply. Evasions and objections noted at their appropriate places.

Does this process appear to you long and careful? I do not conceal the fact that it is, and should be so. But then, it gains for us an
inestimable advantage—that of thorough method. This necessary
quality cannot be bought cheaper.

and intentionally concealed until the 'proper time for the disclosure of each.[1] The example of other departments of popular eloquence is against Doddridge's rule: their masters do not pre-announce any heads of discourse. This practice casts over the whole discourse an artificial and premeditated air, which must be detrimental to its movement and emotion. It seems to advertise the hearer in advance that all the preacher's seeming artlessness and impulses are artificial. It takes off the edge of curiosity, producing some of the same evil effect, which the study of a meagre abridgment works upon the student of science. It confines and cramps the genius of the speaker, which, when animated by effort and sympathy, might otherwise strike *impromptu* upon thoughts nobler than any which were premeditated.

Such are the arguments of the two parties. The latter seem to me to have the right, especially since it is easy to obviate the force of all that is urged by the first. It is true that people often show a singular and perverse ingenuity in missing the true point of the most plainly announced proposition ; but I showed you, that the proper place to guard against this is the explication which leads to the proposition. If this is what it should be, it will leave no possibility of mistake for any one who attends. The speaker, again, should so speak as not to produce restlessness in his hearer : if this arises, no mode could be easily conceived more effectual for disappointing the real ends of discourse, than to set the hearer to counting the coming heads, to see how much

---

[1] De Orat., Bk. ii.

longer he was to be wearied. I required that the proposition should be so announced as to obtrude it effectually upon the attention of all. It is this which will give the sufficient clue to any part of the discussion, if the method is really perspicuous. This method should so develop itself to the hearer, as the discourse proceeds, that its members shall be obvious; and it is this very disclosure of the structure which should stimulate and charm the attention. Rhetorical discourse should be a beautiful, living growth, which results in setting its full-formed product before the delighted spectator, obvious in the harmony and completeness of the parts. It is not an anatomical synthesis which gives us a ghastly skeleton upon which to build some dead model. And finally, if recollection of the sermon is desirable for the hearer, let him be aided in this by an animated recapitulation at the close, instead of a dry pre-announcement at the beginning. The former, as we have seen, will possess the immeasurable advantage of recalling the parts of the discourse, not as dry bones, but as full-formed, warm and glowing members. For these reasons I should dissuade from the formal recital of heads at the beginning of the argument, except in a few cases, where didactic accuracy is the object, rather than rhetorical impression.

•But you will not consider me here as retracting anything that I have urged in favour of right method. The preacher is imperatively bound to have this, primarily for himself, and ultimately for his hearers. His own perception of his arrangement should be perfect when he begins to speak; his hearer's view of it should be correct when he is done. The development of his subject must be a development of his method also, and the latter must be so lucid that it will be impossible for the intelligent listener to misconceive it. He is thus enabled to carry away all the substance of the discourse in a compact arrangement.

LECTURE XVI.

PERSUASION.

RHETORIC is familiarly called the "art of persuasion," and there is a popular sense in which the whole work of the orator is suasive, in that it aims to produce a practical determination of the hearer's will. But man is a creature of understanding and of affections; his soul not only sees, but feels. We infer, therefore, that the rhetorical discourse should deal not only with the intellect (to produce mental conviction), but with the affections to direct the motives.[1] The former part of our work we call argument, the latter, in its special sense, persuasion. While those moral emotions, to which alone the sacred orator may lawfully appeal, are all rational affections arising only upon a view of truth in the understanding, yet there are facts and laws belonging to man's emotive system which must also be regarded in dealing successfully with it. Hence the necessity for this department of our science. When we consider how man is prompted to act, we perceive that the true cause of his volition is always from him-

---

[1] Quinctil., L. iii., c. 5, §§ 1, 2: Facultas orandi consummatur natura, arte, exercitatione; cui quartam partem adjiciunt quidam imitationis; quam nos arti subjicimus. Tria sunt autem, quæ præstare debet orator, ut *doceat, moveat, delectet.* Hæc enim clarior divisio, quam eorum, qui totum opus in res et in affectus partiuntur.

self, or from within. The objective inducement to choice is but the occasion; the soul's own view and feeling are the efficient cause of action. The activity of his nature, as guided by his own intelligence, projects itself toward its appropriate object, and this spontaneous appetency is the true *motive* of choice. The etymological relation between the words "emotion" and "motive" gives correct expression to a truth. It is the emotions which immediately move the will. To produce volition it is not enough that the understanding be convinced; affection must also be aroused. The object held before the soul must be shown to belong to the category of the true, and also to that of the good; for where the latter aspect is not present to receive the appetency of the soul, the truth of the object is as powerless to produce movement as though it were fiction. No man is induced to arise and go to the modern Ophir by the most convincing assurance that it contains abundance of waste earth or stones. This is no more to him, although admitted to be certain, than the idlest dream of Utopia. But when he has credible testimony that there is gold there, and that "the gold of that land is good," he may form the purpose of going. This is because gold is to his nature an object of desire. If you would induce your hearer to adopt a given course, you must not only prove to his wisdom that it is the proper means to its end, but you must show to his heart that the end is desirable. Hence all suasive discourse, whatever its particular topic, may be reduced to two elements—that which places the proposition in the category of the true, and that which shows it in the category of the good. Both elements are essential to the oration. The latter may be present only by implication, but unless it is virtually present there is no rhetorical discourse.

Although this is so obvious, you will still find a general prejudice against what is popularly termed an "appeal to feeling." Men argue that truth should be the guide of the righteous man's actions, and not mere emotion. They imagine that because the understanding is the directive faculty, its decisions are always correct, and the impulses of feeling are blind. Hence they conclude that he who appeals to their understandings deals honourably and beneficially with them, while he who appeals to their feelings is seeking to abuse their natures. And especially do they judge the latter expedient unworthy of the preacher of the gospel, whose message is infallible truth, and whose professed motive is absolute disinterestedness. Let us examine this prejudice.

I think it may be accounted for by two facts. The soul is often abused by an appeal to irrelevant and improper feelings. The hearers are sinners, whose emotions are in a state of moral disease. The false orator who, to gain some end, aggravates that disease of heart in some direction, has indeed done their nature a cruel wrong. But there are also relevant and proper feelings. The strength and prevalence of these are not a fault, but a virtue of the soul; so that he who enables us to enhance them is as obviously our benefactor, as he who enlightens our understandings. If the prosecutor of a man accused of crime should urge his judges to convict him because he was their ancient enemy, appealing to hatred and the lust of revenge in their breasts, this would be most criminal; but if the advo-

cate, while demonstrating by proof that the accused was
a proper object of moral indignation, should appeal to
that sentiment, to the love of justice, and to the benevolent desire for order and the safety of innocent citizens,
to procure his condemnation, this would be legitimate;
for the truth itself teaches us that these are proper
motives for a magistrate, and consequently their prevalence in him is his virtue. When men condemn the incitement of right emotions because we are liable to be
abused by the incitement of the wrong ones, they very
strangely forget that, by the same argument, they might
condemn a just appeal to the understanding; for is not
the reason often abused by logical sophisms? Indeed,
the appeal to logic should be regarded with even more
suspicion than the appeal to feeling, when we regard
the second fact, which is the following: The sophism
imposed on the understanding is far less likely to be
detected by the victim. By the very reason that it has
been successfully imposed, he remains unconscious that
it is a fallacy; he makes no effort to apply the logical
criteria by which its falsehood would be exposed; because, having accepted it as sound argument, he does
not dream that there is any cause for desiring to test it.
But those *criteria* do not usually apply themselves without his volition. The conscience, on the other hand, is
an intuitive and imperative faculty: she pronounces
her unchangeable verdict, and as soon as the din of
passion subsides, it is heard, and it recalls the heart at
once to a sense of the right. Thus, the sophistical appeal to emotion is in most instances unavoidably and
speedily detected; while the sophistical appeal to the
understanding is likely to escape discovery just in the

degree it is mischievous. Does not this fact, while it naturally accounts for men's jealousy of the former, show that there is more reason to be jealous of the latter? There are two thieves: the first steals frequently, and he is always so maladroit as to be detected and punished; hence he has an execrable reputation. The second steals far more frequently, but he is so skilful a knave that he is not even suspected; whence his name is very fair; but he is the more dangerous rogue of the two. The truth, then, lies in this simple question: Granting that the understanding is the directive faculty of the soul, I ask, to what does it direct? You answer: To man's proper good. True; and this good is the object of desire. Whence it appears that desire is what the understanding has to guide. Without the movement of right desire, its directive function is as vain as that of the needle on a ship which is becalmed.

The attempt to propagate suitable emotions is, then, lawful for the speaker; yea, there is no argument which does not implicitly do it. You will reason with men: "This conduct is for your interest." You may profess to have restricted yourself to simple evidence; but just in the degree in which your argument is conclusive, you make a virtual appeal to self-love. You demonstrate: "This course is for the good of our neighbour." You have made an appeal to benevolence. You show: "This act is dangerous." You resort to your hearer's fear. Again, every man practices this rhetoric of persuasion upon himself. We are continually aware that our right affections are too low for their proper objects. We feel that it is not only right, but obligatory, to use expedients for their enhancement, and we recognize him as our moral benefactor who assists us to effect it.

Since the legitimacy of the art of persuasion depends upon our resorting to the appropriate feelings, the first question to be answered is : To what class of emotions may the preacher appeal? I reply, only to the moral and spiritual. If the emotions of taste and of social life are evoked, it must be only for the purpose of reaching the former by their means. Only one word of argument is required to show that the sensual and malignant passions must never be aroused; for this would be to do positive evil under the pretence "that good may come." The damnation of such teachers is just. But, more, the one ulterior end of preaching is the holiness of the hearers. Now, moral motive alone leads to moral volition, whence it is clear that the preacher who satisfies himself with stimulating the natural sensibilities of taste and social affection has really done nothing toward his proper task; while he runs an imminent risk of deluding men with the vain counterfeit of natural emotions about religion, in place of true religious emotion.

In dealing with the moral and spiritual affections, the preacher has one capital advantage and disadvantage. His disadvantage is that he finds all these affections perverted in fallen man. The susceptibilities for love of God, legitimate self-love, love of man, love of holiness, repentance, hope, fear, moral complacency, are not destroyed (they are fundamental traits of his constitution as a rational and responsible creature), but they are radically corrupted in all their actings. His feeling toward God is either open enmity, or a deceitful, sentimental admiration for his natural perfections. His desire of well-being is inordinate self-love. His repentance is guilty remorse. His fear is the fear of hatred. His moral complacency is degraded into pride. His hope is selfish delusion. Conscience alone, God's witness in the soul, retains her integrity, although the *medium* of her vision is partially obscured, and her verdicts often unheeded. The preacher's chief hope, then, is to deal with the conscience and to arouse her action. How can he successfully employ the other affections, which, if awakened, will act only in a perverse direction? His suasive work, then, would be hopeless without his capital advantage. This is the promised power of the Holy Ghost, quickening the dead soul and new-creating its diseased affections. Here is the sacred and glorious distinction between the posture of the true, gospel minister, and of the secular orator—that this spiritual agency is real and almighty, and that the objective truth and good which the servant of the gospel places before the perverted heart are made the instruments of this promised, divine inworking. Whenever the Spirit breathes, the ·icy bonds of spiritual death are dissolved, and the hearer's soul is thus enabled to respond legitimately to its proper, spiritual inducements. Human skill in the work of persuasion must obviously be in strict subordination to this divine agency, and in strict conformity to its instrument, divine truth.

1. The most essential maxim of the art is thus suggested to us in a light which requires no further argument. Study the structure of man's religious emotions as portrayed in the Bible. No human knowledge of the human heart can approach the value of this divine dis-

closure of its workings under the application of the truth. And we discover here, doubtless, a part of God's purpose in giving us in Scripture so many pictures of the religious affections of renewed and of unrenewed men. He designed to instruct his ministers how to deal with those affections. Ponder these pictures. Discover the springs of motive there disclosed. Apply those incentives to feeling which are there represented as effective. Expect men to be rightly moved, as you see them moved there, and no otherwise.

2. You must remember these two facts, that an increase of the moral emotions cannot be made a direct and immediate object of volition, and that their deficiency is a moral defect, implying reproach against him who exhibits such lack. These two statements, when explained, will together teach us some important rules. First, then, it is plain that a man cannot by a mere, direct act of volition, cause himself to love what he does not love, or to regret what he does not regret. This is sufficiently evident from the fact that these emotions are themselves related to volition as cause to effect. The effect cannot determine its own cause. The emotion of love, in some degree, must be *a priori* to a volition to seek its object in love. Only an existing regret for a fault can prompt a wish to feel regret for it. It is, therefore, unreasonable to make a direct preceptive demand upon the emotions, as we do upon the attention. When we wish to establish conviction of a proposition in our hearer's understanding, we directly challenge his attention to our proofs. This is reasonable, for attention may be immediately directed by his volition. But it is with the emotions as with the nerves of involun-

tary motion in the body. If the labourer strikes amiss
in wielding his instrument, we properly command him
to direct his blows differently; they are guided by his
will. If the physician finds that his patient's heart
beats too rapidly, and is consequently wearing out his
life with a nervous fever, it is simply foolish to bid
him quiet its beats by his will; for the nerves by which
it acts belong to another system, on which volition does
not act. What, then, can the physician do? He can
command his patient to employ the voluntary muscles
of his hand, mouth and throat, to receive and swallow
a potion of *veratrum*, or some such drug, which by its
medical virtue stills the over-action of the heart. It is
thus, only indirectly, that the patient can employ his
will to control the organ. So, the pulsations of man's
spiritual heart do not obey a direct volition of his will;
he can only bend his attention to the consideration of
those truths and facts which, through the healing
touch of the divine Physician, occasion a healthy beat of
the soul.

The other fact is, that deficient or wrong moral emotions are proper subjects of reproach, for they are sins.
When the preacher proposes to communicate to his
hearer the proofs of a given proposition, he thereby
implies an imputation of ignorance; the very undertaking assumes that the hearer is less informed of this
evidence than himself. But this is no just reproach
against the hearer, because it is the preacher's business
to be better informed than he of sacred truth. If the
religious teacher is not, he is unfit for his profession.
To assume such deficiency of knowledge and opinion,
and to announce expressly the purpose of correcting it,

are therefore no discourtesy to his audience. So, likewise, it is reasonable to make a direct requisition upon
their attention. But to advertise your hearer that you
design to make him feel more adequately is to accuse
him of delinquency. To announce to him that you
aim to enhance his gratitude is to charge him with in-
gratitude. It is not unnatural that he should repel the
accusation, and steel himself against your appeal. It
appears hence, that while the purpose to convince the
understanding may be pre-announced, the design of
moving the heart may not be. You will not misconceive me as denying here the sinfulness of wrong affections, and the duty of testifying against these, as against
all other sins. When your design is reprehension, that
which is wrong must of course •be reprehended, whatever may be the offence. I intend only to show you
the indiscretion of beginning an attempt to conciliate
and allure right affections with what is necessarily felt
as an implied assault.

Hence I draw these rules : That the purpose of persuading should not be pre-announced : Let the work
be done, and not advertised.[1] And that it is useless to
urge right feeling by mere hortation : Let the preacher
present, instead, those truths which are the objects of
moral emotion.

The presentation of the objects of right affection is
both by argument and by description. Since the soul's

---

[1] Cicero de Orat., L. ii., c. 77, § 310. "Et quoniam (quod sæpe
dixi) tribus rebus omnes ad nostram sententiam perducimus, aut do-
cendo, aut conciliando, aut permovendo, una ex omnibus his rebus
res præ nobis est ferenda, ut nihil aliud nisi docere velle videa-
mur," etc.

seeing is in order to its feeling, and it only feels as it sees, no foundation can be validly laid for an appeal to the emotions without argument; and the evidence alone is often enough to set before the soul that which becomes the object of its emotion, in the most vivid light. Accordingly, there is a species of moral and religious argument which, while severely logical, affects the intelligent hearer with profound feeling. Such was the preaching of Jonathan Edwards and of Thornwell; and such spiritual logic is the noblest basis upon which to build all the other parts of sacred eloquence.

But in many other cases, descriptive painting must be employed to present to the soul affecting images of the truth. It is in this work especially, that the faculty of imagination must be employed. And now that I have uttered this much-abused word, let me protest at once against your receiving it in the perverted, popular sense. By imagination I do not mean the miserable facility of clothing commonplace thoughts in borrowed tropes. This habit, instead of evincing imagination, is more frequently an indication of its absence, and of a mind weak and beggarly in its creative power. Nor do I mean that trait of mind sometimes denominated by the word "fancy"—an aptitude for seeing picturesque resemblances between ideas and the visible objects of nature. This also is no index of constructive power. The imagination is rather the recreative faculty: it is the power of combining the elements of conception furnished by the memory into organic forms which, as wholes, are new. It is that faculty by which the soul constructs complex images out of the separate parts, with truth and distinctness. The constituent parts are indeed old, being ideas derived from perception; but the wholes are, for that mind, proper creations. While the complex images are only conceived, and not seen with the senses, they are, to the vigorous imagination, life-like; they have, to the consciousness and emotions of the soul which forms them, all the force of realities. It is by the force of this representative faculty that noble and strong souls affect themselves, by anticipation or by retrospect, with powerful moral emotions. For instance, the wise and magnanimous patriot, by forecasting the distant but certain dangers of his country, affects himself in advance with a zeal and grief and desire, as ardent as those which duller souls can feel under the actual experience of the present calamity. It is this anticipative passion, kindled through the imagination, which nerves his soul to prepare, to watch, to strive, to bleed for his country's defence, while others are as yet unconcerned, and are perhaps accusing him of extravagance. It was thus that St. Paul's masculine and sanctified imagination painted to him a picture of the future but unseen ruin of souls, so moving as to fire his heart with that love and zeal which, to meaner and colder natures, appeared lunacy.[1] It is from this emotion, in view of absent and future objects, that all man's virtuous activities as a being of forecast proceed. And the sentiment of beauty at beholding a smiling landscape is not more immediately the æsthetic effect of visual perception, than is rational emotion concerning absent objects the effect of imagination.

Such is the nature and such are the value and power

---

[1] 2 Cor. v. 13 ; Luke xix. 41–43.

of this imperial faculty of the soul. The descriptive power is but an application of it. In this work the poet or orator only translates into words that picture which is bodied forth before his own conception. This remark justifies the following practical precept, that in order to describe well the speaker must first conceive well to himself. If you would cultivate this power, you should first represent to yourself the faithful and exact and lively image of that picture which you wish to convey to your hearers; and then, holding it fixed before the conception, merely recite to them in true and vivid terms the essential outlines of what you see. Your task is simply that of Rebecca the Jewess, when she stood looking from the loophole to describe to the prostrate knight, Ivanhoe, the assault which was passing before her eyes. Looking into the window of your own conception, you merely read to the listeners without what you see written there by the pencil of the imagination.

Descriptive eloquence must combine perspicuity of images, definiteness of outline and brevity. Tediousness or prolixity is more fatal to movement and effect here than anywhere else. Description is a species of substitute for mental vision; like vision, ·it must be rapid, almost instantaneous. Yet a certain particularity is requisite, for general outlines are ever vague, and vagueness cannot affect the soul. The master-hand, therefore, usually constructs its pictures by selecting a few particular traits which are suggestive of the whole filling up, and drawing them with a rapid and yet definite stroke. It is thus the sacred historian portrays the horrors of famine in Samaria.[1] Having stated

---

[1] 2 Kings vi. 24–29.

briefly the extravagant prices paid for two repulsive articles of food, he rapidly details the horrid compact of the famished women for devouring their own children, and its breach. This ghastly incident at once unveils to us, without other description, all the woes which filled the famine-stricken city. Still more forcibly does He who "spake as never man spake" reveal to us in a single sentence the outline of the siege of Jerusalem by Titus.[1] We seem to stand upon the western declivity of Olivet and see the verdant zone of vineyards which encircled the city, blackened with the Roman circumvallation, the streets resounding with the clangour of faction and the wails of dearth and pestilence, the final assault, the defenders crushed beneath the falling ramparts, the foundations upturned by the ploughshare, and then the brooding silence of desolation.

---

[1] Luke xix. 43, 44.

LECTURE XVII.

PERSUASION.

3. THE phenomenon of instinctive sympathy is the orator's right arm in the work of persuasion. To sympathize is to be affected with our fellow-man, and because we see him affected. It is, as it were, a spiritual infection by which he impregnates us with his feeling. It is the secondary rainbow more faintly reflecting the glow of the first. The effect is immediate and instinctive: we feel simply because we see our fellow-creature feeling. Now, then, if you would make others feel, you must feel yourself. "*Si vis me flere, dolendum est primum tibi ipsi.*"[1] Let the preacher's own soul be fully penetrated and aroused by sacred emotion. The heavenly flame must be kindled first in

---

[1] Horace, Ep. ad Pisones, line 102.

Cicero de Orat., L. ii., c. xlv., § 189. "Non mehercule unquam apud judices aut dolorem, aut misericordiam, aut invidiam, aut odium excitare dicendo volui, quin ipse, in commovendis judicibus, iis ipsis sensibus ad quos illos adducere vellem, permoverer." C. xlvi., § 191: "Ipsa enim natura orationis ejus quæ suscipitur ad aliorum animos permovendos, oratorem ipsum magis etiam quam quenquam eorum qui audiunt, permovet."

Quinctil., L. vi., c. ii., § 26. "Summa enim (quantum ego sentio) circa movendos affectus in hoc posita est, ut moveamur ipsi. Nam et luctus et iræ . . . etiam ridicula fuerit imitatio."

your own bosom, that by this law of sympathy it may radiate thence into the souls of your hearers.

I warn you emphatically, moreover, that this emotion in the speaker's soul must be genuine and not simulated. The mere appearance of ardent feeling, however artfully it may be imitated, will fail of producing the effect. There is an infallible intuition in man's heart by which he detects the reality or falsehood of the appearances of emotion; and those whose feelings are least sophisticated by artificial culture, even children and ignorant persons, have this insight only the more fully, perhaps, for that reason. Sympathy is a species of spiritual contagion. The painted automaton, when seen at a distance, may appear to glitter and to move itself like a living man; but when we touch it, we perceive at once that there is no life. I am so persuaded the rule is universal, that only genuine emotion can propagate a sympathetic effect, I do not doubt it is true even of the mimic eloquence of the stage. The consummate actor moves the spectators only because he has so realized to himself the sentiments and passions natural to the part he is acting, that his own proper personality is, for the time, merged in and superseded by that of the hero whom the poet's imagination has created. He actually feels and lives the history as his own.[1] The great

---

[1] Some distinguished actors, in mimic combats, fight *ex animo*. One was known, in a suicide scene, actually to stab himself. The charm of Garrick's acting was in his perfect and sincere realization of his character: he was, indeed, for the time, not an *actor*, but a real agent. It is related that a countryman was taken by his London friends to see Garrick in his favourite part of *Hamlet*. The city people were curious to learn the opinion of their unsophisticated friend concerning the entertainment. He was loud in his praise of the minor actors,

classic authorities with one voice assert both the possibility and necessity of this sincere passion. Cicero quotes Democritus and Plato as declaring that no one can be a good poet without ardour of the spirits and, as it were, a divine afflatus of passion. We have seen his testimony above, that "this kind of oration which is designed to move the spirits of others moves the orator himself even more than them who listen." [1]

---

but greatly surprised them by his silence as to the great star. They asked him at length if he did not admire the representation of *Hamlet*. "What," said he—"of the young man whose father was poisoned? I thought nothing strange of his taking on greatly at such a crime, of course." The plain man had not apprehended that Garrick was acting at all, but supposed that he alone was a real character among the mimics, so complete was the assumption of the natural passions of the part.

See also Cicero de Orat., L. ii., c. xlvi., § 193. "Quid potest esse tam fictum quam versus, quam scena, quam fabula? Tamen in hoc genere sæpe ipse vidi quum ex persona mihi ardere oculi hominis histrionis viderentur e sponda illa dicentis:

'Segregare abs te ausus, aut sine illo Salamina ingredi
Neque paternum adspectum es veritus?'

Nunquam illum '*adspectum*' dicebat, quin mihi Telamon iratus furere luctu filii videretur."

M. Bautain (*Art of Extempore Speech*, ch. iv., § 3) expresses an opposite view, not unnatural to one who only knew the intensely shallow and artificial stage of modern Paris. Says he: "The actor, in a word, is obliged to grimace morally as well as physically; and on this account, even when most successful, when most seeming to feel what he impersonates, as he in general feels it not, something of this is perceptible," etc.

This may be true of French actors; but if it is, it proves them poor actors. The true power of the drama is only felt when the scenic passions are real for the time.

[1] See previous note, and De Orat., L. ii., c. xlvi., §§ 191, 194. Quinctil., L. vi., c. i., §§ 44, 45.

But the emotions which the preacher aims to propagate are the moral and spiritual. It is these, then, by which he must be possessed and animated. In other words, in order to be capable of any power of persuasion, you must be men of ardent and genuine religious affections. You must be men of faith and prayer; you must live near the cross and feel "the powers of the world to come." We thus learn again the great truth that it is divine grace which makes the true minister.

For acting through the law of sympathy upon your audience, certain practical cautions are necessary. The disclosure of your own emotion must not too far outrun the temper of the congregation, lest it should appear to them from their cooler position extravagance. The effect of such an impression would be that the chasm between them and yourself would be widened, instead of being closed by their elevation to your level. If, then, the audience is calm at the beginning, the passion of the speaker must be restrained. The disclosure of your emotion may be either a direct display or an involuntary betrayal. The happiest effect is produced in the latter case, where the orator is manifestly labouring to keep an ardent tide of passion under restraint, but it bursts somewhat over its barriers in spite of his self-command. This suggests to the auditors at once the sincerity of his feeling and the exceedingly weighty and moving nature of the subject by which he is possessed. They are thus powerfully prepared to be moved by it, even before they come to a comprehension of its moment. As the apostle declares concerning an impulse more immediately divine, "the spirits of the prophets are subject unto the prophets." The preacher should never permit his emotion to overmaster his faculties; it should rather elevate and strengthen them. When passion becomes a helpless agitation, destroying the poise and self-command of the memory, understanding and imagination, precipitating the preacher into disorder and mental anarchy, the impression of power at once gives place to that of impotency; and his audience, instead of being wielded by him, begin to pity him or to be disgusted by him.[1] "Therefore use all gently, for in the very torrent, tempest, and, as I may say, whirlwind of your passion, you must acquire and beget a temperance that may give it smoothness."[2]

4. The highest skill of the orator is displayed in employing the great law of suggestion in his hearers' minds, to extend his power over their emotions and to give warmth to their apprehensions of sacred truth. You must remember that this law includes not only perceptions and conceptions, but emotions also. A perception or conception may suggest a separate emotion by the tie of association, or one feeling may suggest another, as truly as the sight of a *memento* may suggest the image of an absent friend. Your own consciousness will furnish you with striking instances of this fact. One has lately received some painful intelligence, by which he has been deeply afflicted. But his equanimity has been again restored by the lapse of time. His eye now falls upon some

---

[1] Bautain, ch. ii., § 1. "But if sensibility must be strong, it must nevertheless not be excited to excess, for it then renders expression impossible from the agitation of the mind." . . . "Christian feeling is never intemperate, never disorderly."

[2] Hamlet's instructions to the players.

spot, or some utensil of daily use, and forthwith his mind is tinged with sadness and pain without any conscious cause. The effect is at first unaccountable to himself, until he remembers that his attention happened to be occupied by that place or object, at the moment when the stroke of the calamity reached him. The feeble tie of association, formed by a mere, momentary juxtaposition before his mind, has so linked the perception with the emotion, that the sight of the one revives the other, even without any thought of the original and real cause of the grief. The power of mementoes and of places over the soul is to be explained by the same law. The sight of the home or playground of our childhood suffuses our hearts with a tender and pleasing melancholy, even before memory has placed before us the images of those beloved persons who peopled them.

Now this well-established fact implies another, upon which indeed the subsequent association depends— that when the soul is possessed by an ardent feeling, a part of its warmth is reflected upon any object which coexists with it, however distinct and indifferent it may otherwise be. The mind when thus heated becomes, as it were, a furnace which communicates a portion of its glow to anything which is then introduced within it. It is this fact of which the masterly orator avails himself, to quicken the feeling of his hearers toward any truths which otherwise would be uninteresting to them. He finds them callous to the spiritual affections which his message should awaken; if he leaves it thus, however perspicuous he may have made it to their understandings, it will lie cold and fruitless in their minds. What can he do? He seeks to awaken some congruous natural emotion, legitimate in its moral character, and kindred to the holier feeling which he would implant, and while the soul is glowing with the former he thrusts in the sacred truth. Thenceforward it is imbued with some of the warmth which animated the hearer; it attracts the quickened attention; it begins to be impressive to the soul. Thus, for example, have I seen a skilful orator arouse the parental love of an obdurate, ungodly man, by his domestic portraiture; and when the rugged soul was all melted with this, the only soft emotion native to it, the preacher so pressed home the claims of his parental responsibility to his children's souls and the guilt of parental neglect, as to fix pungent conviction of sin in the hardened heart. So, natural fear, awakened by a graphic picture of the sinner's danger, may communicate its colouring to the timely charge of transgression, and quicken the sense of its justice into wholesome alarm of conscience. Natural grief, evoked by a touching picture of bereavement, may be made to impress the Redeemer's precept that we shall "lay up our treasures in heaven," or to make us feel the preciousness of gospel consolation and hope.

Do you ask how occasion is to be found for arousing these appropriate natural emotions? I answer, this must be done by the preacher's descriptive power. The passages which present these moving pictures may often be legitimate developments of his subject. Or else they may be introduced as illustrations of logical thought or definition, presented in the course of his argument. And here is the last element of value in well-chosen illustrations, which I promised, when speaking of them, to unfold to you. They not only define to the mind

the point of the argument, and so facilitate its comprehension—they not only associate the light of its evidence with the vivid pleasure of an apt but unforeseen
resemblance—they awaken congruous emotion, from
which the coëxisting truth borrows to itself warmth
and colouring. And this is the crowning reason why
the power of happy illustration makes its possessor eloquent. Your own good sense will tell you that if your
descriptive pictures are disconnected with the thread of
the discourse, if they are thrust violently into the course
of your argument, if they arouse irrelevant or discord-
ant emotions, you will wholly fail of your intended
effect. They will be felt to violate unity, and to dislo-
cate instead of welding the discourse. They must come
in naturally and easily, and without betraying a set
purpose of assault upon the hearers' hearts.

But it is now my duty to impose strict limits upon
the use of this means. I have already taught you to
distinguish between the moral and spiritual affections
on the one hand, and the natural and æsthetic emotions
on the other. The preacher's suasive work terminates
exclusively upon the former. It is the propagation of
them which constitutes sanctification. The enthusiasm
of social passions or gratified taste is not Christianity,
and has no tendency in itself to purify the soul. But
he who substitutes it for real, spiritual culture is cheat-
ing immortal souls with a mischievous illusion. I beg
you to note also that an object which is really religious
in another of its aspects may be so presented to the natural taste or passions, that the interest excited by it shall
be as godless and as merely carnal, as though it were
utterly foreign to sacred truths. The rational attributes

and providence of God, or the glories and terrors of the judgment-day, are so painted by some preachers, that the sentiments awakened are no more Christian in fact, than if they had been excited by the description of a cataract or an ocean in tempest. Thoughtless men fancy that, because they are speaking about religious things,[1] they are speaking religion. Remember, then, that these emotions are only means to a better end; we must employ them merely as steps to rise to the emotions of the conscience. The only purpose which can justify an appeal to them in religious discourse is that of forthwith attaching them to sacred truth, which the preacher faithfully presents along with them. If he fails to give them this direction, if he allows his hearers to expend themselves in the mere luxury of natural sentiment and sympathy, he is both deluding and abusing their hearts; for he assists them to deceive themselves with a substitute for true spiritual affection, which is worse than worthless, while he deteriorates and expends their susceptibility by an excitement which is unwholesome, because fruitless. The practical result of this perversion of the art of persuasion is always moral corruption.

The mischievous error of addressing the taste and social sentiments, instead of the affections of conscience, is illustrated by the effects of the Romish worship. Its

---

[1] Pilgrim's Prog., Part i., ch. xix. *Ignorance.* "I am always full of good motions that come into my mind to comfort me as I walk." *Christian.* "What good motions? pray tell us." *Ign.* "Why, I think of God and heaven." *Chr.* "So do the devils and damned souls." *Ign.* "But I think of them and desire them." *Chr.* "So do many that are never like to come there. 'The soul of the sluggard desires and hath nothing.'"

great purpose is to substitute the enthusiasm of the imagination for the culture of moral principles. It must be confessed that this effect is produced with consummate skill. The experience of ages of paganism and of corrupt Christianity has been applied, by the most accomplished cunning, to devise the means for stimulating the superstitious fancy and intoxicating the senses. All the imposing and alluring charms of architecture, music and pantomime are employed for these ends. And everything in the gospel story which can awe or delight the natural sensibilities is ingeniously displayed in the most dramatic forms : the corporeal anguish of the Redeemer, the pitying love of woman typified in her sweetest ideal as the " Mother of God," the stern heroism of apostles, the awful might of miracles and ghostly principalities and powers, the material flames of purgatory and hell; but the great, spiritual truths by which the soul lives or dies, of which this history is but the shell, are carefully left out of view. Existing facts teach us what has been the effect of this gorgeous ritual upon piety and morals. While the taste is cultivated, the conscience is plunged into foul delusion. The most splendid rites of worship and the blackest vices have dwelt together under the same consecrated roofs ; and the communities which are most accomplished in the pomps of their ceremonial are the most debauched.

Now, there is a species of Protestantism, existing to some extent among all denominations, which is obnoxious to the same accusation. Its preachers substitute for the rites of a superstitious worship the pomp of a sentimental eloquence. They descant, indeed, upon the facts and doctrines of the Bible, but they omit all that is awakening and purifying to the conscience; they display only that which is beautiful to the taste, or pathetic, or sublime. The type of sensibility which they evoke is merely human and fanciful, and their preaching is but a rhetorical mimicry of the more candid and more impressive machinery of Rome. It cannot be denied that the images, in which the sacred principles of spiritual religion are clothed, are capable of being developed into a magnificence and beauty transcending all the imaginings of superstition; and it is not difficult for the ambitious and selfish mind to overlook the radical truth, that it is not the æsthetic grandeur, but the moral and spiritual principles in these pictures, which alone make them doctrines of salvation. We are told, for instance, "that it is appointed unto men once to die, and after death the judgment." What imaginative painting could more fascinate and harrow the fancy, than that which describes the accessories of a death-bed? The shuddering listener may be made to thrill at the thought of the pangs by which the silver cord is loosed, unimagined by living man and indescribable by mortal tongue; the irrevocable sundering of ties of love from which the worldly heart has drawn its very life; the spirit's plunge into the dread mystery of the nether world; the aspect of the living man frozen into a ghastly corpse; the gloom, the chill and the corruption of the grave, with its loathsome worm and dust. But what have you done when you have spell-bound your hearer's fancy with these terrors? You have but stimulated the instinctive love of life—a passion at best only social or selfish, in its prevalent element merely animal, and common to him with the beast that writhes and shrieks under the hunter's steel. All this is naught unless you make it the introduction to the truth that "the sting of death is sin, and the strength of sin is the law," and to that victory over the grave given through our Lord Jesus Christ; for it is the latter which teaches us the whole significance of death to the rational soul.

But "after death is the judgment." To depict the grandeur of this final consummation, the Scriptures array material images whose terror and majesty infinitely transcend all the phenomena of nature and the uninspired imaginings of man. The preacher may suppose that he finds here a precedent, which authorizes him to stimulate the natural fear and fancy to their utmost tension. He therefore exerts all his pictorial power, and brings forth his most pompous stores of language to represent the vast and astounding events which will usher in that great day. He so paints the opening graves and gathering hosts of quickened dead, the paling sun, the blushing moon and decadent stars, the ocean of fire which floods the continents and exhales the seas, and so makes them hear the echo of the archangel's trump, that their blood runs chill with delicious horror. They are the entranced spectators of the catastrophe of this world's drama. But, I ask, is this the whole intent of God in this apocalypse of the final consummation? If these material images are all destined to be literally fulfilled, what are they but symbols of solemn moral facts? of the quickening of the slumbering conscience, of the voice of the accusing *Law*, of the unveiling of that divine holiness and glory before which the world with its vanities will shrivel into an atom, and sin will stand unmasked in its hideous blackness? Such a material portraiture has not even poetic truth; for it leaves out the chief elements of the dread transaction, and misrepresents its true impression on the real actors. When the justice of God, like a spirit of burning, shall have taken hold upon the awakened conscience of the sinner, and when eternity with all its issues shall be set before the eyes of his resurrection body, it will be the great conceptions of sin and of righteousness, of a broken law and a divine satisfaction, and of the just awards of infinite rectitude, which will occupy and overpower his mind. These images of material magnificence and terror will then be cast out of the place which they have usurped. "In that day it will be SIN, and not a flaming world, which shall appal the soul."[1]

To awaken the enthusiasm of taste or of instinctive passion is only legitimate, then, where we employ it as means for infusing heat into sacred truth, and thus arousing the moral emotions. The ulterior aim of the sacred orator must be at the conscience alone. Unless these natural affections which his rhetoric awakens are speedily superseded and eclipsed by the spiritual, to which he makes them subservient, they are only mischievous counterfeits. Not only the ambition and vanity of preachers, but the temper of the hearers seduce them into this error; for man naturally loves excitement for its own sake, and there is nothing which he so much hates as to be challenged to forsake his sin. He is grateful, therefore, to the orator who at once provides for him the sentimental luxury, and who suggests this

---

[1] Nat. Hist. Enthusiasm, p. 57.

substitute for the abhorred duty of *repentance.* You will ever, I trust, resist this temptation, and keep these appeals to the natural but unregenerate affections in their proper place.

Of all this art of persuasion he is the greatest master who seems to have none. Let your aim be to persuade men in Christ's name, and not to be praised for skill in persuading. These two distinct ends many preachers confound. You saw that the power over others' hearts depends upon your own disinterested and genuine emotion. You must so hunger for the salvation of the souls before you, that you shall desire to make the effect of sacred truth fill them, to the exclusion of yourself. You must be willing to be nothing in their eyes, and to let your effect be everything. He is not the true preacher who sends his hearers home exclaiming, " How eloquent the minister to-day; how beautiful his imagery; how artful his arrangement; how skilful his argument and his persuasion !" But he is the true sacred orator, who dismisses them so possessed and overpowered by God, that they have forgotten the creature who was the channel of the truth. The message should hide the messenger. To make you masters of the emotions of others, then, self-seeking must be annihilated, and self-renunciation must have its perfect work. It is divine grace which makes the effective minister.

LECTURE XVIII.

PREACHER'S CHARACTER WITH HEARERS.

THE hearers' apprehension of their minister's character is a most important element in his power of persuasion. If I be reminded that this is a truth belonging rather to pastoral theology than to rhetoric, I shall reply, that the element is one which it is impossible to separate from the effectiveness of sacred oratory. The pastor's character speaks more loudly than his tongue. This consideration is immeasurably more weighty in the case of the sacred than of the secular orator. Aristotle[1] announces this maxim, that the latter must establish with his auditors a character, first, for discretion, or knowledge and judgment; second, for probity; and third, for benevolence, or good-will toward them. If the speaker is suspected of ignorance or infirmity of judgment, his advice cannot carry weight and his arguments will be despised. If he is evidently intelligent and shrewd, but of doubtful integrity, the plausibility of what he advances will be felt; but the more ability he shows, the more will the people fear to commit themselves to his opinions; for they have no guarantee of moral principle that he is not employing these forces of his genius, manifestly so powerful, to

---

[1] Rhetoric, B. ii., ch. 1.

entrap and injure them instead of to benefit them. His advice, moreover, will probably be corrupt, unworthy of a virtuous people, and, because immoral, foolish in the end, even if it be kindly meant. If to the assurance of his mental ability to judge with discernment, and of his probity, guaranteeing the faithful and righteous use of his knowledge, be added a conviction of his affection and benevolence toward his hearers, prompting him ardently to desire their benefit; then they feel a strong presumption, in advance of the consideration of his arguments, that they should adopt his opinion. In popular phrase, he who has secured the reputation of these three qualities " has the ear of the people :" they are prepared to hear him favourably before they know what he will say.

The personal glory of success in his office should be the least of the ends which the pastor has in view; yet success should be desired for the gospel's sake. Among those who reach a respectable mediocrity and are not obstructed by some glaring blemish of manner, the difference between the acceptable and popular, and the unsuccessful minister, is chiefly caused by this character. The former succeeds, because he has made his people love and trust him. His judicious social intercourse, his virtues, his affectionate zeal in their welfare, and especially his sympathy with their sorrows, have won their hearty confidence. The doctrines we preach are naturally distasteful to the heart of man, and foolishness to his understanding. We are required to spend a life in the iteration of the same truths, until all the charm of novelty is gone. The most brilliant mind would fail to retain the attention of a charge, during a whole ministry, by the mere force of·mental interest: the attractions of love and confidence must be added. Without a sacred weight of character, the most splendid rhetoric will win only a short-lived applause; with it, the plainest scriptural instructions are eloquent to win souls. Eloquence may dazzle and please; holiness of life convinces.

Now, the fact that the preacher's work is spiritual enhances a thousandfold the force of the maxim of the pagan philosopher. Your professed motive, young gentlemen, is not mere patriotism, but something unspeakably higher and purer. Your ends are not temporal and finite, but everlasting and immense. They are, indeed, humane; for the good to which you seek to persuade men is one so splendid and rich, that the soul faints with excess of joy before it fully comprehends it; the evil from which you seek to rescue them is one so frightful, that the heart shudders at the first apprehension of it. But your work is far more than humanitarian: you are the messengers of that supreme and infinite God "of whom and through whom and unto whom are all things, to whom belongs glory for ever and ever." You are the appointed instruments "to make known by the church the manifold wisdom of God unto the principalities and powers in heavenly places." To you is committed the honour, before men and angels, of that display made in redemption of the most sacred moral perfections of God. The sword of the spirit which you handle is two-edged: it kills where it does not make alive. The cordial which you offer to the lips of dying men is a "savour of death unto death" if it is not made a savour of "life unto

life." The time and opportunity allowed you to rescue
the perishing are both precarious and limited; for the
objects of your zeal are "standing in slippery places,"
over the flames of perdition. The professed motive of
your ministry is at once the most disinterested, tender,
urgent and sacred by which a human soul can be
swayed; for as the prospective woes which excite your
compassion toward your fellow-men are the most frightful, the divine blood and grace which you exhibit are
the most hallowed objects which man can conceive.

It is exceedingly obvious, hence, that there would be
a monstrous solecism and guilt in your marked incompetency for such a ministry, in your dishonesty, or in
your inhumanity in it. What is the inconsistency, the
falsehood of that man who fills such an office heart-
lessly for hire or applause, or merely because it is his
promised task, and his credit does not permit its entire
neglect! How utterly must the enacting of such a lie
before your hearers blast every good effect of your pretended persuasions! Your position as gospel-herald,
then, exacts of you the qualities of discretion, probity
and benevolence, in a far higher sense than they are required of the secular orator, and by far more solemn
motives.

1. Your competent knowledge and good judgment
must be such a soundness of mind as will command the
respect of all men, with a real mastery of the theology
of redemption. A frivolous, weak, illogical mind will
detract from the weight of all that you could say for
religious truth. Even if this indiscretion is shown by
the minister in his secular affairs, week-day intercourse,
and non-professional opinions, it will endamage the effect

of his pulpit labours.   You owe it to your divine Master to show such sound· discretion always, that no man can have pretext, when you assume toward him the position of spiritual monitor, to remind himself of any childishness in your secular affairs, coxcombry or levity in society, or crudity in literary opinions.   If you thus weaken your own message to him, you are an unfaithful, not to say a treacherous, servant.   But especially in your own department, that of evangelical history and doctrine, you are sacredly bound to display such competency, such maturity of opinion, such faithful and honest research, as will make every fair-minded hearer respect your theological *dicta*.   Here you must show such good sense and acquirement, as will make your most cultivated hearer feel that you are a respectable and trustworthy guide in your own field.   Does any one object to this as a hard saying?   Does he complain that I hold him responsible for those gifts of genius and that peculiar ability which nature alone bestows?   I so far admit this statement as to avow that a fool has no business in the sacred office, whatever may be his zeal or his opportunities for training.   But plain, manly good sense, inspired and dignified by true piety, will always come up to my standard.   You have no call to affect the universal genius, "the admirable Crichton," master of all possible arts.   You need not pretend to talk agriculture, physics, politics, belles-lettres, fine arts, with the experts in these various branches of knowledge; but you may honestly avow, when they are the subjects of conversation, that you have not judged it your business to master them, and may keep your mouth closed.   Such an attitude is always respectable.

But when the votaries of these arts and sciences approach the theology of redemption, show them that there you are master of them all. To do this, you only need constant and faithful study of your own department, and this, I repeat, it is your clear duty to bestow.

2. That virtue which in the secular orator is probity, or political integrity and truthfulness, must rise in the sacred teacher to sanctity of character. This will include, of course, a spotless honesty and fidelity in all earthly relations and transactions. " A bishop must be blameless." [1] But this integrity every common Christian is expected to show; many unrenewed men can claim it. The pastor must rise far higher; he must exhibit a symmetry and elevation of Christian character, an exaltation above all carnal ambitions, which will make him venerable and lovely in the eyes of his flock. Such a character clothes his instructions with a weight and sweetness which no talent or learning can give. The hearers feel that they have the guarantee of a purity which it would be both folly and crime to impugn, for at least this conclusion, that the opinions the good man utters are certainly believed by himself after his most faithful investigation.

3. The third quality, good-will, must rise above the humanity and the benevolence of the good citizen to an ardent love for souls. The pastor should be recognized as one who affectionately hungers for the spiritual good of his charge. His admonitions should be received by them as the outpourings of a compassion which cannot be restrained. He sees the worth and danger of their

---

[1] 1 Tim. iii. 2, etc.

souls in the light of eternity, and his eloquence is inflamed from the very altar of God.

This character is sustained partly by the pastor's demeanour out of the pulpit, by his daily and sustained anxiety to save souls, and by the constancy of his labours for that end. If a solemn sermon be followed by an idle, worldly week, the people will feel that the apparent earnestness of the preacher is professional; and if he be yet more exceedingly fervent, they will only applaud his skill as an actor the more, disbelieving while they applaud. Here, let me say, is a sufficient argument for " preaching the gospel from house to house." We sometimes excuse our reluctance to this arduous work by pleading that there is nothing we can say in the household, or the private interview, which we have not said with more connection and force in our sermons; that if we introduce the topic of personal religion, we shall but awkwardly utter, in a " parlour sermon," what has been so much better said already in public. The answer is, that, however constrained, awkward and lame our private appeals might be, they would gain this capital point—they would convince men that we were in earnest in our pulpit fervours. The gospel admonition we addressed to our young, unbelieving friend might be so embarrassing to him and to us, as to leave no conscious impression except one of pain. But on the next Sabbath he would listen with new ears, for he would have had the evidence that we meant all we said.

The demeanour in the pulpit must also confirm the sincerity of the preacher's affection for souls. Every tone, and look, and gesture, from the moment he enters the pulpit until he leaves it, the structure of every sentence in his sermon, should reveal a soul in which levity, self-seeking and vanity are annihilated by the absorbing sense of divine things. No counterfeit will avail here, but the living faith and spirituality which are cultivated at the throne of grace, in the chambers of the afflicted and dying, and by the study of God's word.

The effect of the preacher's known character and earnestness upon his hearers is aptly illustrated by a discriminating writer, from the case of those early Methodists—Whitefield, the Wesleys, and Fletcher of Madely. He asserts that the key to the peculiar effect of their preaching was its obvious actuality. Low as was the state of religion when they burst upon the Christian world, evangelical preaching was not unknown either among the Dissenters or the Anglican clergy. But no such impression was produced by it. A few of these devout men presented the same truths with apparent sincerity and with limited effect. But the difference between the emotions of the larger mass of hearers, and those of the vast congregations swayed by these great evangelists, was like that difference which the military recruit experiences between his feelings in the mock-battle of a review, and in an actual engagement with the enemy. In the former, there are marchings and counter-marchings, there are all the pomp and circumstance of war, there are clouds of sulphurous smoke, and the ear is astounded with the thunders of artillery and the rattle of small arms. The young soldier is not a little excited; he pants with toil, he thrills with ardour, he is eager to see his party repulse their pretended adversaries. But still he is conscious that it is only a splendid farce! How different his emotions when at length he meets an actual enemy in battle, and recognizes in the adverse lines foes who really seek his blood! Again he marches and retires; bodies of men again wheel and manœuvre before him; aids gallop with orders; the guns roar; the war-clouds enwrap him in their sultry folds as before, but he also sees plain proofs that these are no longer blank cartridges which are fired. The earth is ploughed and the forests are cut with bullets, and as he glances along the line, he sees here and there a comrade, who drops his musket and either limps away, or sinks upon the earth with a cry of anguish. This is war in truth! Now again he is excited, he pants, he is ardent for victory, he thrills with passion, but it is a terrible reality. Such was the conviction, such the awakening, of the men who fell under the spell of a Whitefield's sacred eloquence.[1] The obvious sincerity and earnestness of a living faith in the preacher made the Law, the curse, the hell, dread realities to them, which in the hand of other preachers, had only moved them as a serious fiction.

The amiable Cowper has drawn, in the second book of his *Task*, the picture of what a pastor should be in character and preaching, so venerable and lovely that I cannot forbear commending it to you as your ideal:

> "There stands the messenger of truth: there stands
> The legate of the skies! His theme divine,
> His office sacred, his credentials clear.
> By him the violated law speaks out
> Its thunders; and by him, in strains as sweet
> As angels use, the gospel whispers peace.
> He establishes the strong, restores the weak,

---

[1] Isaac Taylor's "Wesley and Methodism."

Reclaims the wanderer, binds the broken heart,
And, armed himself in panoply complete
Of heavenly temper, furnishes with arms
Bright as his own, and trains, by every rule
Of holy discipline, to glorious war .
The sacramental host of God's elect."

*   *   *   *   *

   " Would I describe a preacher such as Paul,
Were he on earth, would hear, approve and own,
Paul should himself direct me.   I would trace
His master-strokes and draw from his design.
I would express him simple, grave, sincere;
In doctrine uncorrupt, in language plain,
And plain in manners; decent, solemn, chaste,
And natural in gesture; much impressed
Himself, as conscious of his awful charge,
And anxious mainly that the flock he feeds
May feel it too; affectionate in look
And tender in address, as well becomes
A messenger of grace to guilty men.
Behold the picture."

Is this, my young brethren, your conception of what the pulpit orator should be?   Well will it be for you and for your flocks, if this portrait, drawn by the sanctified culture and taste of a great poet, from the living models, a Newton and a Cecil, shall engage your whole approval and stimulate your aspirations !

LECTURE XIX.

STYLE.

I NOW approach the third department of our course, called in the regular classical treatises *Elocution.* I would remind you again that they employed this word, not in that limited sense of utterance and gesticulation to which the present American usage seems to restrict it, but in a meaning inclusive of style, figures, utterance, gesture; of all, in a word, which pertains to the outward expression of thought and feeling. Let us begin with style.

This word (derived from the *stylus,* or pen, with which the writing was performed) denotes the right use of words as vehicles of thought. It is not my purpose to repeat to you the discussions of this subject, or the classifications of the different kinds of figures and tropes, or the rules for their use, contained in the ordinary books of rhetoric. I assume that you have acquired this knowledge in your colleges and academies. My object will be to add some directions appropriate to your peculiar work, for the formation of style and the right use of language. But before I proceed to this, I must beg you to bear with me, while I recall your attention to the cardinal qualities of all good speaking and writing. These are so fundamental in importance that you cannot be too well assured of your familiarity with them. They are *grammatical purity, perspicuity, energy* (or as Dr. George Campbell terms it, *vivacity*), *elegance* and *number*.[1]

Grammatical purity is that syntactical correctness which is conformed to the standard of the present, national usage of approved English writers and speakers.[2] It carefully avoids barbarisms, solecisms and obsolete and newly-coined words and construction. The usage which is your rule must be, not an antiquated one, but that of the best contemporary scholars. It must be the usage, not of writers of questionable taste, but of those who are admitted by all to be undisputed models. It must be, not a sectional usage, but that which is equally recognized among educated men in all parts of the land.

To secure perspicuity the first requisite is clearness of thought. Next, let home-bred, vernacular words be preferred, and all unnecessary technicalities be avoided. Let words be employed uniformly and exactly in their recognized meanings. This canon of perspicuity is violated often from carelessness of thought and indistinct-

---

[1] Quinctil., L. i., c. v., § 1. Omnis oratio tres habeat virtutes, ut *emendata*, ut *dilucida*, ut *ornata* sit (quia dicere *apte*, quod est præcipuum, plerique ornatui subjiciunt). Cicero de Orat., L. iii., c. x., § 37. "Quinam igitur est modus melior, quam ut Latine, ut plane, ut ornate, ut ad id, quodcumque agetur, apte congruenterque agemus?"

[2] Quinctil., L. i., c. vi., § 44, 45. Superest igitur *consuetudo*. . . . Quæ si ex eo, quod plares faciunt, nomen accipiat, periculosissimum dabit præceptum, non orationi modo, sed (quod maius est) vitæ. . . . Ergo *consuetudinem* sermonis vocabo consensum eruditorum; sicut vivendi, consensum bononum.

ness of conception, as well as from ignorance of the exact shades of sense affixed by classic usage. But some writers outrage it from an unwholesome affectation and conceit. They imagine that by using a known word in a sense differing by some shade of meaning from its current one they display their ingenuity and refinement. You will find such writers, for example, taking especial pains to talk of the "utterances" of the Holy Spirit when they mean the things uttered. Whereas, in classic English "utterance" is an abstract noun, signifying a power or quality of speech. These writers speak of "philanthropies" when they intend benefactions, while correct speakers of English express by the word "philanthropy" a humane temper or quality. They delight to use the abstract for the concrete, and to talk of "ruined immortalities" when they mean ruined souls. This is a most perverse sin against perspicuity; and much of this species of pretended fine writing as truly needs to be translated into the language of sensible Englishmen, as though it were in a foreign tongue. Let your subtile discrimination be displayed, not in perverting by a nice shade the meaning of words, but in retaining the very shade given them by good usage. Perspicuity is promoted by a due intermixture of brevity and amplification. It avoids long and intricate sentences. It eschews ambiguous words and constructions, and is especially careful to evince the designed relation of every pronoun, so that doubt of it shall be impossible to the attentive hearer. Perspicuity forbids the speaker ever to keep the sense of a compound sentence suspended to its close. Even the periodic sentence, which holds the construction (not the meaning) suspended to the end, is ill-suited for oral address.[1]

Energy (or vivacity) is to be gained by preferring concrete to abstract, and specific to general terms. Applaud not abstract magnanimity, but the living, magnanimous man. Speak not of the *genus homo* as depraved or as guilty, but of the men before you. Speak not of them, but to them, and that in the second person and in the singular. Say, "Thou art the man." Energy requires the greatest conciseness compatible with perspicuity. It demands metaphor in preference to simile, and judicious synecdoche and impersonation.[2] King David, when he would describe the virulence of the slander of his enemies, says: "Their teeth are spears and arrows, and their tongue a sharp sword." How would this be enfeebled were it expanded into a regular simile, which should describe "the words of malice issuing from their mouths as lacerating his good name and comfort as spears, arrows and swords lacerate, gall and wound the body of an adversary!" He who would have energy of style must sternly exclude every epithet which is not essential to the expression of his

---

[1] Cicero de Orat., L. iii., c. xiii., § 49. Quibus rebus assequi possumus, ut ea quæ dicamus intelligantur? *Latine* scilicet, dicendo, verbis usitatis ac proprie demonstrantibus ea quæ significari ac declarari volemus, sine ambiguo verbo aut sermone, non nimis longa continuatione verborum, non valde productis iis, quæ similitudinis causa ex aliis rebus transferuntur, non discerptis sententiis, non præposteris temporibus, non confusis personis, non perturbato ordine.

[2] Deinde videndum est, ne longe simile sit ductum. Syrtim patrimonii, scopulum libentius dixerim: Charybdim bonorum, voraginem potius. Facilius enim ad ea, quæ visa, quam ad illa quæ audita sunt, mentis oculi feruntur.—*Cicero de Orat.*, L. iii., c. 41, § 163.

thought. He must employ the untechnical and vernacular words which the people easily understand. He must be suggestive rather than exhaustive in the development of ideas. In compound sentences, energy will be promoted by placing the shorter member last. In every sentence, the word which is entitled to the emphasis should be placed in the position of greatest prominence. This is usually at the beginning, at or near the end, or at the *cæsura* of the sentence.[1]

Elegance of style is gained, first, by careful attention to the previous qualities. Next, euphony must be consulted, by avoiding the frequent recurrence of the same sounds (a vice always grating to the ear) and by the customary use of those words and sequences of syllables which are musical and liquid, in preference to those which are heterogeneous, guttural or sibilant. All coarseness of allusion and suggestion must be shunned;

---

[1] Aristotle, Rhetoric, b. iii., c. x., teaches us that polite diction is secured by three means: Metaphor, antithesis and energy. The rhetorical metaphor (c. xi.) is that which makes the symbol *energize—i. e.*, it imputes to it, by metaphor, attributes of life, as Homer's "arrow longing to strike."

C. xiii. The diction of the writer he regards as less energetic, but more accurate and full. That of the speaker should be in the "agonistic style." This is less accurate in detail, disjointed, rapid, representing images as the outline picture does.

Aristotle here gives us a happy description of what I have called the suggestive style.

Hear also Cicero de Orat., L. iii., c. 25, §§ 97–99, warning the public speaker against a luscious nicety: "Genus igitur dicendi est eligendum, quod non solum delectet, sed etiam sine satietate delectet. . . . Ea quæ maxime sensus nostros impellunt voluptate, et specie prima acerrime commovent, ab iis celerrime fastidio quodam et satietate abalienemur. . . . Sic, omnibus in rebus, voluptatibus maximis fastidium finitimum est."

no trope or illustration must be admitted, however apt, which degrades the sentiment of the discourse; no broken metaphors or other disorders of thought and structure must be allowed. Yet it should be remembered that there is a polish which is too uniform, and an elegance which is sickly. It were better, if either fault must be committed, that the public speaker should sacrifice elegance to energy, than this to that. As the musician interposes an occasional discord in his sweetest strains, that the contrast may enhance the harmony, so in those phrases and sentences which require a strong emphasis, some harsh syllables may well have place: this redeems the style from effeminacy and heightens the euphony.

The fifth quality of rhetorical style is number. I use this word here in the sense of the prosodist. Says Aristotle, the oration must have rhythm, but not metre. Cicero, recognizing the propriety of number in the prose-speaker, advises that two or three of the same feet shall follow each other, and that then some other feet shall be introduced, in order that the speaker may not fall into a disagreeable mimicry of metre.[1] This always

---

[1] Aristotle, Rhetoric, b. iii., c. viii., Cicero de Orat., L. iii., c. xlvii., § 182. Let the student inspect the most impressive passages from the standard English orators; he will find that the rhythm which is so obvious to the ear, and so characteristic of the strain of eloquence, is caused by an actual sequence of metrical feet, with frequent variations. I give, as an instance, a noted passage from Rev. Samuel Davies' grand sermon on the Judgment. The feet are marked for your assistance:

Ō tre | mēndŏus | doōm ! | Ēvĕry | wōrd ĭs | bīg wĭth | tērrŏr, | and shoōts | ă thūn | dĕrbōlt | thrōugh thĕ | heārt. | "Depārt: |

offends the ear, because it suggests the appearance of inappropriate and abortive effort. The occurrence of the modern rhyme in prose discourse is a positive sin against euphony. But when the oration flows in short but frequently varied chains of equal or equivalent feet, this adds great expressiveness and beauty to the style. Nature recognizes it: all primitive languages, like the

Awāy | from mў prēs | ence! Ĭ | cānnŏt | bēar sŏ | lōathsŏme ă sīght. | Ĭ ōnce | ĭnvĭ | tĕd thēe | tŏ cōme | tŏ mē," | etc.

We have here, first, two *trochees* and a final long syllable; then three *trochees*, three *iambics*, and a final long syllable. Then follow two iambics and an anapæst; then three *trochees* and a *choriambus*. Next we have *five iambics* together; and this, the only strain in the passage which fails of the epic rhythm and majesty, confirms Cicero's precept, that not more than three or, at most, four feet of the same kind should follow each other without a change.

Take the following admired passage from the sermon of the Rev. R. Hall against Modern Infidelity. Does not every ear perceive a different rhythm, suited to express the different sentiment of reprehension? We find a different sequence of feet:

Ĕtēr | năl Gōd! | Ŏn whāt | are thĭne ēn | ēmĭes | intēnt? | Whāt āre | thŏse ēn | tĕrprĭs | es ŏf guĭlt | and hŏr | rŏr thāt | fŏr the | sāfetў | ŏf theĭr pĕrfōr | mĕrs, reqŭīre | tŏ be ĕnvēl | ŏped in ă dārk | nĕss whĭch | the ēye | ŏf heāv | ĕn mŭst | nŏt piērce? | etc.

The order here is three *iambics*, one *anapæst* and two *iambics*. Then one *spondee*, two *iambics*, one *anapæst*, two *iambics*, two *trochees*, one *pæan* 4th, an *anapæst*, two more *pæans* 4th, and five *iambics*.

The student will observe how uniformly these masters of speech comply with Aristotle's rule to close the sentence with a long syllable. Hall's biographer has left us a curious fact, that the author had written at the end of the passage "penetrate" for "pierce," but in reviewing it he struck his pen through it and substituted "pierce," saying, "That is too long a word." His correct ear demanded the closing long syllable.

Hebrew, tend, by their orthography and accent, toward a regular *arsis* and *thesis*. Many critics have supposed that the first continuous recitation of every people was in metre, and that their first composers were always poets or bards. In this sense, if they are correct, poetry is more natural than prose. All music has its rhythm, which is essential to melody. There is something naturally pleasing and impressive to the human ear in the reverberation of a regularly recurring emphasis. It seems to make the strain palpitate with sensibility, like the voice of a living heart. The different feet are, moreover, expressive of their different sentiments. The "*fortis iambus*" breathes vigour, haste, excitement; the *spondee* suggests pensive and meditative ideas; the *pœan* and *choriambus*, by their roll, express some advancing majesty. By clothing your prose with number, you add therefore to its expressiveness as well as to its euphony. Aristotle disallows to the orator the use of the heroic rhythm (composed of *spondees*, *dactyles* and *anapœsts*), as too stately. *Iambics* and *trochees* he deems too lyrical and colloquial. He therefore recommends that the several *pœan* feet and the *choriambus* be prevalently used. But the former feet are so domesticated in every part of the English language that it is vain to deny the orator their use; and the lyrical character of the shorter feet, to my apprehension, evinces their fitness for the rhetorical rhythm, which, like the lyric poem, is so often required to express animated emotions. The Greek philosopher enjoins that the sentence (and each important member thereof) must always end with a long syllable. This is necessary to enable that syllable to bear the closing cadence of the voice. We may be

allowed to modify this law, as was done by the Latin
hexameter, to the extent of making the last syllable
uniformly long by position, whether it was so by quantity or not; and indeed English sentences and clauses
are harmoniously ended, like that metre, with a *dactyle*
and *spondee*.

These five qualities—grammatical purity, perspicuity,
energy, elegance and rhythm or number—will constitute
a fine style. Let me remind you that most young
speakers, in attempting to form themselves, have more
need than they are aware to fix their attention upon the
rudimental and simple qualities of style. In your efforts
for improvement you are in danger of beginning too far
in advance. Grammatical accuracy and perspicuity—
the virtues which lie at the foundation and which also
contribute so much to elegance—are not so commonly
found in English speakers as is supposed. Until your
style is endued with these more homely and solid
virtues, an attempt to deck it with the lighter graces
will be tawdry and poor. Such an error excites a disgust, like that which we feel at seeing a beggar tricked
out with cheap finery, while her person presents the
lack of comfortable and necessary raiment. If correctness and perspicuity are present, the style cannot be
bad. Indeed, so true is this, that a writer who is
strongly characterized by these plain excellences will,
without any other graces, gain from most readers, as
Dr. Franklin has done, the applause of elegance. Let
me urge you, then, to look well to these modest virtues
of style, before you indulge a higher ambition. Lord
Chesterfield, himself no mean orator, testified, in his
Letters to his Son, that while every man has not genius,

every man of common sense can gain a correct and lucid, and therefore a pleasing style. Is not any minister of the gospel, then, positively guilty who neglects to acquire this means for commending his Master's word?

The first requisite for good writing or speaking is good thinking. Clear, discriminating and careful thought must precede the attempt to compose. Let the matter to be expressed exist distinctly in the mind, and it will clothe itself in its most appropriate verbal dress, provided the speaker's taste and memory have been trained by the reading of good models and by exercise. I would recommend, then, that after satisfying yourself of the ideas which you desire to express, you shall suffer them to utter themselves, as nearly as may be. In the act of composition, let not your minds concern themselves chiefly about the verbal dress of the thought, but about the thought itself. The clear and just conception will not fail to clothe itself in lucid words. Language is only a *medium* for the transmission of ideas. The glass which is most transparent is the best. It is only when we look through it without perceiving it, as though the aperture were vacant, illuminated space, when the light passes through it without colour or refraction, when we are obliged to resort to tactual sensation to verify its presence, that we call the window-pane a perfect *medium*. So that style is best, which least attracts the hearer's attention from the thought to itself. If there were a perfect orator, men would come away from his discourse without having any conscious recollection concerning the qualities of his style; they would seem to themselves to have been witnessing, by a direct spiritual intuition, the working of a great mind and heart. It follows also that, in the act of composition, the pen should be allowed to move as rapidly as the mind craves. I do not assert that only rapid composition can be nervous; for the speed which is natural to one mind is very different from that of others. What I would urge is, that you shall not halt in the career of thought to debate the propriety of a term or a construction, to cast about for words or tropes, to scan the effect of the phrase which suggests itself. Correctness or elegance thus acquired would be won at too heavy a cost. The ardour of the mind would be effectually chilled by so many harassing cares; the inspiration, the *afflatus* of enthusiasm generated by the heat of the soul's action expands and exalts all its powers. Give way, then, to the propitious gale when it begins to breathe, and be assured that the language will be as happy, in which your mind will clothe its teeming ideas at such an hour, as its thoughts will be fruitful and nervous. If your investigation and meditation have been thorough and your training in composition diligent, write as rapidly as the impulse prompts. Do you suspect that a loose construction or inelegant word has dropped from your pen? Do not regard it then, but sweep onward with the gale: the time for correction comes afterward.

This remark suggests the great importance of revision. When the writing is completed, it should be subjected to the most searching and laborious examination. This work is irksome, because the *afflatus* is now gone and the charm of novelty is no longer felt. But he who would become a correct and elegant writer or speaker must bend himself with determination to the repulsive task. Every thought should again be con-

sidered. Every clause should be scanned. The style
should be dissected, first, with reference to grammatical
purity and perspicuity, then with an eye to elegance,
energy and rhythm. In one place, you will detect a
faulty construction. Correct it. In another, you will
find a pronoun with an ambiguous reference. Make it
as lucid as the sunbeam. There you will find a harsh
word. Replace it by a euphonious synonym. You
will perceive that a given sentence has its meaning suspended or unnecessarily inverted. Reverse the statement, and make the expression of the thought direct.
Another sentence will be seen to contain two elements
of thought really independent. Divide it. Here is a
trope or illustration which suggests an association out
of harmony with your subject. Suppress it. There is
a redundant epithet, a pleonasm or repetition. Erase
it. Here a mixed or broken metaphor has intruded
itself. Let it be moulded into harmony. There a
figure or an illustration suggests itself as truly apt.
Insert it.

Remember that the object of this painful revision is
not mainly nor chiefly the perfecting of the composition
in hand; your aim is to acquire thereby a ready accuracy in the employment of language for all future compositions. The work is, in this aspect, a species of literary *post mortem* autopsy. When the physician dissects
the corpse of his deceased patient, in order to verify or
correct his *diagnosis* and to test the manner in which
the remedies have operated, he does not propose any
benefit to the subject. For him means are too late; he
is dead. But the practitioner seeks thereby to prepare
himself for treating more successfully many future pa-

tients. Such will be your chief aim in the dissection of what you have composed. You will acquire, for subsequent efforts, mastery over the elements of a good style. It may have seemed to you that I imposed on you contradictory obligations. On the one hand, I told you that a perfect style was the result of attention to many varied and delicate points, affecting not only every thought, but every word. On the other hand, I forbade you to pause over these *minutiæ* in writing. The reconciliation is found in this labour of revision. By it the powers will be so disciplined that art will become easy, and accuracy and elegance will become natural to you. The mind will be drilled to the habit of right expression. Just in proportion as its exaltation and fire increase, will the nicest refinements of true style suggest themselves spontaneously. A pure style will become the easiest and most native dress of vigorous thought.

Nothing has caused more embarrassment to young speakers than the unfortunate notion that public speaking must be generically different from talking. Many have been the pupils of the rhetorical art, who have experienced the fate of *M. Jourdain* in Molière's *Bourgeois Gentilhomme.* He had been speaking prose from his childhood without effort, and without knowing prose from verse. After his learned master had taught him technically, he could only speak it ill and with labour. So men do not know that speaking is but talking; they could do the latter very well and naturally until they attempted to do it by artificial rule. Now one experiences no difficulty in stating or narrating, after his own customary way, what he thoroughly comprehends.

Why should rhetorical discourse be less easy, except as the embarrassment of publicity agitates the powers at the outset? It is because of the perverse idea which is adopted, that when one speaks he must needs employ a contracted phraseology, a different structure for his sentences, an opposite turn of expression, to all which he is unaccustomed. I affirm that speaking is but serious, earnest, correct and elevated talking. The facile, direct, unpretending structure of sentences which we employ in our conversation is the proper one for the oration. The thing which we have to do is not to cast this, our wonted method, away, and attempt one perfectly antipodal and unwonted, but to purify and ennoble that which is natural to us. You are embarrassed in your rhetorical style, because you are David in King Saul's armour. The free and graceful limbs of the mountain boy are unaccustomed to move in greaves. Take, then, your own crook and your sling and smooth stones out of the brook. You will not advance to the combat slouched, nor halting, nor with clownish antics, for the scene and occasion are august, but you will move with that very freedom which you learned in the fields at home. When one desires to pass from one point to another, what is easier to him than to walk? But if you were mounted upon the *cothurni* of ancient tragedy, you would move awkwardly and would perchance trip yourself and fall ludicrously before the spectators. Strip off your *cothurni*, descend from your stilts, let your mind advance in that mode which nature has taught it, remembering only the decorum and seriousness proper for one who moves to a sacred object, and in the presence of the great King.

But let me not be understood as sanctioning by this precept a style meanly colloquial, familiar or low. The natural style and phraseology must be purged of all looseness of syntax, of all familiar abbreviations and provincialisms, of every grovelling allusion. The language of the pulpit should never be undignified, and it is well that it should have in appropriate places elevation, solemnity, grandeur. But these are the opposites of artificial pomp. The noblest passages in the English classics will be found to be the most simple in structure and the least inflated in expression.[1]

In style, as in action, the best teachers are good examples. You should, therefore, form yourselves by the study of the great models, both in prose and poetry. There are, in our day, so much printing, and so much reading, and so much of that which we read is as mean and crude in style as it is worthless in sentiment, that we are in constant danger of having our taste corrupted by infection. We must dwell much with the great masters, in order that we may inhale with them a more healthy atmosphere. We should read them with the closest attention both to their thought and expression. Our aim should be not servile invitation, but a knowledge of the proper application of the principles of

---

[1] See, for example, the speech of Satan in the Paradise Lost:

> "What though the field be lost,
> All is not lost. The unconquerable will
> And study of revenge, immortal hate,
> And courage never to submit or yield,
> And what is else not to be overcome;
> That glory never shall his wrath or might
> Extort from me," etc.

See a still nobler instance in Psalm lxxxix. 7-9.

style, and an infusion of their elevated simplicity, warmth and strength.

The virtues of style which I have explained should be common to all public speakers. But the message of the preacher is peculiar, whence it naturally results that certain special qualities are exacted of him. These I would call *seriousness*, or *gravity, scripturalness* and *simplicity*.

But before I proceed to discuss these, let me urge the value of that quality of *popularity*, if I may so term it, which the style of the pulpit should have, in common with that of the *forum* and the senate. All public speakers should employ, as nearly as the dignity of subjects will allow, the dialect of the people, and use their vocabulary. It is true that every science must have some nomenclature of its own. But the preacher should use technical terms of theology as sparingly as he can. Some of these are so necessary, the ideas which they denote are so rudimental to a knowledge of redemption, that they should be the possession of every hearer of the gospel. Every preacher should feel that it is an important part of his public instructions to convey to the minds of all an exact and familiar conception of their meaning. Such are the words, guilt, satisfaction, justification, faith, new birth, repentance, sanctification. These and similar terms, I repeat, ought to be made in such a manner the common property of all hearers, that they should be no longer technical. But, in other respects, the minister should avoid pedantic or scientific terms. There is a deeper reason for this than the ignorance of a large part of every congregation concerning the language of books. Whenever you

accurately translate a technical idea out of the phrase of
art into the vocabulary of common life, if it is done without impairing its dignity, you confer a great benefit upon
the understandings of the better informed also. There
is a strong tendency in men's minds to accept a familiarity with the sound of a technical word, instead of
true acquaintance with its sense. Because they recognize the often heard phrase, they fancy that they have
a due comprehension of the idea, when in fact their
attention is only mechanical, and their understandings
are nearly passive. But when they miss the familiar
shibboleth, and the idea is defined to them in words untechnical, unheard before in this connection, and yet
correct and plain, they are compelled to exercise a real
intellectual discernment, or, at least, to discover their
ignorance of what is taught. Such language also clothes
old truths with a freshness which is delightful to the
mind and ear.

BUT the style of the pulpit must surpass that of secular orators in seriousness or gravity. The moral, spiritual and divine truths which exclusively occupy the preacher, the sacredness of his professed motive, and the momentous stake which his hearers have in the transaction,—all show that levity of thought or manner would here be an odious fault. Jocular images, satire and sarcasm are not the sword of the spirit. They may amuse or irritate, but they do not make the heart better. Would any one plead that the former. may be legitimate to arouse the attention, and the latter to chastise crime? The answer is, that an expedient for gaining the ear, so heterogeneous to the tone of sacred truth as a ludicrous jest, will make an impression more adverse to the flow of sacred emotion than inattention itself. Satire and sarcasm are inconsistent with that pitying love, which should animate the appeals of a sinner saved by grace to his doomed fellow-creatures. Sarcasm is usually the language of malice. It is claimed as an exception, that we hear Isaiah satirizing the folly of idol-worshippers, Elijah mocking the priests of Baal, and our Saviour scourging hypocrisy with the lash of sarcasm.[1] This is true; but they were inspired and

---

[1] Isa. xliv. 14–17; 1 Kings xviii. 27; Matt. xxiii. 24.

extraordinary preachers: our more humble position should teach us to resort very sparingly to such weapons. You may also remind me that I have myself pointed to the wit of apt illustrations as an admirable element of their force. But this is serious wit, not jocular; stimulating, but not excoriating. I am also ready to concede that there is often a trait in the images of an original and masculine imagination, which approaches near the confines of humour; but this trait, although it may provoke the involuntary smile, is not levity: it often lies hard by the fountain of tears and the abysses of deepest moral emotion. In these instances it is the fact that the element of serious wit or humour is involuntary, yea, unconscious, which is its defence: the moment it appears to have been intruded into the sermon with intention it becomes an odious sin.[1]

The second peculiarity of pulpit style should be scripturalness. This includes two points: the sermon should be rich in apt scriptural quotations, and its whole language should be imbued with the tone and characteristics of our time-honoured version. Such a style is to be

---

[1] " He that negotiates between God and man,
      As God's ambassador, the grand concern
      Of judgment and of mercy, should beware
      Of lightness in his speech. 'Tis pitiful
      To court a grin when you should woo a soul;
      To break a jest when pity would inspire
      Pathetic exhortation; and to address
      The skittish fancy with facetious tales,
      When sent with God's commission to the heart.
      So did not Paul. Direct me to a quip
      Or merry turn in all he ever wrote,
      And I consent you take it for your text,
      Your only one, till sides and benches fail."—*Task.*

preferred by the preacher for every reason. The literary merits of the English Bible as a "well of old English undefiled" make it the best possible model for the student of sacred knowledge. In this venerable book we have embalmed that standard speech of the race which is at once pure, classic and popular. The associations and mental habitudes of the people which have gathered around this version commend it to us as a standard. It is more universally read by Protestants than any other religious book; so that it is to be presumed its language is most familiar and intelligible to them. The most tender and solemn associations of every pious mind are linked with its words; their very rhythm is sacred music to the ear. The preacher who imbues his style with their savour will be sure of having the charm of appropriateness.

But this scriptural style does not consist in a servile aping of a few Bible phrases current among religious people; for this would but render you trite and fulsome. Nor does it consist in an ingenious patchwork of the more quaint images culled from the symbolical parts of the prophets and poets; for this is but pious pedantry and sober trifling. You must read and study the Bible with perpetual diligence, until your whole thought and feeling are imbued with its tone. It will be a profitable exercise to commit to memory extended passages of the highest rhetorical beauty, that the recitation of them to yourself may serve to inspire and invigorate your souls, and fix, as it were, a higher key-note for their strains. There is a difficulty, which no attentive writer can have failed to appreciate, in using the finest Scripture quotations: the contrast was too strong between their majesty and the poverty of his own succeeding words. It will be a useful exercise to you to admit such a citation into the body of your writing, and then return and labour to elevate your own composition, without mimicry, nearer the level of the borrowed strain. You will thus discover what are the traits which you lack to make your style worthy of the Scripture model beside it.

The third requisite of pulpit style is simplicity. I use this word in its moral as well as its literary sense. In manner, simplicity is the opposite, not of art, but of artifice; and in motive it is the opposite of conceit, vanity, ambition and every affection inconsistent with the spiritual sincerity and zeal on which I insisted under a previous head. It excludes, of course, bombast, grandiloquence, prurient ornament, affectation and intricacy of style. It requires simplicity of structure; because a composition which is to be spoken by the voice and caught by the ear as uttered, or else not understood at all, must be more direct, lucid and brief than the essay which can be read and read again. In long and involved sentences, the speaker's voice cannot easily manage and sustain the inflections which are requisite to give expression to the sentiment. In listening to such sentences, the hearer's attention is overtaxed to carry so complicated a structure and meaning. This simplicity employs an unambitious vocabulary. I will not enjoin the preacher, as some have done, to expunge every word which the humblest hearer finds unintelligible; for one of the uses of the teacher is to extend his pupils' vocabulary. But there should be no affectation of hard words. The minister's style should be usually level to the meaner capacities, because the cultivated can understand and be saved by a simple style, but the ignorant cannot profit by an inflated style. The latter can benefit only one class, the former both. Indeed, every person of true learning and taste approves a simple style for such a topic, as not only most useful to the ignorant, but most pleasing to himself. Simplicity implies, finally, a profound singleness, directness and purity of motive in the sacred orator.

Unless I am much mistaken, this holy simplicity needs to be strongly enforced, because the opposite vice is far gone. A reference to classic standards will show that much we now hear from the pulpit would be condemned as bombast by an Addison, a Swift or a Pope. Even Dr. Samuel Johnson, the proverb of his day for inflation, seems natural and terse by the side of many who are now admired. Let us compare ourselves with the great ancient masters of style as to the number of words, the intricacy of structure, the useless epithets and the prurient ornament; let us look, for example, into that most elegant of Latin composers (Horace), as distinguished for the perfectness of his diction as for the hatefulness of his morals, and we shall see that we are as far behind him in true elegance as in simplicity.

The careless haste with which men now write and read the floods of rubbish which pour from the press fosters the same vice. He who has much thought uses compact and pregnant words. As the art of writing much with small materials is extended, complexity and verbosity must prevail. Expansion of shallow ideas goes farther and farther; real triteness of thought is concealed under increasing extravagance, which seeks a cheap applause by striving to outdo itself and its rivals.

A mercenary, luxurious, material civilization surely depreciates the taste of a people. Simplicity of character is lost. That manliness of soul, which proceeds from labour, struggles with difficulty, and intercourse with nature, is gone. The frivolous and sensual race demands the same rank luxury and frippery in its literature which it loves in its animal enjoyments. We know how, in the corruptions of imperial Rome, the masculine eloquence of the republic sank into the puerile and tawdry bombast of the Byzantine style. If the profligate luxury and degrading bondage introduced by the "decline and fall" of the great modern republic do not result in the same effects, the laws of nature must be reversed.

Hence, the conviction has grown upon me, that we need to be recalled to what will seem to this exaggerating age a severe simplicity. I would that each true minister of the gospel might stand forth as a Tacitus amidst the pruriency of this degenerate race. But when I seek this result I am far from waging war against rhetoric, ornament, skill, or polish. I would not have you confound a simple with a low and common style. The truest art is that which has become perfect nature. It does not supplant or exclude, but only perfects nature. The finest statue is that on which the strokes of the chisel are unseen, and the marble appears most like the flesh which grew. The finest picture is that in which the beholder is not reminded of the brush and the cunning mixture of colours, but seems to see the living man standing out from the canvas. So, if preaching be considered as an art merely, he is most perfect in the art in whom the hearer perceives no art, but hears Nature pouring forth her soul in her own spontaneous simplicity. An objection, then, against artifice is that it is a sin against true art. Much that is now heard with admiration from the pulpit is as thoroughly condemned by mere rhetoric, by the pagan Horace's Epistle to the Pisos, or the comedian's instructions to the players in Hamlet, as by Christian principle and feeling.[1]

But let us proceed to direct considerations. The soul is such that all its powerful operations are simple. Complexity in its acts implies the feebleness of all. Multiplicity of objects distracts the attention, and by distracting, weakens. It is the single, rushing, mighty wind which raises the billows of the great deep; a variety of cross breezes only ruffles its surface with insignificant ripples. A moment's reflection upon the powers of the mind explains this. They are quick, but they are not infinite; there is a narrow limit to the number of separate images which men can comprehend in the same moment. If the attention is perfect, every word addressed to the ear makes a demand for sensation, perception, memory and some higher acts, either of comparison or imagination, or both. How many things to be done by the mind for the due comprehension of each sentence! Hence, every superfluous word taxes the mind with an unnecessary labour, and calls it away from the thought. The verbose speaker, therefore, builds obstacles to the comprehension of his ideas, and, as it were, offers his hearers a *premium* for inattention. It is for this reason that brevity is necessary to

---

[1] Quinctil., L. i., c. ii., § 3. Nam siqua in his ars est dicentium, ea prima est, ne ars esse videatur.

energy. To use any phrase, ornament or epithet which is not necessary to the bodying forth of the main idea, is a sacrifice of effect. Every labour of attention, perception and comprehension, expended upon that excrescence, is so much subtracted from the force with which the mind should have grasped the main idea. Prune your language, then, with a severe hand. When we wish to strike a blow which shall be felt, we do not take up a bough loaded with foliage; we use a naked club.

I suspect that the correctness of these views is confessed, even by the consciousness of persons of the most perverted taste. However they may laud their literary idol, they cannot conceal from themselves, that their listlessness grows more and more dreary under the most brilliant flashes of his rhetorical pyrotechnics—that the more his sparks are multiplied the more feebly they strike. There is, indeed, a large class of listeners whose minds are so utterly shallow, and who are so unconscious of the real nature of eloquence, that they are pleased with the mere lingual and grammatical dexterity with which surprising strings of fine words are rolled forth. Their idea of fine speaking seems to be, that it is a sort of vocal *legerdemain*, like that of the juggler who twirls a plate upon the end of a rattan as no one else can— an art in which the skill is measured solely by the difficulty, and the· perfection consists in connecting the largest quantity of sounding words so that they shall have a certain semblance of meaning and melody. With minds so childish he who can carry this loquacity to the greatest height will, of course, be most admired. But I trust that none of you are capable of an ambition for this low and ignorant applause.

I would also argue more definitely, the preacher's topic and motive demand this simplicity of manner and style. He speaks:

> "Of man's first disobedience and fruit,
>   Of that forbidden tree whose mortal taste
>   Brought death unto the world and all our woe;
>   With loss of Eden, till one greater Man
>   Restore us and regain the blissful seat."

He professes to stand between the living and the dead. He deals with the attributes of a jealous and majestic God, the destiny of souls to immortal bliss or woe, the tomb, the resurrection trump, the judgment-bar, the righteous Judge, the glories of heaven and the gloom of hell, the gospel's cheering sound, the sacred tears of Gethsemane, the blood of Calvary and the sweet yet awful breathings of the Holy Ghost. The preacher's mission is to lay hold of perishing men, and by the love of the Redeemer drag them from the pit. His only motive is disinterested zeal, and if he harbours any other, he is compelled for decency's sake to conceal it and affect the former.

Now, the first element of good taste is appropriateness. Grand and weighty themes least admit fanciful ornament. The tracery which might be graceful around the pediments of a cottage would be tawdry if applied to a lofty temple. This must be majestic and severe in its simplicity. What a demand is there here for profound and ingenuous feeling also! How unspeakably inappropriate every artifice which betrays the impulse of self-display! The preacher, to be consistent with his professed attitude, should be instinct with earnestness. But who does not know that the eloquence of native emotion is always simple? When the wail of the bereaved mother rises from the bedside of her dying child, it has no artifice; you have heard it, and know that our art cannot equal its power! When the story of his wrongs bursts from the lips of the indignant patriot, and he consecrates himself upon the altar of father-land, it is in simple words. When the despairing soul raises to his Saviour the cry, "God be merciful to me a sinner!" he speaks unaffectedly. Let me urge it, then, with all the emphasis which language can convey, that an unaffected and direct style is the very first dictate of propriety and good taste for him who speaks of the gospel. To turn away the mind's eye for one moment from these overpowering realities, toward the artifices of rhetoric, is the most heinous sin against rhetoric. It is as though the man who desired to arouse his neighbour, asleep in a burning house, should bethink himself of the melody of the tones in which he cried "FIRE." It is as though the champion, fighting for his hearthstone and his household, should waste his thoughts on the beauty of his limbs and attitudes.

Do I advocate, then, a simplicity so bald as to exclude every figure? By no means. A certain class of figures is the very language of nature. Such we should use in their proper place. They are those figures which, every one sees, are used to set forth the subject and not the speaker. They are those which the mind spontaneously seizes when enlarged and strengthened by the earnestness of its emotions, and welds them by the heat of its action into the very substance of its thought. Such ornaments are distinguished at a glance from the epithets, tropes and similes which the artificial mind collects with its eye prevalently turned all the time to its own meed of applause. Within the strict bounds of this directness and simplicity, there is ample scope for the exercise of genius and imagination. Indeed, it is when a vigorous logic and truly original imagination are stimulated by the most intense heat of emotion, that the noblest simplicity of style and, at the same time, the grandest imagery are combined.

There is with me no stronger conviction, than that the speaker should never attempt to rescue his discourse from baldness and tameness, by resorting to tropes collected with deliberate design. The moment an ornament is felt to be introduced with " malice prepense," it becomes a deformity. There is a rule of architecture propounded for some styles by the greatest masters which we might profitably adopt. It is that while every essential member of the structure shall be so proportioned as to be ornamental, no ornament shall be admitted which is not essential to the construction, no bracket which has nothing to strengthen, no column which has nothing to sustain. The proper sources of rhetorical beauty are, next to true genius, in the warmth of an honest, earnest emotion, and a clear, logical apprehension of the truth discussed. Unless our ornaments come spontaneously from this, their proper mint, they will inevitably be counterfeit. When, therefore, the preacher finds, after he has done all in the composition of his sermon which clear definition, affluence of knowledge, just arrangement and sound logic can effect, that his work is still tame and cold, it is worse than useless for him to seek for artificial imagery. He should seek

Christian feeling. He needs to sacrifice, not at the shrine of the Muse of eloquence, but at the altar of the Holy Ghost.

Remember that men have a perception of consistency which is intuitive with them. Education and culture are not needed to confer this; they may rather blunt it by sophisticating the judgment and mental habits. That which is heartless and calculated will inevitably be detected. But when the hearer perceives artifice he will impute it to a selfish motive, and for him there is an end of right impression. You may plead that your expedient is prompted by a well-meaning desire to commend the gospel. He will not believe you; he will urge with truth that the natural language of disinterestedness is simplicity, as the natural garb of vanity is artifice; he will persist in imputing the latter as your motive.

Observe here, also, that if from our perverted training an artificial manner has become second nature to us, this will not prevent the mischief. To the perception of the hearer who has not been thus perversely trained, it still seems artificial, and he naturally concludes that it is purposely such. It is not enough, then, for you to say that it is really " your manner;" that in you it is no longer artificial, but a second nature. You should inquire how it became " your manner;" whether by giving free course to an ingenuous and ardent love for souls, or by listening to the whispers of conceit and the seduction of applause in your imitative season.

But what hearer is so dull as not to feel, when innate perception detects this heartlessness, that if the preacher really believed what he proclaimed, and felt what he professed for dying souls, he could have neither time nor heart to think of self-display? There will be a conclusion, perhaps scarcely conscious, yet influential, that either this speaker does not believe his own words, when he tells him of his hanging over hell-fire and of love divine stooping to his rescue, or that if he does, he must have the heart of a serpent to be seeking the trivial indulgence of vanity in the presence of truths so sacred and dire. And, indeed, my young brethren, how repulsive is the selfishness of him who, believing these gospel themes, can desecrate them to the tricking forth of his own rhetorical fame! I have seen somewhere this story of Parrhasius (I know not that it is authentic), the gifted but selfish and unprincipled Greek painter, that when he was engaged upon one of his master-pieces, the Prometheus chained by Vulcan to the crag of Mount Caucasus and consumed by an immortal vulture, he purchased a venerable and noble old man from among the Olynthian captives sold by Philip of Macedon, as a model. When he had brought his painting to such a stage that he was ready to give the finishing touches.to the face of the figure, designed to express a mortal and yet an undying agony, he bound his victim on a rack beside his easel, and there tormented him to death with a nice and delicate deliberation, that he might catch the exact lineaments of the death anguish, and transfer them to his picture. Do you shudder at the cruel, the fiendish ambition of this pagan? He could coolly witness, yea, cause, the mortal pangs, and despise the entreaty of a fellow-creature, hapless and helpless, venerable and innocent, that he might perfect with the shadows of his woes the work upon which he built his selfish fame! By how much is that man less heartless, who deliberately traffics in the terrors of eternity to deck and trim his reputation; who gathers the groans and the gloom of the pit of eternal torment, and dips his pencil in the blackness of his fellow-creature's despair to add impressiveness to his work of self-display; nay, who dares to lay his hand on the glories of the cross and the sacred pangs of Calvâry, at which guilty man should only shudder and weep, to flaunt them before a gaping crowd as the trappings of his skill? Nothing can rescue him from the condemnation of a cold and cruel impiety save his unbelief; he can be excused only on the plea that he regards these dread facts as serious fables.

Must your auditors believe, then, that the pastor who, out of the pulpit, is a humane and courteous gentleman, who shows himself sincerely ready to relieve the temporal ills of his fellow-men, is thus savagely heartless? No; they will adopt the other alternative: they will conclude, it may be half-consciously, that you are not in earnest. Thus, artificial preaching gives pretext for infidelity. He who speaks thus will never be made the power of God and the wisdom of God to salvation to them that believe.

The remedy for this fault must be sought in the cultivation of the heart at the throne of grace, in the increase of our faith and in the revivifying of our love. When we believe and feel like a Davies, a Whitefield, an Ambrose, a Paul, then we may preach like them. Only a genuine piety will produce a genuine simplicity. An artificial simplicity, while rhetorically more correct, is, in the sight of Him who searcheth the heart, but a more refined and skilful sin. Let me guard myself

here.   Do we seek the virtue of simplicity in style, do
we forego prurient, excessive and ill-assimilated ornament, only because our more cultivated taste tells us
that this is the truer art and the readier way to win a
higher praise for eloquence?   Is this the only feeling
which animates our condemnation and contempt, when
we reprehend our more ignorant and misguided com-
rades?   If this be so, then, while we may be acquitted
at the bar of our science, at the bar of conscience we are
still found guilty of the impiety.   Let us fall before our
Master and say, " Woe is me, for I am undone, because
I am a man of unclean lips, and I dwell among a
people of unclean lips."   Send, O Lord, "a live coal
taken from off the altar, and lay it upon my mouth;
and say, Lo, this hath touched thy lips, and thine
iniquity is taken away and thy sin purged."

LECTURE XXI.

ACTION.

FROM style we pass to *action*. By this we intend all those functions of the body, by its organs and members, which convey to the audience the orator's thoughts and feelings. I shall treat this subject under the two heads of *utterance* and *gesture;* the first relating to the management of the voice, the second to the posture of the body and the employment of its limbs and features as aids to expression. You are all familiar with the exalted estimate of good action uttered by Demosthenes. The classic masters concur in making it, at the least, the half of the orator's power. Our experience has taught us all what is its potent and enchanting effect, when it is made the vehicle of truly eloquent sentiments. Let me not be understood as encouraging the attempt to substitute a fine action for these. "As the body without the spirit is dead," so action without just thought and emotion is an empty counterfeit. But as the spirit without the body would be invisible and impalpable to us mortals, and incapable of all converse and influence, so the most powerful thought without rhetorical action is inefficient in oral discourse.

It is not my purpose to enter into full details upon these subjects. One reason which forbids is the brevity of our remaining time; another consideration is the belief that detailed and technical rules on this head can never make an orator. In truth, the main foundation for right or wrong action has been laid long before you come here, in the mode of reading to which you were trained in the primary school, and in the habits of utterance formed in the society amidst which you were reared. The great teachers of correct expression are the mother and the master of the reading-school. And then it must be your own ear, taste, heart and intellect which shall teach you the right emphasis and gesture. He who has the gift of native ear and sensibility will learn how to speak from listening to good models. There is no other tuition which is efficient, and there is, for such a pupil, no other that is needed. But yet attention and diligence may do much to amend our faults and to perfect our taste. It is with this view I am to point out to you briefly the elements of rhetorical action. I treat first of utterance.

Speech is addressed to the ear. Its first requisite is, therefore, audibility: we must so utter it as to be heard. This simple remark will suggest to your good sense the rule as to the general gauge of loudness. The voice should be always loud enough to be heard throughout the audience, and, except in animated passages, it should not be much louder. To secure that result, it is well to direct the eyes generally toward the farthest circle of hearers; for the voice will naturally adjust itself to the distance of those we address. This rule is useful also in guarding us against the distraction of our attention and the loss of our thread of thought, by noting too closely any individual countenance or trivial event in the audience near us. But there is an element more essential to audibility than loudness: this is distinctness. By distinctness I mean these traits: clearness or purity of tone, due deliberation or separation of the syllables, and especially careful articulation. The public speaker must never move so rapidly as to huddle his syllables. While he observes due accent and emphasis, he must give space for the distinct enunciation of both the vowels and consonants of all unaccented syllables. There is a tendency growing in this our material age to a curtness and hurry of enunciation, which threaten to destroy the melody and the very identity of the English as a spoken language. This fashion is to disregard the characteristic vowel-sounds of all syllables except the one which bears the accent, and to reduce them to the *e* mute of the French or to the *shewa* sound of the Hebrew. Such speakers pronounce the adjective "capital," for instance, as though it were "*cáp'tle;*" "cardinal" in their mouths is "*cárd'nle,*" "memory" is "*mém'ry,*" "governor" is "*gúv'n'r,*" "innocent" is "*innic'nt.*" This detestable usage would reduce our noble tongue to a torrent of sibilant dissyllables. It is the vowels which are heard: they constitute the real voice of language; the consonants are but the checks or stoppages which the tongue, teeth, lips and palate impose upon the stream of sound. To suppress or diminish the vowel-sounds tends, therefore, to substitute for the music of the flowing river the perpetual gurgle and clatter of the valves of the mill. Rhetorical melody resides in the vowelsounds. If you would possess this charming grace of speech, the vowels must be each one distinctly uttered.

It is true that the consonants give the articulation: they give to human language that grand peculiarity which distinguishes it from the cries and songs of beasts and birds, and thus renders it symbolical of an infinite diversity of thought, while the merely vowel-sounds of the animal world only express a few instinctive passions. Both vowels and consonants should, then, receive their full enunciation.

Next to distinctness of utterance perhaps the most essential requisite is orthoepy. The shade of sound, given to letters and combinations of letters, must be that established for each word by polite usage. The accent (on words of more than one syllable) must be placed on the syllable appointed for it by the same standard. In a word, the whole enunciation of the public speaker should be such as marks the man of breeding and polish. If your hearer is himself a gentleman, his taste requires this culture in the man who claims to instruct him; if he is a peasant, its possession always confers influence over him.

Let me now commend to you the same truth which we found so fruitful when considering the question of style. Speaking is but talking dignified. Therefore a natural utterance is cardinal to good elocution. Notice how intelligent and well-bred people speak in conversation; how they indicate the divisions or punctuations of their thoughts; how they express their sentiments by emphasis; how they vary their utterance to correspond with the varieties of their emotions: here you have your lesson. It is a model to be modified, indeed, by the facts that as an orator, you speak continuously, upon a grave subject, and to a crowd, instead of one person or

a few. You will add gravity and dignity to your utterance; you will emit a greater volume or breadth of
sound; you will, in animated passages, employ those
intonations of passion which, in social conversation, can
rarely find their proper occasion. But, above all, be
natural; with these modifications, speak as unaffected
people talk. Away with all affectations of tones and
emphasis. Let your ear and taste be trained by good
usage, and then, having possessed your mind and heart
with the "thoughts that breathe and words that burn,"
let them find their own intonations.

Especially do the natural tones of unaffected persons
display the beauty and charm of flexibility. When we
listen, for instance, to the animated conversation of children or young persons in their seasons of freedom, we
perceive that the outline of the sound is as mobile and
undulatory as the surface of the sea when gently agitated with billows. There is no approach to monotony.
The variety is as endless as the diversified play of sentiment in their bounding hearts. This quality of flexibility the orator must practice in all directions. To
comprehend these, you must be acquainted with the
powers of that wondrous instrument, the human voice,
whose structure bespeaks so clearly its Creator's skill.
It is susceptible of diversity in no less than seven different respects, and each of these is most expressive of
sentiment. First, the tones of the voice may differ in
pitch. This is the difference described popularly by the
words "high or low," and in the language of art by the
place of the note upon the musical scale. Those who
have any acquaintance with music know that it is not
any interval of pitch whatsoever, which constitutes a

"tone" in the scale, but three certain intervals of fixed
degree, called "tones major," "tones minor" and "semitones." And the octave, or ladder of seven descending
or ascending intervals, which is the universal standard
of melody, is composed of five major and minor steps
and two half-steps or semitones. Now, in speaking, just
as much as in singing, changes of pitch in the voice,
when they occur, should be conformed to this natural
musical scale—that is to say, when the speaker raises
or depresses the pitch of his voice, he should raise or
depress it by some musical interval, or, in other words,
by the space of one or more tones of the octave. This
is essential to melody. When Nature would express inquiry, quick surprise, sharp decision of will, and other
vivid sentiments, she teaches us to raise the pitch of the
voice upon the significant word or phrase. The greater
the rise, the more vivid is the expression. Thus, the
rising inflection in an ordinary interrogation will not
ascend above that musical interval known to musicians
as a third, or a step composed of one major and one
minor tone. In an expression of amazement, or sharp
negation, it may rise through a fifth or even a whole
octave. A depression of the pitch through a third
marks the period of a sentence. The prevalence of a
depressed pitch gives to a passage the expression of
gravity and solemnity. The transition by minor intervals (intervals composed of minor tones and semitones)
is the natural expression of pensive, pathetic and sup-
plicatory sentiments.

When we speak of inflections of pitch, we imply, of
course, that the speech, like the piece of music, has its
dominant key-note, from which the voice ascends or

descends along the scale, and to which it returns. This
key-note, besides, is more prevalent in speaking than
in singing: the speaker returns to it and dwells upon
it more constantly. Now, different voices are classed
according as their prevalent tone is found lower or
higher upon the musical scale, as bass, tenor or falsetto.
The first is impressive and majestic, but more liable to
monotony, and it costs the speaker an exertion more
dangerous to the health of the organs of speech to make
it audible to a multitude. The falsetto voice is both
grating and effeminate; and he must have no mean
powers of thought and emotion, who can give his hearers
the pleasure of eloquence with such an instrument of
expression. The tenor voice is therefore usually to be
preferred for public speaking. He whose prevalent
pitch is in this intermediate degree, but who is occasionally capable of a wide compass, from the deep thunder of the bass to the clear clarion-note of the alto, has
the happiest vocal power. The tenor tones are purer,
more resonant and more penetrating than the bass.
You see an evidence of this fact in the manner in which
one calls a person from a distance: he naturally elevates the pitch as well as the loudness of his voice.
Every speaker should therefore cultivate his tenor
tones and use them as his customary key-notes. He
should so speak as to project his aspirations well forward into the fauces; for the organs are thus made
capable of tenfold exertion without detriment to their
health. And especially should he eschew the mischievous trick of affecting solemnity of voice, by sinking it into a guttural bass and suppressing the expiration to the larynx: he who thus swallows his tones will

almost provoke the judicious hearer to say amen! to the disease which he will infallibly contract.

The second capacity of variety which the voice possesses is the *dynamic*—the change of force. This is expressed popularly by the words " loud and soft." It is a different quality from that of pitch ; for the practiced vocalist can utter a note low and loud or high and soft. It is partly by the dynamic change that we effect both rhythm and emphasis. The accented syllable, or the emphatic word, receives more force. Loudness is recognized as the natural expression of anger, triumph, confidence, dogmatism, earnestness and the animated sentiments generally ; while the softer tones are suitable for quiet narration, didactic statement and the expression of the gentle emotions. There is no caution more necessary for the ambitious young speaker, than that he must not be high and loud throughout his discourse. It is not the absolute pitch or dynamic force, but the relative dynamic increment, which pіoduces the impression of power and animation. He, therefore, who was already loudest where the sentiment was quiet, has deprived himself effectually of the power of expressing his rise to more vivid sentiments. Let me also commend to you the all-important rule : Begin softly.[1] Use no more voice at first than is necessary to be audible to the rear benches. Appropriateness usually requires this, because the thoughts and sentiments of the introductory passages are usually calm. Movement demands it ; for if you begin at your loudest, there is then no

---

[1] See the strong concurrence of the Abbé Bautain in this rule, *Art of Extempore Speech*, chap. xx.

louder voice to be employed as you approach your climax. Especially does the economy of your own health and strength exact this policy ; for a sudden and powerful exertion of the voice at once roughens it, irritates the larynx and induces a hoarseness equally distressing to hearer and speaker. But if the organs are warmed to their work gradually until the circulation of the blood is quickened, the secretion of the natural lubricating fluids stimulated, and the whole body nerved by mental excitement, then the force may be gradually increased, and powerful and protracted exertions made with marvellous impunity. At no time, however, should the loudness of the voice be increased to an extravagant degree. A deafening bawl, tearing at once the speaker's throat and the listeners' ears, is the natural expression of no moral emotion : it excites only disgust and fatigue, and disqualifies the voice for future use. "Pray you, avoid it."[1]

Third, the voice varies its expression of sentiment by the greater or less *time* which it expends in uttering syllables. This is the element named by the prosodists quantity. The voice is supposed to occupy twice as much time upon a long syllable as upon a short. The relation of a long to a short is that of a semibreve to a minim, or of a minim to a crotchet, or of a crotchet to a quaver. It is this difference of quantity which makes

---

[1] "Oh, it offends me to the soul to hear a robustious periwig-pated fellow tear a passion to tatters, to very rags, to split the ears of the groundlings, who, for the most part, are capable of nothing but inexplicable dumb-shows and noise. I would have such a fellow whipped for o'erdoing Termagant : it out-Herods Herod. Pray you, avoid it."—*Hamlet : Advice to Players.*

rhythm, or number, and on it are founded all metres.
Quantity also enters into accent and emphasis, as a chief
element of that prominence, which these are designed to
give to particular syllables and words. They are also
marked in part by the greater force or loudness of voice
expended upon them. Not only is the short syllable
more quickly pronounced than the adjacent long, in all
discourse, but the stream of utterance, as a whole, flows
at some times far more rapidly than at others. A slow
or deliberate utterance expresses serious thought, meditation or deliberation of mind and sadness. Accelera-
tion of utterance gives vivid expression to animating
sentiments.

But the voice possesses a fourth power by which it
denotes its most forcible emphasis. This I denominate
ictus. It is not the same with loudness, for a syllable
may be made relatively very loud without *ictus ;* nor is
it the same with brevity, for a forcible *ictus* may be
upon a long syllable. It is the sudden delivery of the
breath upon the beginning of the syllable with an explosive force. This is effected by the very quick and
spasmodic contraction of the muscles of the breast and
larynx, ejecting the air upon the opening of the syllable, like the gases discharged from a fire-arm. But the
current of vowel sound thus explosively begun does not
always terminate as suddenly ; it may be continued into
a syllable both loud and long. This quality, *ictus*, is
exceedingly expressive. It signifies, in argumentative
passages, the highest dogmatic certainty, and in emotional,
the most vehement, sudden and determined passions.
The orator should, therefore, take care how he expends
this most peculiar means of expression upon insignif-

icant statements or unimpressive emotions. The word
made emphatic by dynamic force, elevation of pitch and
ictus at once, is his Olympic thunderbolt; he should
beware how he launches it, save when there is a *nodus
vindice dignus.*

The fifth quality of voice is that intrinsic trait so
hard to describe in words, but so manifest to every good
ear, which the French artists denominate *timbre.* It is
not equivalent to dynamic force, nor to pitch, nor to
ictus, but it is the essential characteristic with which Nature stamps each kind of musical sound, whether loud or
soft, high or low, sudden or protracted. It is the peculiar thrill which each instrument has as its own. Let,
for instance, a violin and a flute, or a piano and a trombone, sound the same note in perfect unison of pitch and
with the same loudness. Every ear perceives that there
are two instruments, not one. Why does not the tone
affect the ear as one? It is because the note of a violin
has its own *timbre* distinct from that of a flute, and a
piano different from a trombone's, although in unison
in every other respect. So the human voice has its own
timbre distinct from all the other sounds of nature. The
voice of a male has a different *timbre* from that of a
female. The latter is pitched naturally one octave higher
than the former. But if the male elevates his voice to
the same pitch with the female *contralto*, and puts it in
unison, the difference is appreciable still. What is yet
more wonderful, the voice of each person has its own
individual *timbre*, by which his friends distinguish it in
singing and speaking amidst other voices in unison with
it. This quality may be greatly improved without ob-
literating or revolutionizing it, by judicious practice.

There is still another power of expression by which the note of the voice indicates profound emotion. The human characteristic of man's voice just described co-operates powerfully here. This is the inimitable gift of man; it is the power of his soûl mysteriously speaking through the corporeal, and almost spiritualizing its materiality. If you listen to a mechanical instrument, a bugle or an organ, you will perceive that the musical movement, the change of dynamic force, of time, of accent, of rhythm, may be expressive of emotion, but the sounds themselves, apart from the movement, have no expression. With the human voice it is different; a single note suggests often some sentiment, and awakens it in the hearer. The feeling in man's voice consists partly in its peculiar *timbre*, but it involves also another element, a peculiar tremulousness, a quiver or thrill, to which the heartstrings never fail to vibrate. Nature has furnished every man's vocal organs with the exquisite nerves which respond unbidden to true emotion. Genuine feeling never fails, in natural conditions, to communicate this tremour to the tones. The child has it spontaneously in every outcry of his transport, his grief, or his terror. Artistic speakers and singers expend boundless labour to imitate it, but only with partial success. If profound emotion is felt, the person of cultivated taste and simplicity of character will find himself clothed with that magic power without effort, and the hearts of hearers will be moved " as the trees of the wood are moved with the wind."

The seventh characteristic of voice to which I would call your attention is *purity of tone*. This is most important to the resonance and penetration, to the smoothness and sweetness, of the voice, and to the health and endurance of the organs of speech. The sound which rasps the hearer's ear always rasps the speaker's throat. Purity is not pitch, nor softness, nor loudness, nor *timbre*, for it may be either present or lacking under every variety of these qualities. It is regularity and unity of the atmospheric waves propagated by a given tone. Every ear recognizes the difference of voices in this respect. The tones of the good speaker enter the ear with the roundness, smoothness and solidity at once of a polished marble shaft. The impure voice seems to us a ragged beam, spongy and meagre in its central body, but swelled out and roughened all over with an investment of horrid *spiculæ*. To explain this differ-ence we must resort to the theory of sound. This phe-nomenon, as you are aware, is the result of a series of little atmospheric billows, propagated by a vibration in some elastic body which is in contact with the air. The increase of pitch is caused by the diminished breadth and greater rapidity of these waves. The air, being a perfectly mobile and elastic medium, obeys the impact of the vibrating body, and receives and transmits just so many wavelets or molecular pulsations per second of time, as that body has vibrations. Now, a pure tone is evidently one in which these little billows are each distinctly defined, uniform in size and duration, and unmingled with any competing or cross-movements of the air. Thus, in a piano, a perfect sounding-board, firmly fastened at its ends, transmits to the air the very series of wavelets received by it from the vibrating chord which is stretched across it. Because the board is one and perfect, that series is regular, uniform and single. The result is a tone of perfect purity. But let us suppose the sounding-board cracked; then the stronger fragment will vibrate more rapidly than the weaker; there will be a mixed pulsation of two sets of wavelets propagated from them into the air, and they will impress the ear with a cracked or impure tone. Again, the very same distress is caused to a sensitive ear by sounding together two musical chords which are not in harmonic relation; we feel the same roughness or jar which characterized the single impure tone. This fact confirms my explanation.

It is clear, hence, that purity of tone is the result of the right control of the larynx and lungs, under the guidance of a good ear. The vocal chords or vibrating cartilages of the larynx, whose pulsations propagate sound from the human throat, are controlled in their tension by nerves and muscles of the greatest delicacy, which obey the speaker's will. One cause of impure tone is, doubtless, that the vocal chords are not kept exactly at an equal tension during the emission of the note, and hence a mixed or crossed series of atmospheric wavelets is produced. Another cause is the ejection of too much breath against those chords; so that the current of air from the lungs, instead of flowing through the aperture *pari passu* with the musical waves, is ejected with a hissing or strident effect. The whisper evinces this, which is the most impure of all the sounds of the human voice, and also demands the greatest expenditure of breath. This virtue of voice must be the result, therefore, first, of the possession of a correct ear and healthy organs of speech; next, of moderation in the expiration of the breath; and last, of attention and care in the management of the throat during the emission of sound.

Purity of tone should, of course, be the usual quality of our speech; but an impure tone is occasionally most expressive, and enhances by contrast the melody of the rest. The sentiment suggested by this roughness is, like itself, harsh and startling. A harrowing catastrophe is revealed in a whisper; rebuke and objurgation naturally assume a strident voice. The introduction of such tones at appropriate passages corresponds, in eloquent speech, to the occasional discords, by which the musician enhances his stream of harmony.

LECTURE XXII.

ACTION.—CONTINUED.

YOU all know, young gentlemen, how important right emphasis is to the point and perspicuity of your utterance. I have not claimed that emphasis is an elementary power of the voice, because, as we have seen, the stress which is placed on the emphatic word may be composed of several elements. It may be made of an increase of dynamic power, of a prolongation of the quantity, of an elevation of the pitch, and of the *ictus* or explosive impulse. Where all these expedients are combined we have an instance of the strongest possible emphasis. Now, it is impossible to indicate by mechanical rules where the stress should fall in the utterance of a sentence. The obvious design of emphasis is to make the word or phrase which receives it more salient than its neighbours. The principle which must govern is consequently this : that those words shall receive the emphasis which are cardinal to the meaning of the sentence. Thus, in the words, " Great is Diana of the Ephesians," the emphatic word is *great,* because the main object of the speaker is to direct attention to that predicate of the idol. So in Luke xxiv. 34, " The Lord is risen indeed," the emphatic words are *is* and *indeed;* because the opinion of the apostle has been, " he has *not* risen ;" they now desire to assert the opposite :

"he *is* risen." In Rom. x. 13, "For whosoever shall call on the name of the Lord shall be saved," the context shows us that *whosoever* is the emphatic word, seeing that the point the apostle makes from this declaration of the prophet is, the invitation is common to Jew and Gentile.

It is, therefore, only a correct appreciation of the meaning of the sentence, which can direct you in placing the emphasis. Does not this fact also evince how essential right emphasis is to a pleasing and perspicuous utterance? It is the chief element of just expression. The pleasure which it gives the hearer is not merely sensuous, like melody of voice, but intellectual and moral also, because it expounds to the ear and understanding the thought of the discourse. There is no viler or more lamentable mannerism, therefore, than the recurrence of emphasis by a mechanical, instead of an intelligent formula. Some speakers fall into the custom of interposing an emphatic word between every eight or twelve, without regard to the demands of the sense. Others, with every second or third paragraph, alternate from soft to loud at the impulse of mere bodily habit. The stress and *ictus* of voice may, in either case, fall on the word or passage to which it is wholly inappropriate; and it is hard to decide whether the effect is to the attentive and judicious listener more ludicrous or tiresome. Perpetual vigilance is the only condition of right rhetorical action.

I trust that you now comprehend the means of acquiring that flexibility of utterance which is so great a grace. The voice of the animated speaker should sway with perpetual undulations, as variable as the tides of thought and feeling which gush through it from the soul. It may change, from loud to soft, from rapid to deliberate, from low to high, from didactic to emotional, from protracted to explosive, or from pure to rough. Not only is this variety true to nature and to the sentiment of oratorical discourse, but it relieves the hearer's ears and the speaker's throat, while it charms the attention and beguiles us of the lapse of time. There is a grave error to which energetic minds are very liable: it is that of attempting to be brilliant, emphatic or impassioned throughout the whole discourse. No monotony is so dreary as that of the speech which is monotonously boisterous. Take your model here from Nature. She does not thunder all the year; she gives us sunshine, gentle breezes, a sky checkered with lights and shades, the stiffening gale, and sometimes the rending storm. So no hearer can endure a tempest of rhetoric throughout the discourse. An appearance of unremitting and equal intensity is insincere, for no man's soul actually remains in that state throughout a discourse. Flow and ebb characterize human emotions as truly as the seas, and affectation is always, in the orator, the damning sin. I have already indicated that the impression of movement and climax is not according to the absolute, but the relative force of the action. It is the change from the less energetic to the more energetic, which affects the hearer. Now he who, from the first, has risen to his highest level of animation, has left himself no room to rise farther; he has, therefore, wholly deprived himself of the means for signalizing a new access of awakening ideas or emotion. There are, in some mountainous regions, table lands which are thousands of feet above the level of the ocean, but when the traveller has once ascended into them, he finds them as flat and wearisome, and sometimes as malarious, as the marshes next the shore. Picturesque scenery is only composed of diversified hills and vales.

Need I remind you that the action of the sacred orator should always possess that profound simplicity which we saw was necessary for his style? The reasons which demand it are the same. Their application is so obvious that I need not repeat them; I only renew my emphatic testimony in their favour.

The second part of action is *gesture*. If you will recall the strict, etymological meaning of this Latin word, you will have a correct conception of what I include in it. It is the carrying, the port of the outer man in speaking. Do not now suppose that I am about to give you a code of rules in detail, commanding you to expand the arms when a certain sentiment is uttered, to bow the head at another, to strike downward with the hands at another, to frown at another. Such a set of motions, borrowed from abroad and practiced with premeditation, could only make an insufferable coxcomb. The essential requisite of gesture is, that it must be self-prompted: it must be the unpremeditated expression of the speaker's impulse. I am ready to make two admissions, yea, to claim these two facts as of high importance: that a graceful port is advantageous to the preacher, and that there is a natural sign-language, which recognizes the correspondence of certain gestures and looks to certain thoughts and feelings. But the former must be gained, not by deliberate artifice in the act of speaking, but by the habitudes of good society, by self-control, and by the culture of the principles of sincerity, courtesy, modesty and dignity, which make the true gentleman. A graceful port in public speaking is not, generically, different from the same accomplishment in the parlour. Now, when the youth has only gotten to that stage where he moves, speaks, sits, walks, bows, in calculated and mechanical compliance with the rules he is learning from his dancing-master; when every person of experience is reminded, by every motion he makes, of the back-board and the trammels and the drill of posture-making, do they call his manners graceful? His awkwardness is only illustrated and made more grotesque. He must accustom himself to good society, and especially must he rise above his crude self-importance and conceit, to a temper of unaffected modesty and benevolence, until ease and propriety of movement are as natural to him and as unstudied, as the flutter of the bird and the gambols of the squirrel are to them. Then only is he called a graceful man in society—graceful because he no longer studies self-display and is no longer acting a part. A graceful carriage in the pulpit is to be acquired in the same way; and until you are so habituated to appropriate postures and movements that you fall into them without effort—because you cannot without effort avoid it—you are only the more awkward the more you practice the artifices of gesture.

The intercourse of barbarians by signs, who have no common language, the wonderful art of communicating with the deaf and dumb, and the effects of pantomimic acting, teach us that looks and gestures have, to an astonishing extent, a natural correspondence with ideas.

He who is master of this sign-language has, indeed, an almost magic power. When the orator can combine it with the spoken language, he acquires thereby exceeding vivacity of expression. Not only his mouth, but his eyes, his features, his fingers, speak. The hearers read the coming sentiment upon his countenance and limbs almost before his voice reaches their ears : they are both spectators and listeners ; every sense is absorbed in charmed attention. You may ask me : Should not the preacher study to possess this power ? I answer : Yes, by all means ; but it is the wrong time to study it when you are in the actual delivery of your discourse, because, unless the looks and hands speak the unstudied language of Nature in their pantomime, they are false and displeasing. The foundation for this power of expression must be possessed first, in a quick and just sensibility. The public speaker should then study the gestures of natural feeling by observing the port of children, of gifted and animated women in social converse, and of true orators. When he sees the right motion coupled with the right sentiment by one of these, his own heart will avouch it and his mind will remember it. The satisfaction and sense of power which he will experience, in employing this vehicle of expression for his own animated sentiments, will soon teach him to use his acquisitions without effort. Let him now so master his subject by faithful preparation, when about to preach, that he shall be thoroughly at ease touching his command over it. And let him also master his self-importance, his conceit, his lust of applause, so as to forget himself in his sacred task. Let him throw himself into his topic without taking care

for gesture, and the gesture will take care of itself. I
would testify to you (I pray you note my testimony)
that constraint, awkwardness, exaggeration in the rhetorical action usually proceed from one or both of these
two causes—the embarrassment of the mind from the
consciousness of deficient preparation and mastery of
the subject, or the embarrassment of the self-love from
overweening concern about one's own appearance. Let
your heart be right; let your preparation be perfect,
and your previous social training will suggest the right
gesture.

You will perceive a close analogy between this precept and the advice which I gave you concerning style,
that you should write fluently and without stopping to
chill your vein at that time by debating forms of locu-
tion. But I urged you, after the work of composition
was done, to subject your writing to severe review. The
like review should be made of your action after you
have spoken, and for the same purpose. The manner
of the sermon which has been uttered is, of course, irrevocable; you devote that season of lassitude and repose
which follows the toil of delivery to this process of
severe recollection and criticism, for the sake of future
sermons. While you sit or recline in solitude, recov-
ering your strength, you will recall the inflections and
emphasis of your voice, your posture and the movements of your limbs, the changes of your countenance,
every part of your action, and will pass sentence upon
it. You will be conscious that in one passage your emphasis was erroneous, that in another the force of your
voice was extravagant, that in another your movements
of body were awkward and inappropriate. Every such

recollection disciplines your taste and self-control for future efforts. When you enter the pulpit next, your watchfulness and self-recollection should exercise themselves only as safeguards, not as prompters of artifice. Their influence will be only repressive of erroneous action, not suggestive; for the heart itself should be the only positive prompter of the action. Let the gestures and intonations make themselves, only, under the watch of your self-consciousness.

But you may ask, How can the speaker recollect himself so closely, if he obeys the injunction of generous self-forgetfulness urged in other places? You may suppose that I have been inconsistent in these precepts. But you will find, that a generous and sincere excitement in a well-disciplined soul does not confuse the self-consciousness, but only makes it more distinct and quick. That species of passion which leaves a man ignorant of what he is doing is too extravagant for rhetoric, and is the characteristic of a weak and confused mind. If you find that you are swept along to that extreme, it is because you have not thoroughly mastered your subject by preparation. The brave and able soldier in the heat of battle is as much more self-possessed than at ordinary seasons, as he is more aroused. His senses are not squandered by the fire of his soul, but collected; his excitement only makes every faculty more tense and collected. It should be so with the orator. While his soul flashes with the white heat of passion, it is self-poised and steady as the sun in his orbit. Let me again cite the invaluable testimony of Shakespeare's experience: " He uses all gently, for in the very torrent, tempest and (as I may say) whirlwind of his passion, he must acquire and beget a temperance that may give it smoothness."

As I enjoined simplicity of utterance, so I would require moderation and dignity of gesture. The posture in the pulpit should be steady and erect, but not immoveable. The action should never degenerate into mimicry, or theatrical pantomime. While animated and expressive, it should ever retain the gravity and earnestness of the gospel herald.

There are two expedients of preparation against which I wish to utter my protest. The one is that of going through the action of a discourse before a mirror. Those who practice it claim, that it is legitimate the speaker should use this means to ascertain how his gesture will appear to his audience; that he may in time correct what is awkward. The objection is that the audience is not there; that consequently the speaker does not exactly realize the feelings of the actual orator in the presence of his hearers, and that his gestures will therefore be artificial and false. The moral effect of such preparation is moreover unhealthy. It fosters an unmanly attention to manner rather than matter, and I am persuaded that its tendency is to degrade the style of action. The other usage is that of declaiming aloud in solitude the discourse to be delivered.[1] Here again my objection is that the process is unavoidably artificial; the audience is not present, and the author has not the unaffected emotion which he will feel, if his heart is right before God, in the actual delivery. The only re-

---

[1] Cicero de Orat., L. i., c. 33, § 150: Vere etiam illud dicitur, *Perverse dicere homines perverse dicendo facillime consequi.*

sult of his solitary practice is therefore mischievous. The intonations which he so laboriously associates with each particular passage are deficient, heartless, inanimate, or else exaggerated and fantastical; and when his soul is really thrown into the current of his discourse in its actual delivery, he will find them, if he is to speak at all well, erroneous, and obstructions to be gotten out of the way at the critical moment. If he had devoted all his labour to the preparation of his thought and style, and left the utterance to the prompting of the moment, together with the guidance of his general preparation, the tones would have been fresher and more appropriate. Should not the public speaker have any solitary practice, then, in utterance? I answer, yes; much of it. But it will be better for him to use any other composition whatever for such practice, than the one which he is about to deliver. Oratorical utterance and gesture must be at the moment unstudied, otherwise they cannot have the charm of nature. The object of practice in private, then, is only the general culture of the voice, taste and manner. If you attempt by such means to decide in advance precisely how this particular sentence, or that, is to be delivered, you will assuredly decide ill; because it is a matter which can only be well decided by the natural impulse of the moment.

LECTURE XXIII.

MODES OF PREPARATION.

THE last subject of discussion touching the sermon is the mode of preparation. Three modes are recognized as allowable—writing, writing and memorizing, and extemporizing. I will speak of each of these in turn.

Reading a manuscript to the people can never, with any justice, be termed preaching. Even if the matter and style are rhetorical, the action cannot be, but it is almost impossible that the structure either of thought or language should be such, when the invention is performed in solitude and at the writing-desk. Some men of powerful genius have indeed, by long practice, acquired the talent of so representing to themselves the circumstances of public discourse, while engaged in solitary composition, as almost to overcome this obstacle; they do indeed write as an orator should speak. But these are the exceptions. In the delivery of the sermon there can be no exception in favour of the mere reader. How can he whose eyes are fixed upon the paper before him, who performs the mechanical task of reciting the very words inscribed upon it, have the inflections, the emphasis, the look, the gesture, the flexibility, the fire, of oratorical action? Mere reading, then, should be sternly banished from the pulpit, except in those rare cases in which the didactic purpose supersedes the rhetorical, and exact verbal accuracy is more essential than eloquence.

Yet there is a use of the written sermon in the pulpit, which has given us many respectable and some powerful preachers. These write, with the greatest possible care and with rhetorical structure, a manuscript having two-thirds the length of the intended sermon. After the final verbal corrections, they spend many hours of the intensest toil, not in committing to memory the words written, but in learning the ideas and their exact order. They even fix in their memory the geography of their manuscript (if I may so apply the term), in order that they may know, without search, on what part of any page to find the beginning of a given paragraph or thought, in case the ardour of delivery shall have carried the eye and mind for a season away from the paper. For this purpose they go over their sermon eight, twelve or even twenty times, until their recollection of the order of thought is indelible, and until the whole soul is possessed and fired with the subject. They then take the manuscript into the pulpit and open it before them. The knowledge that they can recur to it at every moment sets them at ease from the fear of losing their thread or hesitating for words. The whole train of thoughts and the face of the manuscript are so fixed in the memory, that few and rapid glances enable them to give almost the very words of the writing; but they do not make any conscious effort to adhere to, or depart from those words. They feel that they can do the former at any instant, for the words are before them, and they were selected with care, for their appropriateness; but if an impulse possesses them to modify the language of any passage, it is also easy to do this. They select with facility either of these alternatives which the awakened and impassioned mind prefers at the moment; and in many places, where nearly the exact language of the manuscript is, in fact, retained, yet the utterance really has the quality of *extempore* eloquence, because there is a process of invention at the time. They use these words not at the mere dictate of eye and memory (they are not mechanically read from the paper, and they had not been memorized for the purpose), but at the dictate of their conscious fitness. They also indulge freely the impulse to add new thoughts and images, suggested chiefly during the faithful study of the completed manuscript. Their thorough familiarity with the whole structure of the sermon, and the quickened condition of their own powers, enable them to venture these additions with safety. They experience also that ennobling *momentum* which Cicero compares so beautifully to the progress of the ship after the oars are dropped. [1] The career acquired from the delivery of the parts carefully prepared bears their minds through that which is added *impromptu*, and enables them to give it coherent elegance and vigour of expression. The result is, that the manuscript of thirty minutes' length is expanded to forty-five. In such a use of the manuscript, also, the eyes are but little occupied with it, and the preacher is at liberty to hold much converse of look and countenance with the auditors.

---

[1] De Orat., L. i., c. xxxiii., § 153.

Now, this process is manifestly not reading: it is free from many of the objections made against that indolent and slovenly practice. •If the liberty of eye and thought and emotion which I have described can be acquired, then this method approaches very near the merit of the best *extempore* preaching.

The second method is that of writing a discourse and committing it to memory *verbatim*, to be recited in the pulpit. I should object to this way, as I did to the read sermon, thât the structure and style would seldom be truly rhetorical. Nor can we expect the action to be good. The mind, painfully occupied with the toil of verbal recollection, cannot realize to itself the subject, or feel the emotions which it should inspire. The air is almost unavoidably constrained, and the utterance artificial. The mechanical labour of committing to memory is sure to entail some mannerism, which is fixed as firmly on the preacher's habits as the words are in his mind. Hence, preachers who have spoken *memoriter* have all displayed some trick or foible, from the famous Père Bourdaloue, who always declaimed with his eyes fast shut, to the present day. This method, like any other which fixes both matter and language in advance, robs the speaker of all those advantages that I shall point out as belonging peculiarly to *extempore* speech. Unless one has a remarkable verbal memory (a gift which I have never seen sufficient reason to regard as indicative of vigour of mind), the exact memorizing of the very words of a long discourse must cost a great amount of labour, and that of the most wearying and irksome kind. The main objection to this method may be practically summed up in a single question : How deficient must that man be in the mastery of his mother-tongue, who judges it necessary to replace that attainment (which should be so fully the orator's) by an expedient so toilsome and injurious ? No man is entitled to call himself a master-workman in the rhetorical art, until he has made language his facile tool by polite and correct conversation, by good reading and by careful composition.

By the last remark I have intimated already my opinion that the true method of speaking is the *extempore*. But do not understand me as sanctioning the delivery of a sermon without premeditation, save in extraordinary emergencies. The extempore sermon is least of all *impromptu*. I mean by it a discourse in which the thought has been perfectly prearranged, but the words, except in cardinal propositions, are left to the free suggestions of the moment. The preparation of the ideas may even be by reducing them regularly to a written form, provided the words written are not imposed upon the memory. Some have recommended that the *extempore* speaker should prepare thus, but, as I conceive, unwisely ; for the verbal dress of the writing-desk, always unrhetorical to some degree, will thus be associated with the ideas just sufficiently to embarrass the speaker, in seeking at the moment of utterance, for the right words. I am so far from recommending *extempore* preaching to you as an expedient for saving labour, that I regard it as demanding the most thorough preparation of all. This is doubtless the reason that it is not more practised by ministers of education who address cultivated audiences.

But the advantages of the *extempore* method are de-

cisive with the man who has a true ideal of oratory.   I
believe that no man makes his nearest approximation
to that ideal except when he speaks *extempore*, or in a
manner which is equivalent to it; for then is his oration a true action, which it never can become by mere
reading or recitation.   The capital advantage is, that the
mind is required to perform over again the labour of
invention, during the actual delivery of the discourse.
It is thus aroused and nerved.   The condition of its
success is, that it must again represent to itself in a living
form the whole thought and emotion of the discourse;
that it must, in a word, recreate it in the act of delivering it.   It is only such a discourse, actually born in its
delivery (if it is a second birth), a living progeny of
the soul, that has true movement.   But he who reads or
recites is only delineating the dead outline of what once
feebly lived in his mind.   The ill-starred experience
of all of us teaches us, that it is possible to do this without having the matter of our discourse penetrate any
deeper into our own souls than the memory, and therefore they cannot penetrate the souls of our hearers; for
the speaker can only affect them with the truth as he
affects himself with it.   Eloquence is not the mere communication of a set of dry notions; it is a sympathy, a
spiritual infection, a communion of life and action between two souls, a projection of the orator's thought,
conviction, emotion and will into the mind and heart
of the audience.   Nothing, therefore, is a true oration
which is not a life, a spiritual action, transacted in the
utterance.

From this position you can easily understand the advantages which are usually and correctly claimed in the

books of rhetoric for *extempore* speech. It institutes a commerce of eye and countenance between the speaker and his hearers, by which they mutually stimulate each other. The mind thus roused, having the advantage of its previous premeditation and thorough knowledge of the subject, grasps it with more vigour than it had ever done in solitude. Indeed, all the powers of the soul are now exalted—reasoning, memory, imagination, suggestion, sensibility. More direct and luminous views of logical truth now flash athwart the subject, like beams of sunlight. Glowing illustrations and images now teem in the imagination. More appropriate and burning words now arise unbidden than he could ever have excogitated in cold blood. The emotions of the hour dictate an action natural, flexible and animated. But were the preacher confined to his manuscript, these suggested words and feelings must have been excluded. If there has been a thorough previous training, when the words are furnished from the impulse of the moment the structure of sentences will be more simple and direct. The natural animation of the orator's mind will deliver him from monotony, give flexibility of style, and protect him from tiresome artifices of intonation. The justice of these views is evinced by that fact which has been so often remarked, that only the *extempore* method is ever attempted in the bar, the senate and the popular assemblage. The good sense of mankind rejects the idea of reading or reciting discourses here, as little short of an absurdity. Another forcible argument for cultivating the power of *extempore* speech is found in the fact, that the preacher is often required by duty to proclaim the gospel in places and times where written preparation is impossible, and where it could not be used if it were provided. The man who remains unable to perform his appointed function efficiently in such circumstances is simply recreant to duty.

But there are serious obstacles in the way of true success in *extempore* speech. I shall not count among these the difficulty of finding words when they are not premeditated, nor the danger of wandering from the right line of discourse, nor the impossibility of having a correct style. These are not the serious obstacles. You will find that mere fluency is the easiest and cheapest of all gifts to which the public speaker aspires. And when I say this, I include in the term fluency not only abundance of words, but a certain degree of correctness in their connection. The orator's difficulty is that it is too easy to be fluent. The difficult thing for the *extempore* speaker is to make his words scarce. You will find (what you may not now suppose) that abundant verbiage will come to you in *extempore* speech with far more facility than the direct, apt and simple structure, and that your constant temptation will be to employ the former for hiding and supplementing your poverty in regard to the latter. You will be tempted to pour out forty words because you cannot, as you are conscious you ought to do, express the thought in twelve. In a word, the great difficulty in the way of *extempore* eloquence is to avoid verbal redundancy, and to make the style compact, nervous and clear. To the inexperienced it seems perhaps paradoxical to affirm that the half-trained preacher finds it easier to construct *extempore*, a long and complicated sentence which shall contain no glaring grammatical error, than a short and direct one which shall adequately express his sense. But it is true, and this is his great temptation. The reason is plain to a little consideration. A complex sentence with many members offers the speaker many alternative ways of protracting and concluding it. Hence, if he cannot on the instant recall the preferred phrase or structure, he can procrastinate the issue, while he discovers some other of these numerous ways for getting creditably out of the labyrinth. But the simple, brief, compact sentence (which is the proper form for oratory) is exacting. It demands the right phrase by its very directness, and demands it at once. It requires to be concluded without dallying. The main obstacle you have to overcome, young gentlemen, in order to speak *extempore*, is redundancy and intricacy.

The danger of becoming confused, and totally losing the thread, is one which can always be overcome by diligence in preparation and by use. The tendency of our self-confident and garrulous age is not in that direction. Would that it were more so! I should hail it as a positively good omen, in these days of self-sufficiency, to see an overweening young speaker break down utterly, as did the great Robert Hall in one of his early essays, and stand dumbfounded before his audience. Far better this, than the self-possession of shallow conceit, the uniform prognostic of triviality and weakness. Such a mortification might cure his vanity and spur his indolence, and teach him something of that solemn diffidence appropriate to so responsible a task. The danger of wandering from the right line of thought may also be easily overcome by diligent preparation, and the self-command it confers. The *extempore* speaker will freely admit new suggestions into his plan : this is one of the privileges which gives its value to the method; but for all that, he will not lose sight of his plan nor forget the due proportion between its parts. The unity of his projected discourse has already that control of his own mind and heart which he designs it to acquire over his hearers, and this will very certainly bring him back from all his oscillation to his main intent, like the needle to its pole. If an *extempore* speech is more rambling than the written, it is only because the speaker has neglected his preparation. Nor is negligence of style a difficulty very hard to overcome. It ought surely to be no impossible thing for an educated man to acquire such a command of his mother-tongue, as to be able to form it readily into simple sentences without error of syntax, especially when the mind is invigorated by the excitement of public address. If you are truly masters of your thoughts, you will have no lack of correct words.

The great danger which attends the *extempore* preacher is that he will, after a time, abuse his facility. The capacity for fluent speech is one which is very easily expanded after the first successes. The multifarious avocations of the pastor often furnish a pretext for self-indulgence, and tempt to the neglect both of general study and of special preparation. The fluent declaimer can, for a time, cover his deficiency of matter by his readiness of speech. He avails himself of this unlucky resort, and further indulges his indolence. His fecundity of mind is lost, his freshness is exhaled, he gradually comes to that final state in which the mind can do nothing but run the dull round of its little circle of commonplaces. Whatever may be the text, the sermon is substantially the same. The Church presents but too many illustrations of this danger. They are sad, and should be awakening to our souls. You see here and there those clerical drones who have long ceased to interest or control any one, and who are only endured by churches which are dying by inches under their charge; yet those who are older than you can remember the bright auspices under which these very men began their ministry. Fluent, animated and energetic, they were followed by admiring crowds; their preaching seemed to be blessed of God; their friends prophesied for them a splendid career. But they learned gradually to abuse their facility, and to relax their studies: the end is what you see. The young minister might well pray, were it lawful, that a premature death might cut him down in this auspicious springtime, rather than that he should reach his autumn, only to disgrace his early promise by this crime. One safeguard against this abuse of the *extempore* method is the constant use of the pen. Every minister must write much, whether he carries anything into the pulpit or not. The best system for most young ministers, perhaps, is to write half their sermons, to make the manuscripts as perfect in every respect as their utmost abilities and care can effect, and then either to leave them in their desks, or use them according to the method I described first. Let the other half of the sermons be premeditated as thoroughly as is possible, until nothing remains to be added to the mental preparation of the matter, and then preached *extempore*. But the constant practice of writing is not a sure safeguard; for you will soon find that there may be *extempore* writing as well as *extempore* speaking. The only certain defence is religious principle, a conscience tender and honest, and a devoted heart, which shall make you continue faithful to your studies to the end.

It remains that I shall state the means by which *extempore* ability is to be acquired. The first upon which I insist is careful writing.[1] The abundant and painstaking use of the pen is necessary to give you correctness, perspicuity and elegance of language, and to make these easy to you. No man ever learns to compose a sermon at his desk in rhetorical language save by speaking *extempore* under the rhetorical impulse; so no man ever learns to speak well *extempore* save by learning to write well. I have already said that the use of this writing is not to prepare words in the closet to be delivered in the pulpit, but to prepare the mind for clothing its thoughts with right words without premeditation of language. This species of training cannot be omitted if you would speak well *extempore*.[2]

---

[1] Cicero de Orat., L. i., c. xxxiii., § 150. "Caput autem est, quod (ut vere dicam) minime facimus: est enim magni laboris, quem plerique fugimus; *quam plurimum scribere*. STILUS OPTIMUS ET PRÆSANTISSIMUS DICENDI EFFECTOR AC MAGISTER, neque injuria."

[2] Quinctil., L. x., c. vii., § 29. "Ac nescio an utrumque, quem studio et cura fecerimus, invicem prosit, ut scribendo dicamus diligentius, dicendo scribamus facilius. Scribendum ergo, quoties licebit; si id non dabitur; cogitandum."

M. Bautain, *Art of Extempore Speech*, ch. iii., § 4. "The pen is the scalpel which dissects the thoughts, and never, except when you write down what you behold internally, can you succeed in clearly discerning all that is contained in a conception, or in obtaining its well-marked scope. You should therefore begin by learning to write, in order to give yourself a right account of your own thoughts, before

Your whole education, reading and social intercourse are, in a certain sense, a preparation for *extempore* eloquence. All should tend to furnish you with ideas, to train your literary taste, and to give readiness and versatility to your powers. Here let me urge that you make every sentence you utter, in your most familiar conversation, a drill in correctness of speech.[1] Speak always with propriety, that it may become as natural and easy for you to speak thus as to breathe. You will, of course, not apprehend me as inciting you to the affectation of clothing your familiar converse in stilted and pedantic phrase : this would be silly in the pulpit also ; but you should speak always clearly and properly, allowing in yourself no grammatical errors, no slouched and involuntary forms of expression. But the other great means is constant and untiring practice. The man who is training himself for the pulpit should scarcely allow a day to elapse without an exercise in continuous *extempore* speech. Do you ask me how a student shall find an audience daily? I answer: Let him speak without one : let him go into the forest, let him select a cluster of trees as his imaginary auditors, let him state audibly and connectedly to them, without book, some series of thoughts with which his mind is

---

you venture yourself to speak. They who have not learned this first, speak, in general, badly and with difficulty, unless, indeed, they have that fatal facility, a thousand times worse than hesitation or than silence, which drowns thought in floods of words or in a torrent of copiousness."

[1] Quinctil., L. x., c. vii., § 28. "Ne id quidem tacendum, quod eidem Ciceroni placet, nullum nostrum unquam negligentem esse sermonem ; quicquid loquemur ubicunque, sit pro sua scilicet portione perfectum."

charged: it may be a narrative which he has read, the outline of an argument he has just learned from his text-books, a line of thought which has been unfolding itself in his mind. Of course he will not attempt, in such an exercise, to work himself up to any oratorical fire (unless it comes spontaneously he will have none), but his object will be only to cultivate readiness in correct expression. He should discard all ambition and pomp of language in these exercises, and make it his chief aim to be perfectly grammatical, intelligible and direct. He should frame no sentence which is not clear, simple and manageable to his own mind. It would be better that he should begin with sentences of a single member, like those in which children make their earliest essays in narration, provided they were correct, than that he should permit himself ever to utter a sentence in whose intricacies he became entangled. Let your practice be always guarded by the wise caution I have already cited from Cicero (p. 339, note): "*Perverse dicere homines perverse dicendo facillime consequi.*" You should speak to your trees audibly and continuously, refusing to yourselves any stoppage, and also consulting propriety of utterance as far as your attention enables you. These exercises, perpetually repeated, will at length make the powers pliable or supple for their work, like the fingers of a practised artisan. Indeed, he who would be an orator must drill himself, until his mastery over classic speech shall be as ready, as easy, as versatile, as that of the accomplished musician over the keys of his instrument. To this untiring private practice should be added such public exercises as circumstances permit. Every proper occasion should be seized to speak *extempore* to an actual audience, but it should be only with the severest preparation. It were better to have no practice, than that which fixes your faults of style and utterance into habits.

The *extempore* sermon, as I have urged, is not less diligently studied than the written, as to its matter. There will be no difference in the manner of collecting and arranging the materials for the two classes. I have, in a previous note, explained to you the convenient expedients for assisting the mind by written *memoranda* in the work of comparison and arrangement. It is an excellent practice to write out the plan of the *extempore* sermon in a " brief," or extended and methodical *syllabus*, where all important ideas are briefly stated in their intended order, but not in the language which is to be employed in preaching. The divisions and subdivisions of this brief should then be indelibly fixed in the memory. Remember in this part of your task, that when the work of recollection is to be performed you may be embarrassed, excited, and perhaps confused. You must stamp your outline on your memory so deeply, that it will be impossible for you to fail in its prompt recall. And especially must the relation of every part to the central idea and dominant impression of the sermon be distinctly apprehended. Then it will be a matter of small moment whether this brief be carried into the pulpit or not. Perhaps the better way will be to accustom yourself, from the first, to dispensing with it, and to facing your audience entirely untrammeled by paper. But if you carry this or any other form of manuscript into the pulpit, you will find the handwriting a thing of no small practical moment. You should write remembering that it must be read by a rapid glance, and the characters should be large, the ink-strokes strong, the words well separated and block-like in arrangement, and the capitals marking the beginnings of paragraphs and sentences prominent.

You will find a number of books of plans, or skeletons of sermons, obtruded upon you as helps in your preparation. These you may safely regard as usually rubbish. They are the work of inferior men, as one might surmise in advance; for a true genius could hardly fail to find something better to do with his powers, than to construct these pulpit crutches for lazy and incompetent people. But whatever the merit of another man's plan, it cannot be borrowed by you. If you attempt it, you will find to your cost that it is the most unsatisfactory of follies to attempt to build a sermon on it. The idea of the plan must be your own conception, or to you it cannot have life. Its invention in your own mind can alone give spirit and interest to your discussion. But when you consider the effect of these illicit helps in enervating your own powers by suspending their functions, you will agree with me, that the habitual use of them is positively criminal. I would warmly recommend, on the other hand, the study of some sermons of the great masters, such as Samuel Davies, John M. Mason and Robert Hall. You should analyze them in every direction, to detect the elements of their power. It would be useful to you, after two or three careful readings of a sermon, to prepare a syllabus of its members and divisions, as a training for yourself in this part of your own work. Imbibe their taste, seek to have

your powers suffused with their spirit and quickened by
their energy and devotion.   The contemplation of a noble model ennobles the soul.

I wish to close this discussion of the different modes
of preparation with one remark, which is the most important of all.   Whatever may be your method, excellence can only be the result of strenuous effort.   He
who labours most on each sermon is usually the best
preacher.   Let me impress you with the high responsibility of ascending the pulpit, and beseech you to form
a lofty ideal.   He who proposes to sway the souls of a
multitude, to be their teacher, to lay his hands upon
their heart-strings, to imbue them with his passion and
will, makes an audacious attempt.   But nothing less
than this is true preaching.   It behooves the man who
attempts this high emprise to have every power of his
soul trained and braced like an athlete, and to perfect
his equipment at every point, with the painful care of
the commander who is about to join battle with a powerful enemy.   He begins the adventure with a solemn
awe, an anxious diffidence, whose palpitations nothing
but a heroic will controls.   The great Athenian statesman, Pericles, the model upon which Demosthenes
formed himself, was wont to say, that so solemn did
he deem the act of speaking, he could not ascend the
bema without an anxious invocation to the immortal gods
for their assistance.   Surely, the minister of a divine
Redeemer should mount his pulpit with a more holy
dread, by as much as he discusses a more sacred theme
and more everlasting destinies.   To preach a sermon is
a great and awful task.   Woe to that man, who slights
it with a perfunctory preparation and a careless heart !

LECTURE XXIV.

PUBLIC PRAYER.

YOU are aware, young gentlemen, that, during the "Dark Ages," the disgraceful incompetency of the clergy resulted, first, in the introduction of forms of prayer, and, second, in the customary disuse of the divinely-appointed ordinance of preaching. The Reformation reversed all this. It has become the characteristic of the Popish religion that it makes the liturgical service nearly the whole of public worship, and of the Reformed that it makes the sermon the prominent part. This difference is imprinted upon the very speech of the people. The Papist says: "I go to mass;" the Protestant, "I go to preaching." Many ignorant Protestants depreciate the devotional acts of the sanctuary too much. I would protest against this unseemly and mischievous extreme. It is for this reason, in part, that I would give great emphasis to the minister's duty of preparing himself thoroughly for public prayer, and performing his part in it with propriety. I trust you will not graduate the relative importance which I attach to the sermon and the prayers, according to the relative space here bestowed on the two subjects; for the principles which regulate pulpit eloquence apply also to the devotional parts of it. I beg you to consider me, once for all, as applying them all to this important branch of your duty.

I deem that the minister is as much bound to prepare himself for praying in public as for preaching.
The negligence with which many preachers leave their
prayers to accident, while they lay out all their strength
on their sermons, is most painfully suggestive of unbelief toward God and indifference to the edification of
their brethren.   When the sermon is appropriate, nervous, finished, but the prayers of the same minister are
rambling, aimless and nerveless, how distressing is the
impression upon every pious heart!   This lamentable
indifference in the spiritual guides accounts sufficiently
for the feeling which the worldly part of our congregations so plainly betray, that in their eyes the sermon is
the only part of the proceeding which can possibly interest them, while the devotional acts are only the wearisome "grace before meat," the irksome form which
detains them from their indulgence, to be evaded in any
way not positively indecent.

Some affect to think that the spiritual nature of the
exercise ought to preclude preparation ; that because it
is the Holy Ghost which teaches us to pray, we should
not attempt to teach ourselves.   This argument is a
remnant of fanatical enthusiasm.   Should we not also
preach with the Spirit?   Why, then, do we not extend the same sophisms to inhibit preparation of the
sermon ?   The answer is, that the aid of the Holy Spirit
does not suspend the exercise of our own faculties.   He
works through them as his instruments, and in strict
conformity to their rational nature.   He assists and
elevates them.   He helps us also in prompting us to
help ourselves.

Bethink yourselves, my young brethren, that it is no

slight undertaking to guide a whole congregation to the throne of the heavenly grace, and to be their spokesman to God. To speak for God to men is a sacred and responsible task. To speak for men to God is not less responsible, and is more solemn. The public prayers of the pastor are apt to be the models of the devotions of his people; when he leads them in prayer he is really teaching them to pray. Prayer is the Christian's vital breath. Prayer is the appointed channel of his whole redemption. How mischievous is that man who by his coldness, inappropriateness, irreverence, vagueness, unbelief, chills the aspirations and obstructs the access of a whole multitude which he should have led up to the mercy-seat!

The many blemishes which we hear in public prayers are to be traced to two sources: first, deficient piety, and, second, deficient preparation. It is this delinquency to duty which gives the advocates of an enforced liturgy all their plausible objections against *extempore* prayer in public worship. We, who claim liberty from such restrictions, and who assert the superiority of the free method of the scriptural saints, are bound to commend our opinion by our practice. I shall recite some of the blemishes by which the Christian ear and heart are most often offended, in order to guard you against them.

It is a grave fault to repeat frequently and mechanically any *formula* of words; as interjections, the names and titles of God, or favourite phrases. Inordinate repetition grates on every ear. These "words, of course," betray either odious mannerisms, or a vacuity of heart in the sacred service which is utterly profane. We sometimes hear the name of the majestic Being to whom prayer is addressed repeated so heedlessly, that it is a literal "taking of it in vain." In a word, the mere commonplaces of devotional language are not the dress in which that soul clothes its desires, which has a true errand at the throne of grace. Such a heart will be very far from going to seek after the novelties and pedantries of language, but the sincerity of its emotions will give a certain freshness to its language of request. This mechanical phrase is obnoxious to every charge of formalism, monotony and lack of appropriate variety, which we lodge against an unchangeable liturgy, while it has none of its literary merit and dignified and tender associations.

He who speaks to God for others is bound to eschew all provincialisms, solecisms, vulgarisms and grammatical errors in his language. He should never be guilty of thrusting into the mouths of worshippers such locutions as the request that God would "solemnize their souls," or that he would "grant to bestow" his grace. You will have need here for great jealousy of the imitation of the current phrases; because usage has blinded even many educated men to odious blemishes, and given these faults a species of pious license. But why should the devotions of those who have some feeling for their mother-tongue be disturbed by violations of her integrity? Does God take pleasure in bad grammar? He has spoken to us in good Greek, thereby showing us that he expects us to address him in good English.

We observe that desire is always definite when it is earnest; our petitions, therefore, should be definite also. But this does not excuse an indelicate or trivial minuteness of detail. The pastor may feel that, in asking temporal blessings, after the example of the petition, "Give us this day our daily bread," he may appropriately ask for "rain from heaven and fruitful seasons, filling our hearts with food and gladness;" but good taste should prevent his descending to such particulars as that the bloom of the peach might escape the spring frosts. To pray nominally to God, but really at a fellow-creature, to flatter or revile in prayer, to insinuate a witticism or sarcasm, to arouse by allusions to party strifes, political prejudices and asperities,— all these are nauseous to a true taste and a genuine piety as well. The man who is really inspired with the spirit of prayer will be incapable of such crimes against propriety. What must be the unbelief and irreverence of that man who can make a pretext of approach to a God so pure, majestic and good, for displaying his smartness or his malice, or for loading the ear of the eternal Judge with flatteries of a fellow-culprit?

Half-educated or spiritually proud men frequently indulge in an indecent familiarity with the Most High, under the pretence of filial nearness and importunity. It is the amazing privilege of justified believers to call this exalted Being their "Father which is in heaven," and, through their divine Advocate, to approach him with filial trust; but this joyful affection should always be tempered with adoring reverence and tender contrition. The proper language for the accepted sinner before the mercy-seat is, therefore, that of profound veneration. Especially are all fondling and amatory expressions, addressed to either person of the Trinity, abhorrent to the truly pious heart. Our affection for the Author of our redemption should be too unique, and elevated by its sanctity too far above all carnal emotions, to borrow their language. The prophets and apostles surely apprehended God, and knew how to praise him better than we; but they are never found addressing Jesus Christ or the Father or Spirit in any of these fulsome terms: they speak only the language of holy adoration.

Vague and aimless language indicates very clearly a vacant mind devoid of true spiritual affections. Too often the prayers offered before sermon are such as to suggest no other real purpose, than to comply with an expected form and fill decently the allotted time. So, the prayer which closes the sermon is often so pointless, that it amounts to nothing more than a mechanical mark for the ending of the ceremonial. Sometimes there is an absence of any intelligible order in the prayers; and we hear petitions for a mixed medley of objects, interspersed with thanks, confessions and praises.

Now, in opposition to all these faults, I would point out to you the proper mode of performing this duty, by referring you to the instruction of our Directory for Public Worship.[1]

---

[1] I. It seems very proper to begin the public worship of the sanctuary by a short prayer; humbly adoring the infinite majesty of the living God; expressing a sense of our distance from him as creatures, and unworthiness as sinners, and humbly imploring his gracious presence, the assistance of his Holy Spirit in the duties of his worship, and his acceptance of us through the merits of our Lord and Saviour Jesus Christ.

II. Then, after singing a psalm, or hymn, it is proper that, before sermon, there should be a full and comprehensive prayer: *First.*

1. Our Standards here discriminate between the grace or spirit, and the gift of prayer. The former is a devout, believing, thankful frame of heart, which " hungers and

---

Adoring the glory and perfections of God as they are made known to us in the works of creation, in the conduct of providence, and in the clear and full revelation he hath made of himself in his written Word. *Second.* Giving thanks to him for all his mercies of every kind, general and particular, spiritual and temporal, common and special; above all, for Christ Jesus, his unspeakable gift, and the hope of eternal life through him. *Third.* Making humble confession of sin, both original and actual; acknowledging and endeavouring to impress the mind of every worshipper with a deep sense of the evil of all sin, as such; as being a departure from the living God; and also taking a particular and affecting view of the various fruits which proceed from this root of bitterness—as sins against God, our neighbour and ourselves; sins in thought, in word, and in deed; sins secret and presumptuous; sins accidental and habitual. Also, the aggravations of sin, arising from knowledge, or the means of it; from distinguishing mercies; from valuable privileges; from breach of vows, etc. *Fourth.* Making earnest supplication for the pardon of sin, and peace with God, through the blood of the atonement, with all its important and happy fruits; for the Spirit of sanctification, and abundant supplies of the grace that is necessary to the discharge of our duty; for support and comfort, under all the trials to which we are liable, as we are sinful and mortal; and for all temporal mercies that may be necessary, in our passage through this valley of tears—always remembering to view them as flowing in the channel of covenant love, and intended to be subservient to the preservation and progress of the spiritual life. *Fifth.* Pleading from every principle warranted in Scripture; from our own necessity; the all-sufficiency of God; the merit and intercession of our Saviour; and the glory of God in the comfort and happiness of his people. *Sixth.* Intercession for others, including the whole world of mankind; the kingdom of Christ, or his Church universal; the church or churches with which we are more particularly connected; the interest of human society in general, and in that community to which we immediately belong; all that are invested with civil authority; the ministers of the everlasting gospel; and the rising generation: with whatever else, more particular,

thirsts after righteousness," superinduced by divine grace. The latter is the ability to express this frame appropriately in words. The former only is necessary for the right performance of the duty of secret prayer; both are necessary for him who would lead the devotions of others. Now, the grace of prayer is to be secured only by a life of personal and private devotion. He who carries a cold heart into the pulpit betrays it not only to God, whose detection of it is inevitable, but almost surely to the hearers also. The pretended gift without the grace is a body without spirit. The dis-

---

may seem necessary, or suitable, to the interest of that congregation where divine worship is celebrated.

III. Prayer after sermon ought generally to have a relation to the subject that has been treated of in the discourse, and all other public prayers, to the circumstances that gave occasion for them.

IV. It is easy to perceive that in all the preceding directions there is a very great compass and variety, and it is committed to the judgment and fidelity of the officiating pastor to insist chiefly on such parts, or to take in more or less of the several parts, as he shall be led to by the aspect of Providence; the particular state of the congregation in which he officiates, or the disposition and exercise of his own heart at the time. But we think it necessary to observe, that although we do not approve, as is well known, of confining ministers to set or fixed forms of prayer for public worship, yet it is the indispensable duty of every minister, previously to his entering on his office, to prepare and qualify himself for this part of his duty, as well as for preaching. He ought, by a thorough acquaintance with the Holy Scriptures, by reading the best writers on the subject, by meditation, and by a life of communion with God in secret, to endeavour to acquire both the spirit and the gift of prayer. Not only so, but when he is to enter on particular acts of worship, he should endeavour to compose his spirit, and to digest his thoughts for prayer, that it may be performed with dignity and propriety, as well as to the profit of those who join in it; and that he may not disgrace that important service by mean, irregular, or extravagant effusions.

play of it only serves to distress and chill the truly devout, to confirm the slumbers of drowsy Christians, to encourage the prayerless tendencies of the ungodly, to place the minds of all out of harmony with the divine truths which are about to be discussed in the sermon. Above all, the help of the Holy Ghost and the inestimable advantage of Christian intercession are forfeited. Thus the purposes of God in ordaining public prayer are disappointed, and this means of edification is turned into a deadening form. How great is the guilt of him who, appointed to be an ensample to the flock, obstructs their access to the throne of grace! The pastor is under sacred obligations, then, to cultivate upon his knees the spirit of prayer. This possessed, the gift of prayer will be taught him by the same principles of taste and propriety which direct his preaching.

2. But, second, the pastor must look to the position in which he stands, as the leader of public prayer, to determine the manner of its performance. He is the organ of the people; not of himself, save as he is one among them. He speaks the mind of the aggregate church in that place. He is to pray in behalf of the church, then, as the church should pray for itself. If a Christian could be found who was the fair type of what his brethren in that place should be, the pastor should speak just as that representative man would, only changing individual expressions into public and common, and the singular member into the plural. How, then, does a soul properly speak for itself to its God? Does it dream of fine language? Does it think of artificial terms of expression? Does it deem that ornaments of style have any place? You well

know that if you overheard that man in his secret prayer, and found him employing such ambitious verbiage, you would conclude at once that he was insincere. So, just as soon as the minister introduces any rhetorical artifice, he betrays the fact that he is speaking to creatures and not to God. He has forgotten what he professes to be about, and is mocking the Searcher of hearts![1] The first requirement, then, is that the language of prayer must be wholly unambitious, unaffected and simple. It must be, not such as is proper from a teacher speaking to his congregation, but just such as is appropriate for an accepted sinner speaking to his God.

From the same position I deduce the rule that the preacher, in intercessions which he represents the people as offering for himself, should indulge in no affected excesses of humility. This would be in reality to have the people tell God in their pastor's presence, how great a sinner they thought he was! The pastor may presume that his people respond to the apostolic request: "Brethren, pray for us," but in giving voice to their prayer for himself, he should put into their mouths no other language than they would use, if interceding for him in his presence. Even in doing this he should avoid the appearance of egotism.

From the same point of view I infer that the pastor should be chary of introducing personal details into his

---

[1] It is said that a newspaper, with laudatory intention, remarked of the prayer of an ambitious young Socinian: "The prayer of the reverend gentleman was admitted to have been the most eloquent ever addressed to a Boston audience." The silly editor uttered a truer sarcasm than he knew; your "eloquent" prayers are always addressed to the audience, not to God.

public devotions. He represents his church as a whole: neither he nor his family, nor any other individual or family, should monopolize that access to the throne of grace which is common to all. Even when a single person is under such peculiar trials as to entitle him to the special prayers of the church, the pastor should not dwell too long upon his particular condition.

Once more, true prayer is the language of faith. None really pray except those who have begun to feel the quickening grace of God; hence it is unnatural that any one should pray habitually and still remain an entire stranger to the filial affections and hopes of the Christian. Prayer, then, is usually the language of God's children, not of his enemies. The pastor is the organ of the body of penitent believers, not of the impenitent. He should use language suitable to a sinner turning from his ways; for this is always appropriate, not only to the awakened sinner, but to the imperfect and penitent child who is continually renewing his "first works." But his strain should be prevalently filial, believing and hopeful, as becomes God's reconciled children.

Since it is God to whom you speak, and not man, your prayers should not be didactic. Doctrinal truths and the facts of redemption are, indeed, the grounds, arguments and guides of our petitions. This will justify such allusion to them, especially in our pleadings, as founds our requests on their proper reasons; but our reference must be subordinate and brief, lest we should seem to preach to God instead of praying to him. There is a painful absurdity in our going about formally to instruct God of his doctrinal truths: it is his part to inform us of these; it is our wants and praises which he invites us to tell him.

3. It is of radical importance that the leader of the church's prayers shall present distinct and definite petitions, and these not numerous at one time. One of the constant sins of our prayers is that we are vague, and therefore feeble, in our desires. We scarcely remember precisely what we asked of God; we do not watch and work for the answer. The pastor should conscientiously avoid fostering this wretched vice of the people's devotions: he should put into their mouths always distinct objects of desire. Prayer is the professed language of want; but want is always definite: he who wants, wants some thing—a distinct thing. The leader of prayer should therefore speak as one who has an errand at the throne, a point to press with God. He should eschew loose generalities of petition, and all that stream of indefinite, goodish talk with which so many prayers are filled, which really expresses nothing save a slumbering faith and a heart void of desire. Nor should the emotions and memories of the people be burdened with many points in the same prayer. Sincere devotion is the most arduous exercise of the soul: it should therefore not be too much taxed at the same time. Ardent desire is, moreover, expulsive in its nature: it claims, for the once, the whole heart for its object. No man is strongly exercised concerning many diverse and remote objects at once; hence a few appropriate topics of petition, handled in an orderly manner and enlarged with judicious amplification, until the mind is fixed and the heart engaged by them, constitute the most edifying prayers.

4. He who leads the devotions of others must study appropriateness of matter. He should ask himself what would be uppermost in the hearts of Christians at that time, if they were supposed to be in a suitable temper. Let that be his topic. It is due from the judgment of charity that he shall credit God's children with that right temper; and he should desire, at any rate, to foster it in them, by leading them to the expression of those desires which it should prompt. He must remember that he is the mouthpiece of the church. What right, then, has he to put into her mouth words which she is not rightfully inclined to utter? If the children of God have one thing upon their hearts, and you force a different one into their petitions, you do them a grievous wrong. Assume, then, that the things which ought to be especially appropriate to the time and circumstances are the things which the Holy Spirit has put into the desires of the people, and give tongue to these. Every prayer should be studied with reference to the present wants of the church: this will also secure variety in your public devotions. When the soul of the people is pressed with particular wants, do not consume their time with the usual routine of adoration, thanksgiving, confession, to the exclusion of their chief errand at the throne of grace, but either abbreviate those parts, or borrow their thoughts from the same pressing objects.

5. "Be not rash with thy mouth, and let not thy heart be hasty to utter anything before God; for God is in heaven and thou upon earth; therefore let thy words be few."[1] The language of prayer should be

---

[1] Eccles. v. 2.

well-ordered and considerate. He who speaks to the Searcher of hearts should beware how he indulges any exaggeration of words, lest his tongue should be found to have outrun his mind, and to have "offered the sacrifice of fools." Both the words and the utterance should express profound but affectionate reverence. The enunciation of prayer should be softer, more level, less marked by *ictus*, less vehement, more subdued. Every tone should breathe tenderness and supplication. There are ministers whose inflections, modulated upon the pensive, minor key, are the native voice of contrite desire. Study to make these tones your own. It is difficult to say which is most unsuitable to this sacred exercise—a hurried, perfunctory utterance, as of one who reads some tiresome or trivial matter, a violent and declamatory manner, as though one had ventured upon objurgation of his Maker, or a headlong and confused enunciation.

6. Above all should the minister enrich his prayers with the language of Scripture. Not everything in the Scripture is appropriate to express devotion, as some pedantic minds seem to imagine, but the language of its spiritual and devotional parts. Besides its inimitable beauty and simplicity, it is hallowed and sweet to every pious heart by a thousand associations. It satisfies the taste of all; its use effectually protects us against improprieties; it was doubtless given by the Holy Spirit to be a model for our devotions. Let it then abound in our prayers. The young minister should store his memory richly with these noble strains, fixing in his mind the very words of the English version. He should memorize perfectly the finest passages from the

Psalms, the Prophets, the Evangelists and the Apostles, and study to make them the apt vehicles of his worship. But let him shun those fantastic and perverse applications of the language of the Bible in which certain classes of preachers so much delight, which wrest figurative or tropical expressions to some quaint sense they were not intended to bear. This has grown, in some, to an odious pedantry: the more strange and far-fetched their applications, the better they are pleased. Such a mannerism can only mystify or else amuse the hearer, and it is therefore glaringly out of place in prayer.

Great beauty, variety and solemnity are gained by employing the numerous descriptive and attributive phrases which are found in the Scriptures for addressing the persons of the Trinity. These forms of speech should be selected with reference to the particular topic of thanksgiving, confession or petition which was to be introduced; for example, either a request or a thanksgiving for temporal good may be begun: Thou, Father, "which openest thy hand, and satisfieth the desires of every living thing."[1] A prayer for aid in self-examination may appropriately begin: "Thou who searchest the hearts, and triest the reins" of the children of men.[2] A prayer for rulers, or against powerful assailants, may address God as "Judge of all the earth,"[3] or as "King of kings and Lord of lords."[4] Prayer for deliverance from war and confusion naturally appeals to the "Prince of peace."[5] Those passages in our prayers which ex-

---

[1] Psalm cxlv. 16.   [2] Jer. xvii. 10.   [3] Gen. xviii. 25.
[4] Rev. xvii. 14.   [5] Isa. ix. 6.

press adoration, or exalted, spiritual emotion, may be best composed of the varied and inimitable forms of doxology contained in the Scriptures. What formula of human invention can ever equal this?—" Now unto the King eternal, immortal, invisible, the only wise God, be honour and glory, for ever and ever, amen!" Or this: "Worthy is the Lamb that was slain to receive power, and riches, and wisdom, and strength, and honour, and glory, and blessing."[1] So, the formulary known as the Lord's Prayer should not only be a guide to the matter of our prayers, but it should, on suitable occasions, be recited in the words of the Gospels. And it is especially adapted to form the close of a prayer of human composition.

In fine, public prayer must never be prolix or tedious. The soul cannot long sustain properly so elevated an exercise. After weariness supervenes, all that remains is a ministration of formalism.

From all this, young gentlemen, you will readily comprehend that this duty will require of you careful and special preparation. The young minister should no more venture into the pulpit with an *impromptu* prayer, than with an *impromptu* sermon. And the prayer after sermon, although usually short, should no more be left to the chance suggestions of a moment of exhaustion, than the longer. Every pastor should practise frequently the art of devotional composition. He will do this, not so much to recite these written prayers in the pulpit, as to train his own taste, and to gather a store

---

[1] 1 Tim. i. 17; Rev. v. 12. And the following: Rom. xi. 33–36; xvi. 27; Jude xxv.; Rev. iv. 8, 11; Rev. vii. 12; Isa. vi. 3; Dan. ix. 4; Ps. viii. 1; c. 5; lxxii. 18 to end.

of devotional language. He should also prepare himself regularly for his duty by noting suitable subjects of prayer and praise with careful deliberation and by preparing acceptable words. And, above all, he should seek to have his own soul in a right frame by fervent, secret prayer.

Let me, in conclusion, recommend to you the little work of Dr. Samuel Miller on Public Prayer. You will find that most of the advices I have given you are borrowed from it. It is a manual of the highest merit for its piety and excellent taste.

THE END.

70737

251
D 115